The Lands and Peoples of East Africa

New Edition

G. M. Hickman B.A. Ph.D

University of Bristol School of Education,
Director, Schools Council Geography 14–18 Curriculum project.
Formerly at Makerere College, University of East Africa
and at the
University of Ghana

and

W. H. G. Dickins M.A.

Formerly Lecturer in the Faculty of Education
Makerere College
University of East Africa.

New Edition 1973
with the help of
E. Woods
Formerly of Alliance High School, Kenya.

Longman

Longman Kenya Ltd
PO Box 45925
Shell and BP House (2nd floor)
Harambee Avenue
Nairobi

Longman Tanzania Ltd
PO Box 3164
Dar es Salaam

Longman Uganda Ltd
PO Box 3409
Kampala

Longman Group Ltd
London and Harlow

This edition first published 1973
Reprinted 1973

ISBN 0 582 60219 X

Printed by Kenya Litho Ltd.,
P.O. Box 40775, Cardiff Road, Nairobi.

To William Dickins

Outstanding teacher and geographer, who
died of pneumonia on the Ruwenzori
Mountains, aged 31 years, this book is
dedicated.

Contents

List of illustrations

Maps and line drawings

Photographs

Acknowledgments

The publishers are grateful to the following for permission to reproduce photographs:

Advertising Photographs Nairobi: 132 (top left), Aerofilms: 155 Palle Artler: 131 (top left), 131 (bottom), 132 (top right), Barnaby's Picture Library: 35 (top), Camera Press Ltd., Russell Court: 44 (top left), 44 (bottom), 64 (Both Pictures), 147 (bottom), 148, Allan Cash: 6, East African Common Services: 114 (bottom right), East African Railways and Harbours Nairobi, Kenya: 35 (bottom right), 39 (bottom left), 40, 53, 55, 58 (bottom right), 61 (bottom right), 63, 67, 122, 134, 145 (top left), 145 (bottom left), 150, 151, Kenya Information Services: 58 (top) 80, 114 (top left), Kenya Tourist Office: 119, Nationfoto: 115, Dr. W. A. Petana: 23, Paul Popper Ltd., 34 (bottom right), 59 (top right), 162, Skyline Advertising Ltd., Nairobi: 160, Tanzania Information Services: 133, Fergus Wilson: 39 (bottom right), 59 (bottom right), 85, 85, 87.

The authors and publishers are also grateful to the many people who have provided material for particular studies, or information for diagrams. They would particularly like to thank the following: P. R. Baker, P. J. Bailey, East African Airways, East African Railways, I. L. Griffiths, P. Hobbs, M. Kamunyu, R. H. Mcbridge, A. Mckee, W. D. Morgan, National Irrigation Board, Kenya, S. Odingo, S. H. Ominde, G. R. Siviour, C. J. Skinner, P. H. Temple, R. White, Williamson Diamonds.

To the student: How to use this book

I The plan of the book

There are *three* parts.

Part I provides the background studies to regional planning and development: rainfall, temperature, soils, communications, i.e. a systematic approach.

Part II Regional studies: case studies of small areas or units representing larger regions or important development themes.

Part III Resources of East Africa: systematic studies of resources e.g. agriculture, industry, trade etc. A regional summary of population distribution.

The authors of this book do not expect you to read it all

It is important to *select* parts of the book that relate to your own country and region; and to do a good deal of *practical* study (i.e. collecting local rainfall or production figures, making field sketches, drawing graphs) relevant to your own district. You will understand other places better if you can compare them with your own.

II How to use the book for studying your own country.

You can begin *either* by reading about a place that you know; *or* by reading the part of Chapter 15 that relates to your country.

The chart at the bottom of this page shows the location of studies relating to each country.

III Different kinds of study material

This book contains

1. *descriptive text* written by the authors

Chapter	Part 1 BACKGROUND					Part 2 REGIONAL				Part 3 RESOURCES					
	1	2	3	4	5	6	7	8	9	10	11	12	13	14	15
Kenya		S	S	Ⓑ		Ⓓ	Ⓘ Ⓙ	Ⓝ Ⓞ	Ⓢ Ⓣ Ⓤ ●			●	S	S Ⓩ	S
Tanzania		●S	S		●	Ⓒ Ⓔ	Ⓛ	Ⓜ	Ⓠ ●		●	●Ⓥ Ⓦ	S	Ⓧ S	S
Uganda		●S	S	Ⓐ	●		Ⓕ Ⓖ Ⓗ Ⓚ	Ⓟ	Ⓡ				S	● S Ⓨ	S

Key Ⓣ Case-study: letter from figure 36. S Text summary

● Special section related to the country shown

2. *case studies of particular places* (see page 45)

The case studies are of little use unless some *general statements* can be developed, that apply to the larger area, i.e. from one industry to industry in general. Sometimes the authors provide the generalisations; sometimes this is left to the students. Examples of generalised 'key' statements are given on

page 72, 1–4 (settlements in Uganda)
page 77 B (how sub region B differs from A)
page 99 Chapter 9, first paragraph (height of land)
N.B. Do not read all the studies. For example there are *four* development schemes in Ch. 12c and others in Chapters 4, 7, 9. Choose *one* or at the most *two*.

3. *detailed study sections* (printed in smaller type)
   These may be omitted or used for advanced study
4. *work exercises* of different kinds in the *Work to do* sections at the end of each chapter.

IV Study methods and ideas for a geographical shorthand.

1. The sections on Work to do at the end of each chapter can be used both for starting to study (i.e. use the questions to start looking for answers in the chapter) *or* for checking and revision.
2. *Note summaries* to bring out *key facts*. For example notes made on the Ahero Pilot Scheme (pages 80–81) might be:

   i Location: (from figure 56) Kano Plains, 14 miles east of Kisumu.
   ii Irrigation: water from Nyanza uplands to be used for 36,000 acres.
   iii Present situation: 2,000 producing rice.
   iv Production similar to Mwea, but *two* crops a year.
   v Reasons etc.

3. *Diagram summaries or flow charts*. These can provide a better picture of the *sequence* of processes (i.e. the stages in growing a

crop or preparing it for market; in mining and processing a mineral etc.) making them easier to remember.
It can also lead to a *generalised statement* or a *model* of a complex situation that would be difficult to describe in words.

Three different ways of making a summary of the sequence and processes used in preparing sisal for export.
Note. Each method is acceptable. However, each could be more useful according to the purpose for which it is needed.

A   *Notes* on processes/stages

1. Sisal cut, loaded in fields
2. Transported to
3. *Factory*
4. Flesh stripped from leaves (decorticated)
5. Washed, dried on wires, bleached.
6. Brushed, graded, baled,
7. Exported

B   A *model* or *flow diagram* that also shows more detail and complex needs.

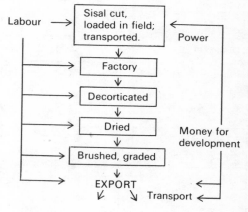

C

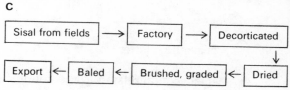

4. *Analysis of weather charts.* There are some starter questions on page 50 (Figure 38); also at the beginning of *The work on the land through the year* page 72.

5. Labelled landscape sketches, line drawings and photographs.

There are many photographs in the book that can be simplified as *line drawings*. Suitable photographs are found on pages 32, 37, 55 (more difficult) 80, 150 (more difficult). Some are simple but bring out important facts. For example, on page 113 the photograph *summarises* important elements in tea production; the upper photograph on page 58 shows the change of crops grown on different parts of a slope, in relation to the availability of ground water. More complex examples of labelled landscape sketches are given on page 60 (Figure 42, sisal) and page 103 (Figure 103, Kigezi).

For a *plan* made from an *air photograph*, see page 155, Figure 98.

Case Studies

The position of the case-studies is shown by a letter in a circle thus:(A) on figure 36 page 46.

Case-studies related to countries:

Kenya:
Letters B D I J N O S T U Z

Tanzania:
Letters C E L M Q V W X

Uganda:
Letters A F G H K P R Y

The cover shows:
(top left) Mt. Kenya seen from Karatina
(bottom left) Tororo cement factory
(top right) A Kenyan dairy farm
(middle right) Below the Nile dam at Jinja
(bottom right) A steamer on the Tanzanian shore
of Lake Victoria
All photographs by kind permission of Professor
Fergus Wilson.

Part one: The background to regional planning and development

Chapter 1: An introduction to East Africa

The object of the first part of this book is to examine, from a geographical point of view, some of the situations that affect economic development in East Africa. Before progress can be made, it is necessary to study the difficulties, and to consider the potential offered by the physical resources of the land.

The East African countries of Kenya, Tanzania and Uganda form a rectangular block which covers an area of 1 670 550 sq km (645 000 sq miles). By comparison with the really large countries of the world, such as the U.S.A. (7 770 000 sq km) this is not large. Nevertheless, the distances within East Africa are very considerable. From the north of

Kenya to the south of Tanzania is 1 930 km (1 200 miles). The distance across Tanzania is nearly 1 000 km (622 miles). East Africa stretches through 11° of longitude and 17° of latitude, about two-thirds of it being in the Southern Hemisphere.

Within these countries live 31 million people, giving an overall density of population which averages about 18 to the sq km (47 to the sq mile). Compared with Java, another mainly agricultural country, with 350 people to the sq km (907 to the sq mile), this seems sparse; and by comparison with the industrial countries of Western Europe (Great Britain about 200 to the sq km (518 to the sq mile), East Africa is not densely populated. Nevertheless, it is very much greater than in a

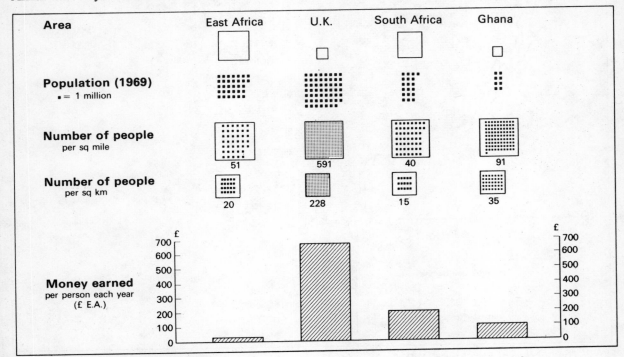

Fig. 1 East Africa: Some comparisons

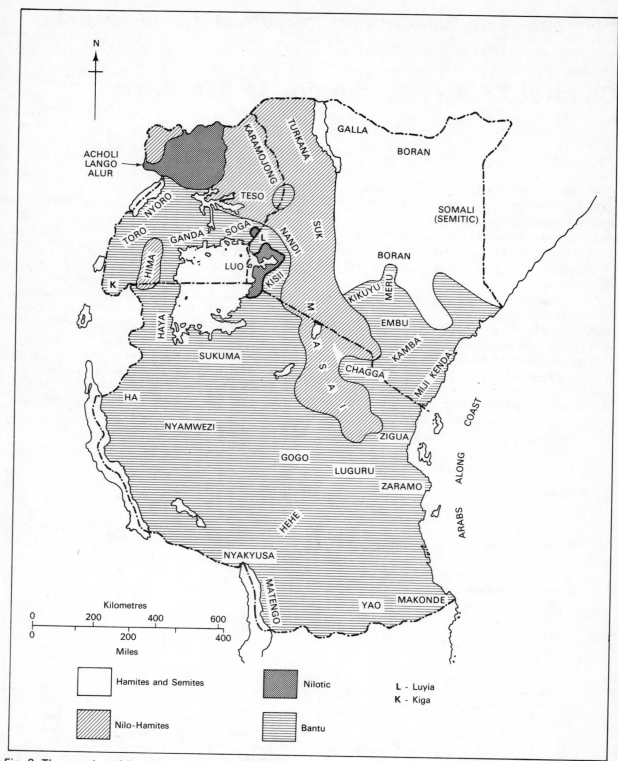

Fig. 2 The peoples of East Africa (N.B. Prefixes have been omitted to make the map easier to read.)

2

continent such as Australia, which has an average* of less than 2 people to the sq km (5 to the sq mile).

The figure for *average* population density hides very wide differences in density within each country. In parts of north-east Kenya there are several sq km to each person. In the area south of Mount Kenya, and in one or two other parts of East Africa, the density is over 400 to the sq km (1 036 to the sq mile). In other words, within one country the population density ranges from very high to very low.

To the individual living in a country, however, areas in sq km and densities of population do not mean very much. What really concerns him is his own personal standard of living. He may think of this as the money that he has in his pocket, or as other kinds of wealth, such as a fertile garden or a good herd of cattle.

The wealth of the people of a country depends chiefly, on three things.

1. The amount of natural resources such as good agricultural land and minerals.
2. The skill of the people and the way in which they use the resources.
3. The number of people who share the wealth.

Fortunate countries, like the U.S.A., have vast natural wealth in relation to the number of people, and make very good use of the resources. There are also countries like Denmark which, although naturally poor, have managed by intelligent hard work to achieve a high standard of living.

East Africa is not very rich. There are resources, both agricultural and mineral, but various factors, such as the tsetse fly and transport difficulties, have hindered their development. The wealth of East Africa, although limited, is sufficient to support the people at a far higher standard. The main problem is to use the land more carefully, and to increase the land available to farming by irrigation and reclamation.

Within the area of East Africa three groups of people are normally recognised, the Africans, the Asians and the Europeans. This, however, does not correspond with any scientific division; it is the recognition of a difference in way of life rather than of race. Strictly, the majority of Arabs, Somali, Galla, Boran and Indians belong to branches of the 'white' or Caucasoid race and so should be grouped with the Europeans. For the purpose of description it will be convenient to take the groups normally recognised, but remembering that the differences are cultural rather than racial.

African peoples make up 98 per cent of the total 31 millions.

(a) The most numerous group is the *Bantu*, a name which strictly refers to language and not to race. Many of the well-known peoples of East Africa are Bantu cultivators, and the map (Fig. 2) on page 2 gives their locations.

(b) The *Nilotic* peoples moved into East Africa from the north and they are both cultivators and pastoralists. The most important representatives of this group in East Africa are the Luo of Kenya and the Acholi of Uganda.

(c) The most obvious characteristic of the *Nilo-Hamitic* peoples is their love of the pastoral way of life. The Masai described in chapter 8 are the most famous of this group, but the Turkana, the Suk and the Karamojong have an equally strong attachment to their animals. Some of the people, particularly the Teso, Nandi and Kipsigis, have begun to give considerable attention to cultivation as well.

(d) The nomadic Galla and Boran of the deserts of Northern Kenya are pure *Hamites*, as are the Somali.

The Arabs have been in East Africa for many centuries, and mainly inhabit the coastal area. Indians and Pakistanis have come in considerable numbers ever since the Kenya-Uganda railway was begun. They came originally to work on the building of the railway, and many decided to stay, going into commerce, industry and various skilled trades. For this reason Indians form a large proportion of the inhabitants of East African towns. The skills that the Asian community has contributed have speeded economic development.

Europeans form only a small proportion of the total population. They came originally from many parts of Europe, especially Great Britain, Italy, Greece, Germany, the Netherlands–and from South Africa. But people now come into East Africa from a large number of countries on short-term contracts. Before Independence they worked mainly as administrators, farmers, teachers and in

*To find *average* density of population the total number of people in a country is divided by its size.
  Uganda 9 526 000 people
    ÷93 802 sq miles = 104 people to 1 sq mile [40 to 1 sq km]
  Kenya 10 880 000 people
    ÷225 000 sq miles = 49 people to 1 sq mile [19 to 1 sq km]
  Tanzania 12 557 000 people
    ÷362 700 sq miles = 33 people to 1 sq mile [13 to 1 sq km]
  Population for 1969: *all* figures approximate.

commerce, but in recent years there has been a big inflow of 'expatriates' serving the East African governments as technical advisers, especially in agriculture.

East Africa contains, as has been seen, a number of peoples who differ racially and in appearance. Add to this that there are differences in language, in way of life, in education and in standards of living, and it will be realised that it is not easy for the different peoples to understand each other's point of view. It is very important that they should do so. If resources are to be developed, and the challenges of the environment are to be overcome, it is necessary that each group of people should contribute as much as it can.

In addition to understanding each other, the peoples of East Africa must understand their countries. These can be looked at in two ways. It is possible to regard one's geographical surroundings as a sort of prison, from which it is impossible to escape, poor land making poor people. On the other hand, they can be thought of as a challenge – difficulties to be overcome rather than given way to. The second way is difficult but rewarding. It requires people to work hard and intelligently, and to take note of the methods of others who have had to deal with similar problems. It demands patience, and willingness to set aside the fruits of one's work, until sufficient money has been saved to buy better equipment. But if it is successful the rewards are far greater.

Chapter 2: Understanding rainfall

In East Africa about eight persons out of every ten are farmers. To some of them the coming or not of the rain can mean life or death, or at least the difference between a full stomach and a long period of hunger. Certain features of the rainfall present problems. Over much of the area it is insufficient; it is often unreliable; and it is capable of doing damage both to crops and soil by the way in which it falls. The people who face these problems must solve them or go hungry.

Factors influencing the amount and distribution of rain

Most school atlases include a map of annual average rainfall. This kind of map is based on the average of the totals recorded over many years. Such a map does not tell us how much the amount of rain varies from one year to another, nor the reliability of its timing during the year.

Rainfall, humidity, temperature, sunshine and air-circulation are some of the *elements* or parts that make up the climate of a place. They are influenced or determined by the interplay of a number of *factors*. These include latitude, height above sea level, and position in relation to the distribution of land and sea.

Study the following diagrams as you read the text. They will help you to understand the process of rain-making.

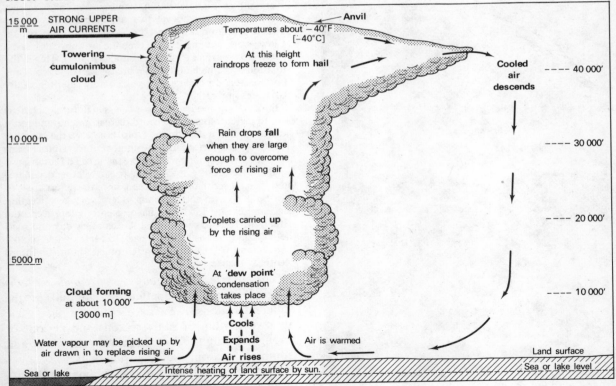

Fig. 3 The formation of cumulonimbus clouds by convection

Rainfall can only occur if the air is cooled, usually by rising, and if there is sufficient water vapour in the air. This process is called condensation.

Condensation may be brought about in three main ways:

1. when intense heating of the ground causes rising air currents (*convectional* rain). Many local thunderstorms in East Africa are of this type. Fig. 3 shows the main stages in this process.
2. when air is forced to rise by meeting higher land (*relief* or *orographical* rain).
3. by the meeting, or *convergence*, of two bodies of air of similar character causing heavy storm rain. In recent years meteorologists have begun to realise that much of the day to day rainfall, and the overall climatic pattern, can be explained in terms of the movement of masses of air.

Detailed study section   (see 'How to use this book') *The section set in small type is for advanced study. Return to this later if you prefer.*

A towering cumulonimbus cloud. Compare its shape with Fig. 3.

Converging air (called *convergence*) occurs when more air is moving into a region than is moving out of it. This happens across the whole of Africa in a broad belt known as the Inter Tropical Convergence Zone (I.T.C.Z.). It develops because the sun, which is almost directly overhead, causes intense heating of the ground so that the air near it heats up, expands and rises. The rising warmed air creates low pressure at ground level, so that more air flows in from other areas to take its place. As the zone of greatest heating moves north or south, following the apparent movement of the sun, so the I.T.C.Z. also shifts north or south over eastern Africa.

The rising air cools as it expands because heat-energy is used up to move the molecules of air apart. If the air rises high enough, cooling causes the water vapour it contains to condense. The extremely small droplets of liquid water thus formed are suspended in the air as clouds, until they combine in sufficient number to form much heavier drops, which can overcome the air's resistance and fall to the ground as rain.

Divergence is the opposite of convergence. Whereas convergence is associated with rising air, divergence is usually associated with sinking air. Subsiding air warms as it descends and this increases its ability to take in and hold moisture. So when air is sinking and flowing away from a particular area, there is less chance of rain being produced.

The situation is, however, complicated by the way air moves at some height above the ground.

Air will only *continue* to rise if it is flowing away (that is, diverging) at high levels. A combination of low-level convergence and high level divergence is necessary to give suitable conditions for rain. (Fig. 3). If convergence occurs at low levels, but at the same time the air above descends, it results in warmer, drier conditions (Fig. 8). This is the situation over much of the drier areas of East Africa. Thus it is the *upper* air movements which really determine daily variations in weather.

Information about the higher layers in the atmosphere is sent to meteorologists by recording instruments and radio carried aloft by balloons. Unfortunately, the weather balloons are expensive and the number of transmitters sent up is too few to obtain a complete picture. The situation is made worse because much East African weather originates in the east, over the Indian Ocean, or in the desert areas of northern Kenya and Somalia. Here very few weather stations exist. Satellites have greatly improved the situation. They pass over East Africa every day and send actual photographs by radio back to earth. These photos show cloud patterns and can tell much about the future weather prospects.

The diagram *Rainfall regions and patterns* (Fig. 4) shows the pattern of rainfall in the different regions of East Africa. Each region has its own rhythm of rainy seasons and periods of drought resulting from the movement north and south of the air masses and wind belts.

The two main wind systems affecting the climate of East Africa are the north-east and the south-east

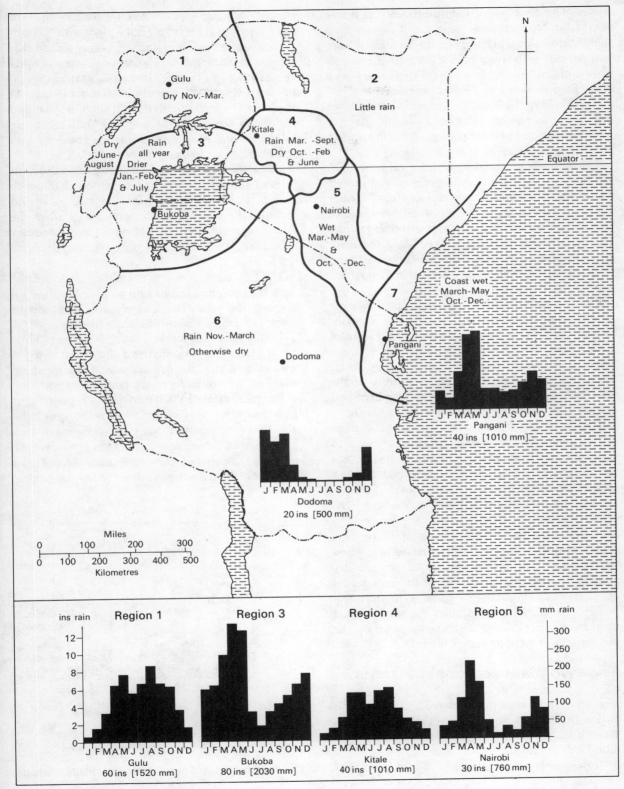

Fig. 4 Rainfall regions and patterns

trades. The zone where they meet receives heavy rain from convectional storms: it becomes a thunderstorm zone. Hence equatorial regions have two periods of heavier rain related to the northward and southward movement of this *convergence* zone. Region 3 on Fig. 4 best illustrates this.

Farther from the Equator the peaks come closer together as in region 1. Farther away still they are so close that there is one continuous rainy season and one long period of drought (region 6).

The simple equatorial pattern (of rain throughout the year with two heavier periods) and that of two main seasons (one wet and one dry) farther north and south might prevail over the whole of East Africa but for the existence of other factors. These are the size of the landmass of Asia, the north to south direction of the East African Coast, and the distribution of high and low land in East Africa itself.

The north-east trades include a northerly air stream from Egypt and the Sudan and a north-easterly stream from Arabia and the Horn of Africa. This air has its origin in the desert zone, and condensation is slight except on the coast. Such conditions extend to other months of the year and account for the aridity of northern and eastern Kenya and of the dry zone of Tanzania.

The south-east trades, a tropical air mass from the southern Indian Ocean, bring heavy rain to most parts of East Africa in April and May, but in the following months the winds tend to blow almost parallel with the coast so that the rain-bearing influences are not felt far inland. The seasonal change in the direction of the winds at the coast is often described as monsoonal. During the period May-October much of Tanzania is covered by air which has blown overland from the dry interior of southern Africa. Hence the long period of drought. The southerly wind is in part responsible for the heavy rainfall of the northern and western shores of Lake Victoria. It picks up the moisture in its passage across the lake.

The two main seasonal patterns

The total amount of rain received and its distribution through the year influence farming greatly. The whole way of life of the farmer is tied to the falling of the rain.

For example, in many areas 500 mm (20 ins) of

rain, if they are spread over twelve months, are not enough to grow crops. But a place with 500 mm falling within the few months of a rainy season may be able to plant and harvest crops. There are other effects too. For example Gulu has 1 500 mm (60 ins) of rain a year and Kampala 1 200 mm (48 ins). At the latter it is well distributed through the year and coffee can be grown. But north of Gulu most rain falls between May and October. The long dry season makes it less easy to grow coffee.

While there are within East Africa *seven* different rainfall patterns, they may be grouped into *two* major types—the first where the rain is spread through the year but with two periods when the fall is heavier than usual; and the second, or Tanzania, type which has only one wet and one dry season.

The following examples show the importance of both the total amount of rain and the distribution through the year. The first place is Rugorogoro Shema, Western Ankole, Uganda (region 3).

In this part of Uganda about 1 000 mm (40 ins) of rain fall each year. Figure 5 shows the two wet seasons and the two dry seasons. How do these affect the way of living of the people?

The total rainfall 1 000 mm makes it possible to grow many crops of which coffee is the most valuable. Planting can be done at the beginning of each rainy season, during which the crops grow until the next dry period when harvesting takes place. This is shown by the planting symbol for sorghum, peas

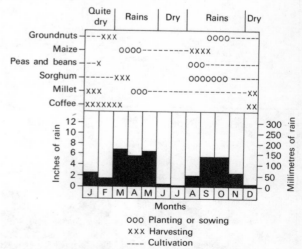

Temperature average for most months in the year is 69°F (20·5°C); a little lower (20°C) in May, June, July

Fig. 5 Rugorogoro Shema, Western Ankole, Uganda

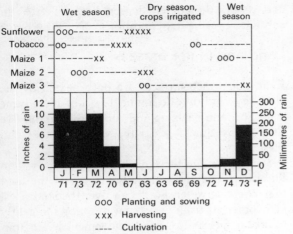

	Wet season	Dry season, crops irrigated	Wet season
Sunflower	000 -------- xxxxx		
Tobacco	00 ------- xxxx	00 --------	
Maize 1	------xx	000 ---	
Maize 2	000 --------- xxx		
Maize 3	00 ------------------- xx		

	Planting and sowing	000
	Harvesting	xxx
	Cultivation	----

Fig. 6 Songea area, Southern Tanzania

and beans in August and groundnuts in September; maize and millet in March and April.

The dry season of June–July is sufficiently long and hot to check the growth of plants. The dry season of December is shorter and does not usually cause so complete a break in plant growth. The two heavy rains fall soon after each equinox.

The people who work on such a shamba have their work spread out through the whole of the year. There is little danger of crop failure and famine and they have a varied and healthy diet.

In the second example Songea (region 6) the total amount of rainfall is similar, just over 1 000 mm (40 ins), but the distribution quite different. Almost all the rain falls during the months November to April so that there is only one wet season planting, of maize in November, tobacco and sunflowers in January and a second maize sowing in February. These crops begin to ripen between March and June. Once the harvest is over there is a quiet period.

For much of the dry season the ground is too hard to cultivate and crops would not survive the six months without appreciable rain. So if the farmer needs to grow more crops he must provide water for irrigation. He looks after a little irrigated maize and beans, and starts the tobacco in watered seed beds. In this way he increases production and spreads his work over more of the year.

In nearly every part of East Africa where there is a long dry season there is a period of anxious waiting before the next harvest (see chapter 8 and Fig. 6).

These two crop-rainfall charts illustrate a method of studying (i.e. discussing and writing about the relationship between crop growth and weather throughout the year).

Rainfall and relief

Relief is another factor that affects the amount of rain that falls. Most of the water vapour in the atmosphere is found in the lower layers. When warm moist air meets higher ground it is forced to rise into regions of lower air pressure. In these regions the water vapour turns to rain.

Most mountains therefore have a higher rainfall than the country surrounding them. This is true of East Africa as a comparison of the rainfall map with a relief map will show. In almost every case the areas of high land such as the Kenya Highlands, Kilimanjaro, the highlands of south-west Tanzania and of western Uganda stand out on rainfall maps as having high totals. There is usually a zone of maximum rainfall above which amounts decrease. That is why the tops of the highest mountains such as Kilimanjaro have less rain than the lower slopes.

The heaviest rain is found on the windward slopes of hills and mountains. Whether the air mass comes from across water or land is therefore important. Very heavy totals are usually received on south and east slopes but in the far west of Uganda the rain falls on western slopes too, because weather systems come from the Congo basin and the South Atlantic Ocean.

On the leeward slopes and the rift valleys below the level of the plateau there is often a dry area or 'rain shadow'. The section across the western Rift

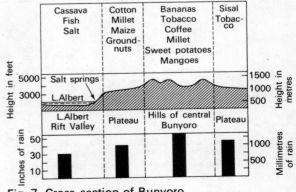

Fig. 7 Cross-section of Bunyoro

9

Valley and Bunyoro (Fig. 7) shows how closely rainfall relates to altitude. The highest rainfall is on the hilly country of central Bunyoro. The lowest is near Lake Albert. Lake Albert is in a rain shadow formed by the hills of Zaire and of Central Bunyoro. About 1 000 mm (40 ins) falls on the plateau between the central hills and the edge of the Rift escarpment, enough to allow the growth of cotton and maize. On the higher hills, there is more rain so coffee and bananas are grown. Hence we have three different ways of life all very close together, and an exchange of products takes place. The fish and salt, the only important products of the dry Rift Valley, are taken up and traded for maize and millet. The cotton-growing people can buy bananas and other goods from their neighbours.

Local rain-makers: mountains and lakes

We now know that mountains make their own weather. They create their own local convergence systems. Highland areas not only receive higher average annual totals than nearby lowland areas, but also a more reliable rainfall.

Because the atmosphere is heated by radiation from the ground, air close to it has higher temperatures than air at some distance above. So, in the diagram (Fig. 8) the surface temperature (Ts) is higher than the free atmosphere temperature (Tf) *at the same level*. The air in contact with the ground becomes less dense and lighter than the free air, and moves up the slope, as a mountain wind which is called *anabatic*. This is why most of East Africa's highest peaks are rarely free of cloud, and why even in months which are generally dry, highland weather stations record showers. In lowland areas

and valleys the cooler, denser, heavier, 'free' air subsides, causing dry conditions.

Land and water breezes

Land and water surfaces are both heated by the sun's rays, but they do not heat or cool at the same rate. The land heats up and cools down about five times more quickly than the water in lakes and seas.

During the day the land becomes warmer than the water. The air is made warmer over the land than over the water. So the air over the land rises, and cooler air from over the water blows in gently to take its place. This gentle movement of air from the water to the land in the daytime is called a water or *sea breeze* (Fig. 9a).

During the night, the land cools more quickly than the water, and so air above the water is warmer and less dense than air above the land. The air over the water rises and the cooler air blows in from the land to take its place. This movement of air from the land to the water at night is called a *land breeze* (Fig. 9b).

On the eastern side of Lake Victoria, both the land breezes and the prevailing wind are from the east, and there are clear skies at night. On the north-west side it is quite different. Fig. 9a shows the situation over the western side of Lake Victoria at night. The prevailing wind is from the east or south-east, across the lake. After the heat of the day the land quickly cools, but the water does not; so a wind flows from the land towards the lake, against the prevailing wind. Thus a small *convergence* is formed, with very heavy rain storms, especially just before dawn.

Much the same 'back-wash' situation develops on the east coast near the islands of Zanzibar and Pemba, with land breezes at night blowing towards the east, to meet the winds from the Indian Ocean blowing towards the west.

Fig. 9b shows what happens on the east side of Lake Victoria during the day.

Although most rain is caused by convergence, rain can occur through other circumstances. For example it also happens at the coast, where the prevailing easterlies are slowed down by friction on crossing the land. The air 'piles up' and is forced to rise, causing some rainfall on the coastal strip.

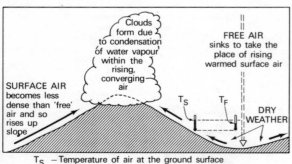

T_S — Temperature of air at the ground surface
T_F — Temperature of 'free' air, some way above ground
— Thermometer

Fig. 8 How montains create clouds

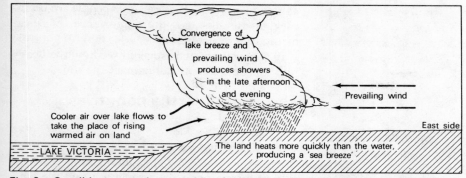

Fig. 9a Conditions over the east side of Lake Victoria during the day (sea breeze)

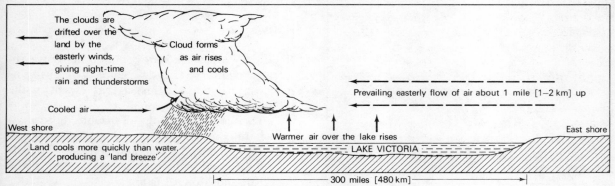

Fig. 9b Conditions over Lake Victoria during the night (land breeze)

Rainfall reliability

So far the main topics of study have been the factors influencing amounts of rainfall and the distribution through the year. Of equal importance for people who gain their living from the land is the reliability of the rainfall. Highland areas not only receive higher average annual totals than lowland areas, but a more reliable rainfall.

If a man plants maize in an area which usually has 762 mm (30 ins) of rainfall, he may reasonably expect a crop. But if the rainfall turns out to be 381 mm (15 ins) that year, or possibly 1 143 mm (45 ins), the crop will either be ruined by drought or washed out by too fierce rains. The following figures illustrate the point that rainfall totals vary considerably from one year to another.

Between the years 1923 and 1947 the average rainfall for Nairobi was 864 mm (34 ins). The highest recorded total during that time was 1 550 mm (61 ins), and the lowest was only 483 mm (19 ins). Similarly the average for Mombasa was 1 194 mm (47 ins), the highest total 1 880 mm (74 ins) and the lowest 889 mm (35 ins). Dodoma,

average yearly rainfall 584 mm (23 ins), has received a maximum of 1 092 mm (43 ins) and minimum of 305 mm (12 ins). Generally speaking the lower the rainfall the less reliable it is.

The parts of East Africa which are most deeply affected are not so much the areas which have the lowest rainfalls, for no one lives there. They are those parts where, in an average year, there is just enough to grow a crop or to provide grass to keep the animals alive. These areas, such as Gogoland and parts of Sukumaland, suffer most from famine. Here the grain store and the reserve cassava crop have real importance. In Gogoland not many years ago half the whole cattle population died as a result of an exceptionally dry year (See also Chapter 8).

Fig. 10 shows East Africa divided into four reliability zones:

1. The dark shaded areas are those in which there is a very good chance of receiving *over* 760 mm (30 ins) each year. Here cultivation can take place without serious danger of the crops being ruined by drought.

2. and 3. The areas with smaller dots have

11

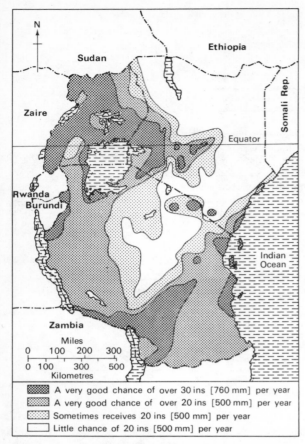

Fig. 10 East Africa: rainfall reliability

The map legend reads:

- A very good chance of over 30 ins [760 mm] per year
- A very good chance of over 20 ins [500 mm] per year
- Sometimes receives 20 ins [500 mm] per year
- Little chance of 20 ins [500 mm] per year

In some parts of East Africa, the people are beginning to understand the importance of these methods of agriculture.

In the next chapter we shall see how the heavy rain of tropical areas can damage the soil.

The rainfall of the countries compared

We can now make a comparison of the countries from the point of view of rainfall and its relationship to farming and the population that the land can support (check back to Fig. 4).

Kenya

Really dry areas are very common in Kenya. In fact, the country has little chance of receiving as much as 500 mm (20 ins) a year except in the following areas:

1. The coast from the Tanzania border to Lamu.
2. The Highlands east and west of the Rift Valley and including the central part of the Rift and Mount Elgon.
3. The Lake Victoria shores. Even here in comparison with Uganda the position is less good as the winds carry more moisture to the north-west shores of the Lake.

The result of this is that Kenya's 11 million population is crowded into a much smaller area than Uganda's and there is little room for expansion. For this and other reasons the densities of population in Kikuyuland are among the highest in East Africa.

The distribution of rain throughout the year is similar to that of Uganda, mostly with two maxima.

Tanzania (mainland)

Tanzania, like Kenya, has large areas of arid country where totals are unlikely to reach 500 mm (20 ins) a year. As in Kenya, the parts at present intensively used are comparatively small in area and are mainly coastal or of fairly high altitude. In addition, however, there are areas of plateau country covered by miombo woodland whose rainfall is fairly reliable and likely to reach 500 mm (20 ins). Much of this miombo area at the moment is uninhabited or very sparsely inhabited for

totals between those of 1 and 4. Most of these areas are capable of growing some crops. They are probably best suited to a mixture of cultivation and animal keeping. In zone 3 the rainfall is less reliable than in zone 2.

4. The area left blank rarely gets as much as 500 mm (20 ins). Much of it receives as little as 250 mm (10 ins) in a year and is almost desert. Generally speaking, this area is unsuited to the growing of crops and is better for pasture where it is usable at all.

About one-third of the surface of East Africa is classed as type 4.

The effect of a very dry season can, in part, be avoided by the use of good farming methods. Careful cultivation can increase the amount of water taken in and retained by the soil. In a drought such farms are often the last to suffer. It is also possible to breed and grow drought-resistant crops.

various reasons. (See chapter 7 and chapter 15.) Although not ideal country for farming, some of it could be put to much better use, as some more recent developments are proving.

In general, the centre of Tanzania and the north-east are very dry except where mountains rise above the general level. Western Tanzania receives some rain from the southern Atlantic.

Except for the coast, the Highlands in the north-east and the Lake Victoria area, practically all of Tanzania has only one period of rain, from about November–December to April.

Zanzibar

The rain of Zanzibar and much of the coast is affected by the monsoon winds of the Indian Ocean. No part of the island is short of rain. *Most* receives over 1 520 mm (60 ins). The heaviest rainfall is found on the *western* side of both Zanzibar and Pemba because of the back-wash effect mentioned earlier.

Uganda

More than half of Uganda has a good prospect of receiving over 760 mm (30 ins) of rainfall each year; and for most of the country the prospect of receiving more than 500 mm (20 ins) is good. The driest areas include the western Rift Valley, near Lakes Albert, George and Edward, the part of Karamoja bordering on the Kenya frontier, some of north Mengo and the Ankole grassland area.

The rainfall of Uganda is unusually high for a country so far from the sea. Lake Victoria and the numerous swamps contribute to the generally high level of rainfall and humidity, and western Uganda is affected by moist air from the Congo basin and the South Atlantic Ocean, as well as by that from the Indian Ocean.

The distribution of rain through the year is of the double maximum type. The two peaks tend to come closer and closer to each other to the north, so that the December–January dry season gets longer. There is also a noticeable difference between the western and the eastern half of the country in the *amount* of rain received in the two peaks. The western half usually receives more rain from August to November and the eastern half from the rains beginning in March.

Thus Uganda, the smallest of the three countries, has a more reliable and better distributed rainfall. Uganda farmers have fewer problems than those who live in some of the less favoured areas of Kenya and Tanzania. This is reflected in the average density of population which is twice that of either Kenya or Tanzania.

General conclusions

The nature and the amount of the rainfall provide East Africa with some of its greatest problems. The present and future use of the land depends very greatly on an understanding of this subject. Tanzania has considerable areas that could be used for agriculture but they will require considerable study and outlay of money. Uganda is even more fortunate in some districts. Kenya has some well-watered land, but is already short of such favoured areas. (See chapter 15.)

Work to do

1. Make sure that you know:
   (a) What is meant by: 10 mm of rain; a rain shadow; reliability of rainfall.
   (b) List those parts of East Africa which have a very good chance of receiving over 760 mm (30 ins) of rain each year.
2. *For your school or home area:*
   (a) Draw a rainfall-cultivation diagram similar to the charts drawn for Rugorogoro Shema and Songea.
   Compare your chart with one of these:
      (i) In the distribution of the rainfall.
      (ii) In the total amount of rainfall. Is your average high or low by comparison with other parts of East Africa?
      (iii) Are your crops similar to or unlike those on the charts in this book? When are they planted and harvested?
      Would you say that from the point of view of rainfall your area is better or worse off than Songea?
   (b) Which of the three factors mentioned on page 6 are most important in controlling the amount of rain in your area? Consider these factors with the help of an atlas relief map.
   (c) Which of the problems connected with

rainfall are found in your area? Write down examples you know of times of unexpected drought, too much rain, etc.

3. Compare the rainfall map on page 7 with:
   (i) A relief map.
   (ii) The map of production for export on page 126.
   (iii) The map of distribution of tsetse flies on page 24.
   (iv) The map of population density on page 164.
   Do these things appear to be related?

4. Which other parts of the world illustrate the following features found in East Africa?
   (1) Relief rainfall.
   (2) Rain shadows.
   (3) Different amounts of rainfall due to differing heights resulting in different types of cultivation.
   (4) A low and unreliable rainfall.
   (5) Monsoons.

5. Cultivation charts in this book are drawn in three different ways:
   (a) Like those in this chapter.
   (b) Like that for Zanzibar–Pemba, Fig. 38 p. 51.
   (c) Like the circular chart (Fig. 59 p. 84) for West Teso.

Make a rainfall-cultivation chart for your school or home area on the patterns of (b) or or (c).

There are many other sets of rainfall figures in later sections of the book, many of them occurring in 'work to do'.

Chapter 3 : Soils and their use

A discussion of rainfall leads easily into a chapter on soils.

Storm rain and soils

Falls of rain are often very violent in tropical areas. The individual drops are large, and the total amount that falls in a short time is high. At Namulonge, near Kampala, a fifteen-minute shower has been recorded during which the rain was falling at the rate of 430 mm (17 ins) to the hour. These violent tropical storms are of very great significance in the agriculture of East Africa.

(i) When a lot of rain falls quickly, the ground soon becomes saturated with water. Once the ground can take up no more, the remainder runs off into rivers, streams or swamps. This water, from the farmer's point of view, is lost.

(ii) Not only is the actual loss of water important but the water in running away can do considerable damage by eroding the soil. When a raindrop hits the earth some of the water and some of the soil splash up. Many buildings have their lower parts discoloured in this way. On a hill this splashing results in soil being carried down the slope. Also raindrops hitting the ground result in a cementing action. This makes it more difficult for the water to sink into the soil. When water does enter it carries with it the finer particles of soil and re-deposits them at a greater depth. After a while, these finer deposits form a barrier to the movement of the water. The water then begins to run off instead of soaking into the ground.

This is the most critical stage of all. If the rain continues to fall, the water begins to flow over the surface of the ground. The greater the amount of the water, the more soil it can carry away with it. Soon, little streams develop which carry away the most fertile top part of the soil and also cut small gullies which are a nuisance in cultivating the fields. The damage does not stop there. The best soils are a mixture of fine and coarse particles. As the water moves it carries away the finer soil particles leaving the coarse.

The soils of East Africa vary very much in the ease with which they can be eroded. There is, however, one general point which can be made. In the highland areas the average slopes tend to be greater than elsewhere. A steep slope helps soil erosion. The highland areas also have the higher and more reliable rainfall of East Africa and are therefore better suited to agriculture. It is just in those areas that soil erosion is likely to be the greatest danger, as a result of steep slopes and a high rainfall.

Water is one of the main agents which make soils what they are. It influences the type of vegetation that will grow and this in turn influences the soil. To a large extent too water affects both the soil-forming and soil-destroying processes. While geological factors are also important, it is becoming clearer that what really decides whether a soil will be productive in East Africa is the amount of water it has in it. Many soils are useless either because they contain too much or too little water.

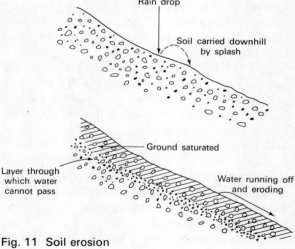

Fig. 11 Soil erosion

Three general statements which are held to be true of tropical soils can be illustrated from East Africa.

1. They tend to lose their fertility fairly rapidly and therefore have to be farmed carefully.
2. They are exposed to climates that can cause them severe damage through soil erosion, even though they are naturally more resistant to erosion than temperate soils.
3. They are less well understood than the soils of temperate latitudes. It is especially true that, although a good deal is known about the soils themselves, very much less is known about the best way of farming them.

Soil fertility

All soils in the world decline in fertility if they are not properly looked after. Soil is not just lifeless dirt. It is a very complicated mixture of rock particles, air, water, humus (a product of decayed vegetable and animal matter) and minute organisms or bacteria. Within the soil these change with depth. The layers produced form what is known as the soil profile. If too many crops are taken off any soil, the delicate natural balance is upset. The soil may then fail to produce crops because of exhaustion. The upset of the balance of the soil may also lead to soil erosion.

The fact that a soil becomes poorer if it is constantly cultivated has long been recognised by farmers in Africa. Methods of cultivation have made allowances for it. For example, in south-east Tanzania the Makonde have maintained the fertility of their soil, which is not naturally very rich, by a kind of thicket rotation. The rotation or changing of crops from year to year is planned as follows:

Year 1. The thicket (very tough, dense and impossible to walk through) is cut down in July and August. In November the cleared bush is burnt. When the rains start in December, a hill type of rice is planted, mixed with maize, sorghum and sometimes cassava.

Year 2. After the crops are harvested, the land is left to grow weeds. Then in December, maize, sorghum and cassava are planted. The rice is left out because even after one cropping the soil has lost some of its richness.

Year 3. Cassava alone is planted, for the now nearly exhausted soil will produce no other crop.

Years 4–10 or 13. The ground is allowed to lie fallow and return to thicket.

Each family clears about 0·6 hectares (1·5 acres) each year, with the help of neighbours, so that 6–8 hectares (15–20 acres) are necessary to keep a family permanently in food.

This is an illustration taken from an area where the soil is not very fertile but to a greater or lesser extent the same sort of land rotation takes place in many parts of East Africa. Even in southern Buganda, where the soil is exceptionally fertile, part of a shamba is usually left uncultivated for a time to allow the soil to rest.

The question of soil fertility is very complex. It is difficult to give an accurate picture for the whole of such a large area as East Africa. Soils change so rapidly that, within a few hundred metres' walk, one may cross four or five completely different types.

The following three factors are important in understanding soil fertility.

1. The rock from which the soil is made

The rock from which the soil is made is called the parent material. The main types of parent material are granitic, volcanic, metamorphic and sedimentary rocks. From these develop many different kinds of soil. Rocks contain within them in varying amounts the chemical substances which plants use for food. Fertility is a measure of the quantity of mineral foods available to plants.

In East Africa the more fertile soils are those formed from volcanic rocks. Lavas contain less quartz (silica oxide) than do other rocks. Granites and sandstones weather into sandy soils because the grains of silica (quartz) are almost indestructible. Silica is not useful as a plant food; rocks with less of it, such as lavas, have larger quantities of other minerals more useful to plants. Mature lava soils are normally more clayey, and it seems likely that they are less easily eroded than the sandy soils in a region.

2. Soil-forming processes

The rock is, however, only the starting point. Much happens to it before it becomes a soil. The rock is attacked, broken up and altered by the agents of weathering. These include the action of rain, micro-organisms and plant roots. The chemical activity of rain water is especially important. In the generally high temperatures the rain water combines with carbon dioxide to form carbonic acid. This acidic rain water dissolves some of the minerals and combines with others as it passes down through the soil. Thus valuable plant foods are carried downwards through the soil and out of the zone where the plant roots can reach them. This process is known as *leaching*. Naturally it results in a soil that is poor because it lacks plant food. In the higher and wetter parts of the highland areas of East Africa, this process is very noticeable.

Too much water can be damaging in another way. Many soil-forming processes are dependent on bacteria to help them along. Most bacteria will not live under water. When a soil is permanently under water, as in a swamp, it tends to become very acid. Even when a swamp is drained, this acidity makes it difficult to grow crops, in spite of the large amount of vegetable and mineral matter in the soil. Fortunately one important East African crop thrives on acid soil. This is tea, which actually requires the soil to be slightly acid in order to do well.

The vegetation also affects the way a soil develops, particularly in supplying humus. Humus is formed from rotted vegetation. Being of vegetable origin, it is an important plant food. A soil rich in humus is therefore frequently a fertile soil. The following simple diagrams show how a change

from natural to cultivated vegetation can greatly reduce the supply of humus.

Fig. 12a shows how natural vegetation takes up minerals and converts them into vegetable matter ⓐ. Eventually plants die and the dead matter slowly decomposes on the ground·surface ⓑ. During this period the dead vegetation protects the soil surface from erosion. As decay continues, minerals are released into the soil to be made use of again. Thus a cycle, known as the nutrient cycle, is established.

Fig. 12b illustrates the way in which the clearing of the natural vegetation and the growing of crops upsets the cycle.

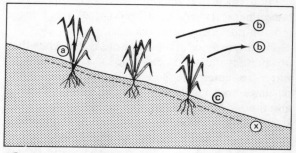

ⓧ = New ground surface

Fig. 12b The nutrient cycle in cultivated crops

As before, the cultivated crop absorbs and converts the minerals present in the soil ⓐ. But instead of being returned to the soil most of the minerals are removed with the crop for consumption ⓑ. Therefore very little goes back to the soil to be available for further crops. Meanwhile there is a real danger that the unprotected soil surface will be eroded ⓒ. If this rapid reduction in soil fertility is not prevented, crop yields decrease rapidly. The Makonde system already described on page 16 illustrates this fact. Obviously new minerals need to be added to the soil in the form of either animal manure or artificial fertiliser.

Humus has other important functions, in that it helps the soil to absorb and store water. Given sufficient time, a constant supply of humus can convert a poor soil into a good one. Age can therefore have a great influence on the fertility of a soil. A very young soil formed from recent rocks such as the lavas of the Bufumbira Mountains is infertile because it has not had time to break down and acquire humus. A very old soil that has been leached for thousands of years is likely to be poor.

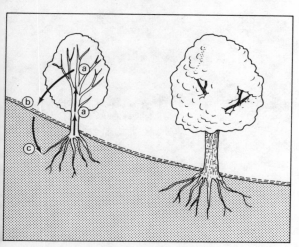

Fig. 12a The nutrient cycle in undisturbed vegetation

17

In fact in this case soil erosion may be a good thing as it exposes new and unleached rock. In the Hera Juu plateau of north-west Tanzania, cultivation takes place on the tops of the ridges because it is there that the soil is being renewed most rapidly.

3. The structure of the soil

Over and above all these other factors in soil fertility there is the question of the structure of the soil. In soils that are in a good condition the individual particles tend to stick together to form little groups known as crumbs. These crumbs are held together by colloids, which are particles so finely divided that they are highly cohesive. Very fine mineral particles can become colloids but the most important source is humus.

The importance of these crumbs is that when they are present the soil is more open. This allows the water to enter the soil easily. Also when the particles hold together in crumbs they are heavier and therefore more difficult to carry away or erode. A soil with a good crumb structure is therefore easier to cultivate; because of its openness it will take in and hold the water it receives, and be less liable to erosion.

Soil erosion

At this point it is possible to understand the way in which soil erosion starts. The beginnings of soil erosion are almost always due to the soil losing its structure, that is, the humus colloids holding the crumbs together are used up and the particles fall apart. Once this happens, the process described on page 15 begins. The individual particles are washed together to form a layer through which the water cannot pass. The water runs off and begins to erode, using the particles it carries as tools.

A soil can lose its structure by various means. A great deal of wetting and drying one after the other can start the process. More important, however, is the fact that it can be caused by human activity. Overcropping and overgrazing can both bring it about.

Overcropping

If a farmer tries to grow the same crop year after year on the same ground, he very quickly exhausts it. This exhaustion brings on the loss of crumb structure mentioned above. The exhaustion leads to two things. First of all the crops grown get smaller and smaller because the plant food available lessens. This means that the protection from the rain given to the ground by the plants becomes less. This, added to the disappearance of the crumbs, helps the process of soil erosion to speed up. Once soil erosion has taken away the better top soil, the plants find it more difficult to grow and the protection becomes less and less.

Overgrazing

The same sort of thing can happen if a piece of land is made to support too many animals. The cattle, sheep or goats eat away so hard at the grass that it has a struggle to keep alive. Sheep and goats are the worst as they eat the grass right back to the ground. Some of the grass dies off and, particularly at the end of a dry season, bare patches appear in

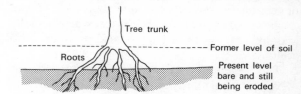

Fig. 13 Soil erosion, Baringo

Typical gulley erosion in the Kondoa district. The gulleys are 4–5 m (13–16 feet) deep.

18

the soil. When rain comes, the bare patches are attacked by erosion and the better top soil is once again removed. Once the top soil has gone, the grass finds it difficult to re-establish itself. The Baringo district in the Rift Valley of Kenya gives excellent examples of this. Large areas of formerly fertile land are now bare and barren. Trees have their roots sticking out of the ground.

Soil erosion is therefore a natural process made worse by man. Many farmers in Africa have not as yet fully understood the danger of soil erosion. In many cases erosion is due to the keeping of too many cattle, because cattle are regarded as the symbol of wealth and importance. In some areas overcropping is due to an increase in population; the land has to be used over and over again without being given a rest. In some areas, ignorance of the fact that fertility can be maintained by changing the crops every year, or adding manure, has helped to bring about damaging erosion.

There are in addition other things which make soil erosion a problem in East Africa. The nature of the rainfall, as described in the previous chapter, plays its part. The steepness of some slopes also is important.

Probably the worst soil erosion in the whole of East Africa is found in the Kondoa district of Tanzania. This will serve as a striking example of the damage that can be done. In passing through the district one sees the hillsides cut by deep gullies. In places the roads are covered with great

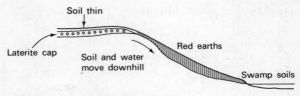

Fig. 15 Soil section, Buganda

patches of sand which have been swept down from the hills during a period of storm. Both the vegetation and the crops are in a poor condition. There is much bare ground.

The gullies are gradually killing the agricultural life of many areas. They are damaging for several reasons. Gullies across the field make cultivation difficult. Where they exist the good soil has gone. In addition the gullies help to lower the water table and the lowering of the water table makes it difficult for short-rooted plants to survive.

Kondoa is useful as a particularly severe example (see Fig. 14). The soil there is not very stable; it erodes easily, the countryside is hilly with fairly steep slopes, and the rain falls with sufficient intensity to do damage without providing the water that would ensure a complete protective vegetation cover. In addition, the density of population is fairly high (31 to the sq km–80 to the sq mile) and the people are very unwilling to be parted from their animals, which they keep in too large numbers.

However, although the evidence of soil erosion may not be as obvious in other parts of East Africa, erosion is nearly always present. Even in Buganda, where the vegetation grows easily and gives good protection, the flat tops of the hills have a much thinner covering of soil than the valleys. Also the tops of the slopes frequently have a less good soil than the bottom where the soil is deeper, where the moisture collects, bringing with it the mineral plant food from higher up.

The control of erosion

The geographer is interested in soil erosion because it affects the wealth of a country. He is concerned with cures for soil erosion for the same reason. Soil-conservation methods are also of interest. They not only preserve the soil from damage: sometimes their use gives a countryside a characteristic appearance. There are several notable examples of this in East Africa.

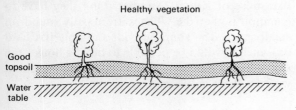

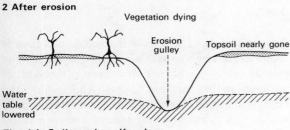

Fig. 14 Soil erosion, Kondoa

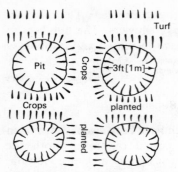

Fig. 16 Soil conservation, Umatengo

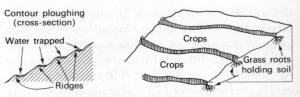

Fig. 17 Soil conservation, Kenya Highlands (left), Poroto and Kigezi (right)

Umatengo

This highland corner of south-east Tanzania has a system of soil conservation which is among the most interesting in the world. It was developed by the Matengo, who had to take refuge in the hills to escape from the raids of the Angoni. They used to hide in caves and it was important that they should be able to cultivate their fields intensively, so as not to have to go too far from their hiding places. On the steep slopes of Umatengo, with a rainfall of 1 520 mm (60 ins), the soil would soon disappear, if there were no anti-erosion measures. Pits are dug about three feet across and the turf is laid in lines across and down the hillside between the pits. The crops are planted on these ridges (Fig. 16). All waste matter is thrown into the pits so that in future years the ground has the benefit of the rotted vegetation. In addition, the pits and the lines of turf across the hillside act as very efficient soil traps.

Mountain areas: Poroto and Kigezi

Similar conditions of heavy rainfall and steep slopes are found in the Poroto Mountains to the north-east of Umatengo and in Kigezi in south-west Uganda. The principle that has been applied is one in very wide use, that cultivation should take place along the contour. Contour ploughing is recommended and used in the Highlands of Kenya. This means that, instead of ploughing up and down hill leaving furrows which help the water run away, the farmer ploughs round the hill keeping each furrow at the same height. Then the little ridges formed by the plough help to stop the water running downhill: each one acts as a small dam (Fig. 17). The Safwa of the Poroto Mountains and the Bakiga of Kigezi do not use the plough but the hoe, so instead of leaving soil ridges they leave a row of elephant grass which catches the soil before it has been swept away (Fig. 17). The important thing is to prevent the water laden with soil increasing in speed and volume. The faster the eroding water flows and the bigger the stream, the more damage is done.

Because this form of cultivation is practised on the hillsides in Kigezi between 1 525 m and 2 440 m (5 000–8 000 ft) and the Poroto Mountains, the areas look rather like a contoured map. In Kigezi the valleys are extremely steep and deep, some of them 610 m (2 000 ft) from top to bottom. As in many parts of Uganda, the valley bottoms are filled with swamp, the edges of which are planted with sweet potatoes. Sorghum, peas and beans are the most important crops on the hillsides on account of the height and cold.

The Poroto Mountains are very similar in appearance but although they also are high (1 830 m, 6 000 ft, and over) and have steep slopes, the valleys are not nearly as large. The crops are like those of Kigezi. Another thing they have in common is that the villages are mostly found on small spurs. The spurs provide the only flat land on which it would be possible to build a house, the slopes being so steep that it is difficult even to walk on them in places.

Summary

Kenya

The area of most serious soil erosion in Kenya is found in the Highlands. This is to be expected. The rainfall is high. Slopes are steep. It therefore requires skilled farming to hold the soil on the land. Until the end of the 1939–45 war the position was not good but now all farmers are more aware of the dangers of erosion.

Increasing population densities are a problem. Maize, a main food crop, is noted for giving little protection to the soil. The greatest expert on soil erosion in Kenya described the problem as one 'which, if solved will make East Africa a happy and prosperous country, but which if neglected or evaded will leave a barren desert in which will skulk a few tattered and starving wretches with their questing goats' (C. Maher). (See also chapter 9.)

Tanzania

Much of Tanzania is unaffected by soil erosion because it is very sparsely inhabited. Where there is a high density of population, there is always a danger that soil erosion will start. This is particularly true when a dense population lives in a hilly countryside. The Kondoa area has already been mentioned. The Mbulu district is a similar hilly area with a large number of animals. The Uluguru and Usambara Mountains also have erosion problems, in the latter area due to overcultivation. Sukumaland has soil erosion problems because of its large population of both people and animals.

Uganda

Uganda, although having a fairly high rainfall, is mainly plateau and therefore suffers less from erosion than either of its neighbours. The rain helps to grow a protective cover of vegetation. In particular the elephant grass which covers much of southern Uganda is an extremely good builder and restorer of soil fertility and structure. The two major mountain areas, Mount Elgon and Kigezi, are also fortunate. The Elgon volcanic soils are rich and they stand up to erosion very well. Kigezi has, for its height, a moderate rainfall, 90 mm (39 ins). This rain fortunately comes in fairly gentle showers and so does comparatively little damage.

The north-east of Uganda is the part most affected by soil erosion. Karamoja is a hilly area with considerable slopes. It is also fairly dry but with sufficient storm rain to do great damage. The people are pastoral and the land is considerably overgrazed. Add to this the fact that the soil naturally erodes easily, and a fairly serious position results. Teso, the neighbouring district, also has a serious erosion problem. The rain falls in exceptionally heavy showers. The numbers of people and cattle have increased very rapidly so that there is overstocking. Cotton, which is the main export crop, is grown extensively but gives the ground little protection.

Work to do

1. Make sure that you know:
   (a) The meaning of the terms soil erosion, fertility, overcropping, overgrazing.
   (b) The names and position of those places where soil erosion is a serious problem in East Africa.
2. For your school or home area:
   (a) Find whether the soil is considered to be rich or poor. Where exactly is the best soil found? Is it on the hill tops, on the slopes or in the valleys?
   (b) Find if there is any evidence of soil erosion, e.g. are there:
      (i) gullies?
      (ii) areas where the ground has been swept bare of soil or vegetation?
      (iii) trees leaning down the slope of a hill?
      (iv) trees whose roots have been laid bare?
   (c) If there is soil erosion, is anything being done about it? What measures does the local agricultural officer recommend to stop it? What will happen if it is not stopped?
3. Compare the areas of severe erosion with the rainfall, relief and population maps.
4. Find out which other parts of the world are affected by soil erosion and why they are affected.

Chapter 4: Temperature and health in tropical countries

All countries in the world that have moved along the path of economic progress have had to deal with the question of the health of their people, their animals and crops. Ill health is one of the most wasteful things in any country. People in poor health cannot work hard. When they become weak from one illness, they pick up other diseases more easily. Also they find it difficult to produce the food that is essential for good health. A chain of events can be started, poor health leading to poor work and on to insufficient food, which in turn leads back to ill health. This forms what is sometimes called a vicious circle.

In many temperate countries it has been possible to break out of the circle. This is partly because the diseases of temperate latitudes have been studied longer and the cures are better known. It is also partly due to the fact that a cold winter tends to keep in check some of the organisms that bring and carry disease. The tropics, lacking a cold season, and especially those parts that do not have a dry period, give no check to the reproduction of the bacteria and insects which do harm to people, their animals and their crops.

In East Africa, as in all parts of the world, temperature decreases with height. This is due to the following facts:

1. The sun does little direct heating. Its rays become heat rays when radiated again from the earth's surface. Heating of *air* is therefore from below rather than above.

2. The heat rays must have something to heat. Near to sea-level the air is compressed by the weight of air above it. At high altitudes it is thin, dry and dust-free. The heat rays are lost without doing much heating. The result is that air is greatly heated near to sea-level and warmed much less at high altitudes. The decrease in temperature that results is about 1°C for every 120 m (1°F per 300 ft) increase in height. This is known as the lapse rate.

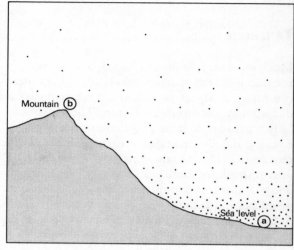

At **a** air molecules are closely packed, and absorb much of the heat radiated from the earth.

At **b** air molecules are relatively scattered, and much of the heat radiated from the earth escapes into space.

Fig. 18 The influence of altitude on the heating of the atmosphere

This has very important consequences. As East Africa is on the Equator, and has considerable mountain areas, it has a wide range of climates. From sea-level to 1 220 m (4 000 ft) the climate is tropical, temperatures averaging nearly 27°C (80°F). From 1 220–1 830 m (4 000 to 6 000 ft) the climate is sub-tropical or warm temperate (temperatures 21°C (70°F) falling to 17°C (62°F)). Above 1 830 m (6 000 ft) the climate is temperate. At about 4 900 m (16 000 ft) the snow line is reached.

Three important modifications must be remembered:

1. In most parts of East Africa the temperature falls during the rainy season or seasons. Clouds help to reflect back the sun's rays, and the rain itself has a cooling effect. Southern Tanzania is an exception to this. It is sufficiently far from the Equator to experi-

ence a very mild winter, when the sun is overhead in the Northern Hemisphere.

2. The humidity is higher near to the coast and around Lake Victoria, thanks to evaporation from the sea and lake surfaces. High humidities have the effect of making high temperatures feel even hotter than they are.

3. At high altitudes the thin, dry, dust-free atmosphere allows a large proportion of the sun's rays to reach the surface of the earth. Although these rays cannot heat the air to high temperatures, they do heat strongly the surface of anything they strike.

Most of East Africa lies below 6 000 ft and therefore shares the health and pest difficulties of all tropical countries. Medical science has had only seventy years in which to study the problems of this part of the world. Thus, although progress is being made, East Africa has a long way to go before it can be satisfied with the health of its inhabitants. Over large areas it is perhaps true to say that it is the insect that has the upper hand and not man. Among the many insects which influence people's lives in East Africa are the mosquito and the tsetse fly. As these are so important, a brief study will be made of those species which are of significance in East Africa. See the detailed study section on page 26.

The mosquito

There are many species of this insect. They are best known as the carriers of yellow-fever and of malaria. Both these diseases have caused a great deal of pain and misery in East Africa. Malaria, in fact, is one of the most deadly killers in the world. Even when it is not fatal, it makes people very ill and unfit for work. It is not found only in the tropics but the parasites inside the mosquito multiply much more rapidly when the temperature is high. In the cooler areas (above 1 520 m, 5 000 ft), malaria is therefore relatively rare.

Below 1 520 m, however, malaria is found almost everywhere where there is water. The climate and relief make it easy for the mosquito to breed. Most of these insects prefer stagnant water. The lack of slope over much of the plateau prevents water from draining away very quickly. Heavy tropical showers leave behind them pools that remain long enough to allow breeding to take place. The leaves

of some plants act as cups in which water can remain and be used in breeding.

Fortunately, most Africans have considerable resistance to the disease in their own areas. Nevertheless, it is probably the largest single cause of ill health. 46 727 cases were dealt with in Tanzania hospitals in 1969. Of these, 768 died. This, of course, does not take into account the many who did not come near a hospital. In East Africa it is the largest killing disease within the infectious group. Even though Africans have resistance to the disease in their own area, they frequently have none to different strains of the disease in another area if they go there to live.

Table 1   Tanzania (Mainland) Malaria Figures

Malaria	1967	1968	1969
Number of hospital deaths from malaria	799	858	768
As per cent of total hospital deaths	8·0%	8·6%	7·4%
Number of admissions to hospital with malaria	48,254	44,242	46,727

Source: Tanzanian Ministry of Health

The tsetse fly

The tsetse fly is an insect rather like a large house-fly, found over much of East Africa. It is the carrier of human sleeping sickness and of a cattle disease, nagana (*trypanosomiasis*). The disease in each case

A hungry tsetse fly, with proboscis plunged into the skin of a human forearm, is pouring infected saliva into the wound.

23

can be fatal and in consequence the tsetse fly is feared over a very large area. Because it kills, the fly has caused great stretches of countryside to be abandoned, some of it very good, fertile land. Its ill-effects, however, do not end there. There are large areas where the fly carries disease deadly to cattle, but not to man. Here it is possible to cultivate the land but cattle cannot be kept. This means that a very important element in the diet is missing, as milk and meat are not available. Furthermore, the absence of cattle is bad for agriculture as the manure useful for keeping the soil fertile is also lost. Thus large numbers of people live in those parts that are free from tsetse. In some cases this leads to overcrowding and over-stocking, resulting in soil erosion.

As in the case of the mosquito, there are many different species of the tsetse fly (whose family name is *Glossina*). There are eight types of tsetse fly found in East Africa. Of these four are of great importance. Each one prefers a definite type of vegetation and climate. Unfortunately, there is a type of tsetse suited to almost all conditions found in East Africa. The only conditions which no tsetse will tolerate are those of cold and drought. Above 1 830 m (6 000 ft) therefore, tsetse is almost unknown. Similarly, there are very few of these flies in those parts of East Africa where the rainfall is below 400 mm (16 ins). But as most of those areas are too dry to be of much use, this is poor comfort. Tanzania is the worst affected of the three countries. About half of its surface is infested. Uganda is also seriously affected. Kenya, because so much of it is dry or high, is comparatively little troubled. See Fig. 19.

The tsetse fly, sleeping sickness and nagana have been very much studied during the past fifty years. The point has been reached where the human disease is being controlled and cured. It is also possible to inject cattle against nagana. But whatever attack is made on the problem, whether by spraying, clearing the vegetation or inoculation, the expense is always great.

Another problem is that only close settlement keeps the cleared land free from fly; yet the number of families needed to do this is sometimes greater than the land can support. Hence the tsetse fly may remain master of large sections of East Africa for some time to come.

A case study in tsetse control

In Uganda much progress has been made in organised tsetse control. The map of south-east Bunyoro (Fig. 20) shows a complicated pattern of group farms, settlement schemes and ranches. The area was cleared of tsetse fly by removing its food supply. This was done by hunting the wild animals on which the tsetse lived and with whom they 'travelled'. By 1955 1 554 sq km (600 sq miles) of Bunyoro had been successfully cleared and were ready to be developed. However, it was easier to clear the flies than to prevent them from returning. The land to the north and west was still infested, and so a way had to be found to keep the tsetse out.

The main method was to clear a belt 5 km (3 miles) wide. In this belt, which is called a consolidation zone or line, the bush environment which the tsetse preferred was removed. In its place, dense settlement by cultivators was encouraged.

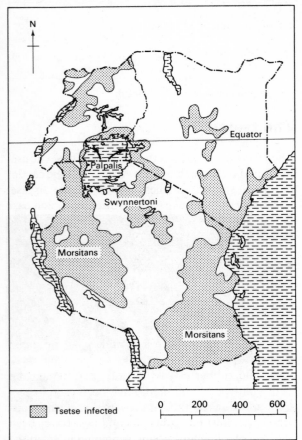

Fig. 19 Distribution of different species of tsetse fly

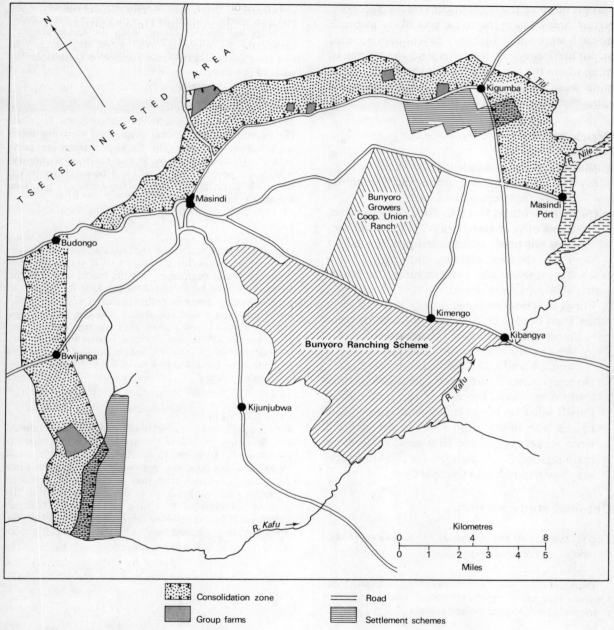

Fig. 20 Tsetse control in south-east Bunyoro

The plan was to bring in more people to make a continuous consolidation barrier which the tsetse fly could not cross. To encourage this movement, two settlement schemes, one at Kigumba and one at Ntoma (not shown), were established. These were not very successful, as the people tended to move away after a time. Eventually in 1964 giant tractors were used to clear the barrier. Since then other settlers from Rwanda and over-populated West Nile have come in. Estates growing sisal, sugar and rubber existed already, and new group farms, shown on the map, have been established.

In addition to this improvement of the consolidation barrier, other techniques have been used. These include, firstly, hunting on a limited scale to reduce the tsetse's food supply and to

25

make it more difficult for them to travel. Secondly, certain areas where the tsetse was likely to break through were sprayed. The sprayers concentrated on the undersides of branches and the trunks of trees, where the tsetse rest during the day. Thirdly, more bush clearing by tractors removed small areas of tsetse infestation.

Work to do

1. Make sure that you know:
   (a) The *equivalent* centigrade and fahrenheit figures for temperatures.
   (b) What is meant by 15°C, 20°C, 25°C, 35°C in terms of your own homes? Is it a cool, hot, very hot time? Is it the temperature felt at 9 a.m., 10 a.m., midday, midnight?
   (c) The rate at which temperature decreases with increasing height.
2. For your school or home area:
   (a) Find out which diseases are the most common and which cause the most deaths.
   (b) Make a list of pests and diseases that attack animals and make it difficult to rear them.
3. No temperature figures for East African weather stations are given here. They can be found in Part Two. Combine rainfall and temperature figures with information given in the text and write an account of the climate of *each* of the main regions. (Page numbers for rainfall figures are shown in italics in the index.)

Detailed study section

The section set in small type is for advanced study. Return to this later if you prefer.

There are eight types of tsetse fly found in East Africa. Of these four are of great importance. Each one prefers a definite type of vegetation and climate.

GLOSSINA MORSITANS
This is the most important of them all. It is at home in the miombo woodland that covers so much of Tanzania. Two great blocks of miombo (see Chap. 7, p. 84) country are found, one in western and one in southern Tanzania. The two blocks are separated by a corridor formed by the Southern Highlands and the dry tongue of land across the centre of the country. *G. morsitans* will not live in the cold above 1 520 m (5 000 ft). It is relatively rare in places with less than 680 mm (27 ins) of rain.

This type of tsetse likes the fairly open conditions of the miombo woods. Shelter from high temperatures is adequate during the wet season when the leaves are out. During the dry season the 9–12 m (30–40 ft) high trees lose their leaves and the tsetse population is considerably reduced in numbers.

GLOSSINA SWYNNERTONI
This tsetse fly has very different requirements. It avoids the miombo woodland and prefers the very dry thorn bush known as *nyika*. The fly feeds mainly on game animals which are plentiful in this more open country-side. Some people argue that it will be necessary to kill off much game in order to free the areas affected from the attacks of the tsetse fly.

GLOSSINA PALPALIS
Glossina palpalis is a tsetse that likes to live near water and in fairly thick forest of trees of a good size. It is therefore found particularly on the banks of rivers and by the shores of lakes, and does much of its damage to people coming down to collect water. The fly is particularly common round the shores of Lake Victoria and the other main lakes. It does little damage to cattle but is the carrier of sleeping sickness. Earlier in the century 200 000 out of the 300 000 inhabitants of the part of Uganda near Lake Victoria were killed by an epidemic of sleeping sickness.

GLOSSINA PALLIDIPES
Glossina pallidipes can inhabit almost any type of country. The fly is not particularly dangerous to man but is exceptionally so to cattle. Even when it is present in small numbers it can do a vast amount of damage. The most annoying fact about it is that one may clear an area completely of another kind of fly only to find that the methods of clearing have had no effect on *Glossina pallidipes*. It just takes over the country from which the other has been removed.

Chapter 5: Relief and communications

The first few chapters have discussed the physical factors that influence the growing of crops and the health of the people in East Africa. The farmer's problems do not end there. He can only sell his goods if there is a demand for them, and his crops must be taken to market. The profit the farmer receives will depend largely on how much marketing costs. The higher the cost of taking and selling the goods, the less profit there is for him.

The cost of marketing depends on two groups of factors:

1. *The physical.* This includes distance, and relief features such as mountains, escarpments and swamps. All these affect the cost of building and running transport (lines of communication).
2. *The economic.* This covers organisation and labour costs, and the type of transport used, whether water, rail, road or air. In addition it deals with such questions as the amount of goods available for transport. No system of transport can pay if there are few things to be carried.

These affect each other but for the sake of simplicity each will be dealt with separately. It should also be remembered that although relief is linked with communications in this chapter, it has an important part to play in other kinds of development. Geological 'accidents' such as faulting and volcanic activity have modified the relief. Land has been raised to sufficient height to create the mountain climates suitable for a wide variety of crops. Later chapters illustrate this. On the other hand, the thick layers of volcanic rock make it impossible to prospect for minerals in the ancient rocks they cover, called the basement complex.

1. Physical factors

East Africa is a very large and varied area. Some of its rocks are over 500 million years old. Others are more recent volcanic rocks and newly formed corals and sedimentaries. Its highest mountain, Kilimanjaro, rises from little more than 600 m (1 974 ft) at its base, to over 5 800 m (19 027 ft).

The following types of relief are found.

The plateaus

East Africa is essentially a land of plateaus but there is still great variety. One of the commonest levels is about 915 m (3 000 ft), but some plateaus are found at 1 530 m (5 000 ft, or at 2 440 m (8 000 ft), and some as low as 183 m 600 ft). In some cases, the plateaus are very extensive. In many, however, rivers have cut down into the surface, leaving the general level flat to the eye but really much broken by valleys. Parts of the plateaus show a definite slope in one direction, the result of tilting.

The history of the development of the plateaus goes back hundreds of millions of years. They are largely formed of very ancient rocks referred to as the Basement Complex, because of their location below all other rocks in East Africa; and because they have been greatly complicated by folding, faulting and given changed form, which we call

A group of inselbergs standing on a peneplain in Karamoja, Uganda. The level of the earth's surface must originally have been higher than the tallest inselberg.

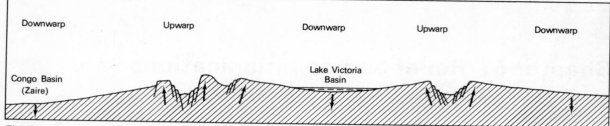

Fig. 21 Section showing the gentle warping of the earth's crust across central Africa

metamorphism. These rocks have been lifted up and worn down many times in a succession of erosion cycles. The result in places has been to leave a series of steps, each step representing the point at which one period of erosion stopped. These levels often appear to be almost flat and have been given the name *peneplain*, meaning 'almost a plain'. The photograph on page 27 shows such a peneplain in north east Uganda. Notice that isolated hills rise above the general plateau or peneplain surface. These residual hills are left isolated, as agents of erosion gradually remove the rock around them. Another name for the hills is *inselberg*, after the German words for 'island-mountain'. They are a common feature of the plateaus of East Africa.

To summarise, the plateaus present certain problems to the builder of roads and railways. The different levels are often separated by steep slopes which make road or rail building difficult. The flatness of the plateau surface might seem an advantage but it also means that in places the rivers become lost in swamps. These are expensive to fill in and even then make bad roads.

The depressions in the plateaus are formed in three main ways: by warping and faulting on a large scale, and by river erosion, usually on a small scale.

Warping and faulting: the rift-valleys

Across Africa in equatorial latitudes, the earth's crust has been gently bent, or warped.

When rocks are as old as the rocks of the plateaus of East Africa, they have usually become hard or brittle as a result of compression. If they are further compressed or pulled apart, they do not bend as younger and softer rocks do, but fracture to relieve the strain. These fractures are called faults. Often faulting produces movement,

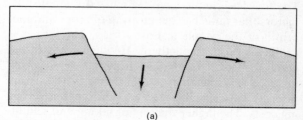

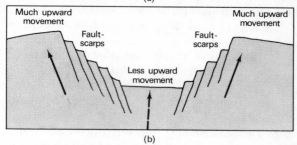

Fig. 22a, b Two possible theories to explain the formation of the Rift Valley

with the land rising on one side and subsiding on the other. The diagram (Fig. 21) shows how the two great depressions, the East and West Rift Valleys, have developed between sets of parallel faults on the crests of two up-warps. So the origin of these rifts is probably *not* simply that the middle part sank while the sides rose as is seen in Fig. 22a but rather that the whole area rose, with the middle section rising more slowly and lagging behind as in Fig. 22b.

The faulting which has produced the rifts is very complicated, with hundreds of faults, often occurring in parallel groups as steps. An example of this can be seen a few miles north-west of Nairobi. (Fig. 23). Probably the Rift Valleys have been moving for thousands of years and are still moving slightly. The earthquakes that are felt from time to time in areas near to the Rift Valleys are proof of this instability.

We now know that there are volcanic mountain ranges rising from the beds of the oceans (Fig. 24).

28

One of the steps on the side of the Rift Valley. The scale is indicated by the village in the centre. Beyond it to the right is a steep scarp, and to the left is the floor of the valley.

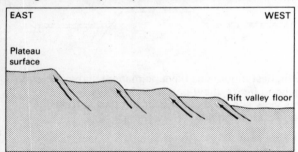

Fig. 23 Step faulting west of Nairobi

They form mid-oceanic ridges which run the entire length, and contain rift valleys in their crests. One of these under the Indian Ocean links up with the rift valley of the Red Sea, and is probably connected with the East African rift system. Many scientists think that the submarine rifts may mark the points from which the continents have drifted apart, so that the existence of a similar rift on land presents an interesting problem. There is evidence that the Arabian Peninsula has swung away from north-east Africa. It may be the East African Rifts are at an early stage in the break-up of continental blocks.

Whatever the full story, rifting has had a marked effect on the communications of East Africa. The change in level along the line of the faults results in an *escarpment*. Some of the largest fault-escarpments in the world are found in eastern Africa. The

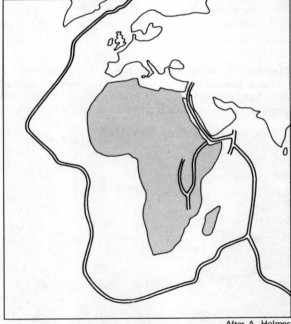

After A. Holmes

Fig. 24 The East African Rift Valley and mid-ocean ridges

size of the escarpments varies from a drop of about 1 220 m (4 000 ft) in Kenya to a step of a few metres in Tanzania. Contact with the Congo in the west has been hindered by the barrier of the western Rift, running from Lake Tanganyika to Lake Albert.

29

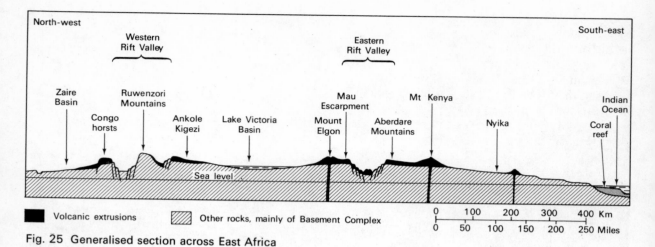

Fig. 25 Generalised section across East Africa

Fig. 26 Theories of block mountain formation

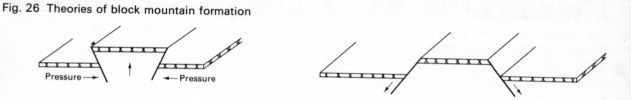

Glaciated landscapes in East Africa. Only the crests of the highest mountains have permanent snow, ice and glaciers. Glacial features include high-level lakes (tarns), jagged freeze-thaw peaks, and valleys whose 'V' form has been worn by ice to a 'U' shape, shown here. This view shows some Ruwenzori peaks. Note the giant groundsel plants in the foreground and the screes on the left hand side of the valley.

The highlands

The Highlands of East Africa are very closely linked with the rift valleys. If the section (Fig. 25) is studied, it will be realised that almost all of the highest parts of Kenya, Uganda and Tanzania are on or near the main areas where faulting has taken place.

There are two reasons for this:

1. Block mountains

In some places block mountains have been formed. They are really rift valleys in reverse, and are probably formed when a block of land is forced to rise above the land on either side. The best example in East Africa is the Ruwenzori Range (which is also warped and tilted) on the Congo–Uganda border. As in the case of the rift valleys, it is not certain precisely what kind of movement took place.

The Usambaras were formed in a similar way, and a cross-section through them near Lushoto (Fig. 27b) shows how the block stands up high above the surrounding plateau.

2. Volcanic mountains and other volcanic features

Much of eastern Africa has been overlain by vast outpourings of lava erupted during the volcanic activity which accompanied rift valley formation. Rifting probably began about 30 million years ago. But a period of intense faulting and extrusion which occurred about one million years ago has been responsible for many important landscape features today. Fig. 28 shows the extent to which lava flowed out to either side of the eastern Rift, covering the ancient rocks of the highly altered Basement Complex. In addition to widespread lava flows of great thickness, there are a very large number of cones and other types of volcanic land form. In western Uganda, activity has produced lava flows, conical mountains and explosion craters, some of which are linked with more widespread activity in eastern Zaire and Rwanda.

The products of vulcanicity may be loosely grouped into liquids, solids and gases. The first two have formed the more obvious landscape features; but gaseous products are occasionally seen as crystals crusted on to other rocks.

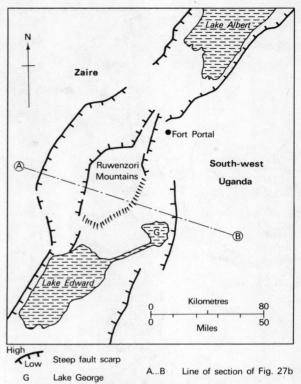

High / Low   Steep fault scarp
G   Lake George   A...B   Line of section of Fig. 27b

Fig. 27a Sketch-map of the Ruwenzori mountains

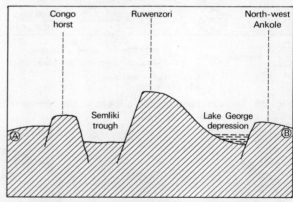

Fig. 27b Cross-section through the Ruwenzori mountains from A to B on Fig. 27a

Detailed study section

The section set in small type is for advanced study. Return to this later if you prefer.

Examples of volcanic relief forms taken from a small area. To the north-west of Nairobi an area bounded by the Rift Valley (Fig. 30) contains examples of all three types of product, and close study reveals many interesting landscape features within a relatively small area.

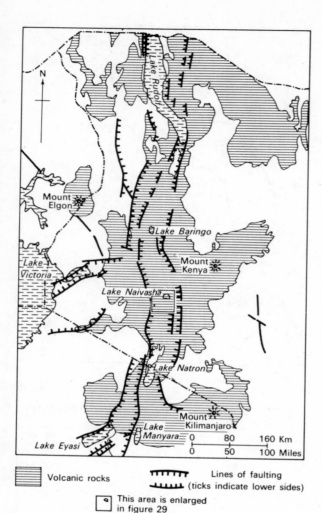

Fig. 28 **The extent of volcanic rocks in the region of the eastern Rift Valley**

Volcanic rocks

Lines of faulting
(ticks indicate lower sides)

☐ This area is enlarged in figure 29

This area is dominated by the volcanic cone of Mount Longonot, which rises from the Rift floor (about 2 070 m (6 800 ft) to a peak 2 777 m (9 110 ft) above sea level on the west side of its rim. The photograph, taken looking west from near the top of the Rift Valley eastern escarpment, shows its main features. The summit of the present volcano is a *caldera*, that is, a deep, steep-sided depression probably caused by the subsidence of much of the cone.

Longonot is a *composite cone*, consisting of alternate layers of ash (volcanic dust) and lava. In the cross-section the caldera is seen to be 366 m (1 200 ft) deep, the inner edges dropping almost vertically from 2 777 m (9 110 ft) to 2 408 m (7 900 ft) above sea level. Fig. 29 shows the shape. The floor of the caldera is about 1·2 km (¾ mile) wide, and is covered with thick bush, in which buffaloes are said to roam. On the inner wall of the caldera, steam jets show that like many others in East Africa this volcano is dormant rather than extinct. Indeed, there is so little vegetation on a circular lava flow erupted from the northern side of Longonot, that activity must have been very recent. Local tradition dates this flow as less than a century old, and at the rate at which plants take root on lava flows it cannot have existed for much longer than this. Some lava flows in Kivu (Zaire) are well colonized after 50 years.

Older lava flows extending on the eastern and southern sides give the volcano a stepped profile, with the surface

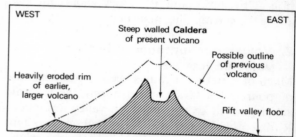

Fig. 29 **Section through Mount Longonot**

Mt Longonot, showing volcanic features, (e.g. lava flows) and erosion gulleys

32

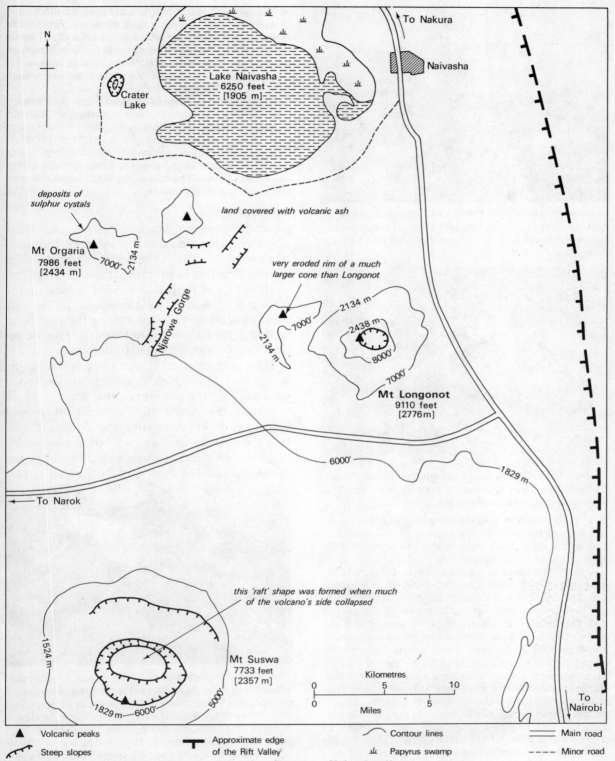

N

To Nakura

Naivasha

Lake Naivasha
6250 feet
[1905 m]

Crater Lake

deposits of sulphur cystals

land covered with volcanic ash

Mt Orgaria
7986 feet
[2434 m]

7000'

2134 m

very eroded rim of a much larger cone than Longonot

Njorowa Gorge

2134 m

2134 m

7000'

2438 m

8000'

7000'

Mt Longonot
9110 feet
[2776m]

6000'

1829 m

To Narok

this 'raft' shape was formed when much of the volcano's side collapsed

1524 m

Mt Suswa
7733 feet
[2357 m]

1829 m   6000'

5000'

Kilometres

0   5   10

0   5

Miles

To Nairobi

▲ Volcanic peaks

Steep slopes

Approximate edge of the Rift Valley

Contour lines

Papyrus swamp

Main road

Minor road

Fig. 30 Some volcanic features on the Rift valley floor near Naivasha, Kenya.

33

View northwards from the rim of Longonot caldera, looking over the subsidiary ash-cone to the recent lava flow which has spread out over the Rift Valley floor.

An injected block thrown from Mt Longonot. It has been broken open to show its crystalline centre. The keys give an approximate scale.

of an individual flow forming the gently inclined 'tread', and its front marking the farthest limit of that particular flow with a steep 'rise', inclined at up to about 35°, the angle of rest of this particular lava.

A fairly late stage in the evolution of Longonot was the building of a small subsidiary cone on its northern side. This conelet has maintained an almost circular crater and both inward and outward facing slopes are steeper than the main cone. On the slope between it and the caldera rim there are a large number of *volcanic bombs*. These *pyroclastics* (a word which means literally 'fire rocks') are more accurately described as 'ejected blocks', since they were already solid when ejected. They should not be confused with a true volcanic bomb which is the result of a mass of liquid lava solidifying as it spins through the air. These ejected blocks are 5–46 cm (2–18 ins) in diameter, and many of them have large numbers of crystals within their baked exteriors.

The highest point of the caldera is composed of ash and pumice, which is like a volcanic glass but so full of gas

bubbles as to be completely different from the other form of volcanic glass, a rock called obsidian. The present mountain rises from the wreck of an earlier, still larger volcano. Low, much eroded remnants of it still exist on the south-west and west sides. Therefore this cone within a volcano resembles that of Meru mountain in northern Tanzania and Vesuvius in Italy.

Pyroclastics in the form of ashes and agglomerates were poured out by both Longonot and its predecessor. This has resulted in vast accumulations especially on the western side, where deposits have formed the 3 050 m (10 000 ft) high Mau Escarpment, composed almost entirely of this type of material. Similar deposits cover the Rift Valley floor, many of which have been deposited under sedimentary conditions in lake waters.

Longonot

Although Longonot lies within a fairly dry zone which probably receives only 635 mm (25 ins) of rain a year, erosion by running water on the sides of this area has been considerable. The gulleys so carved form a distinctive radial pattern on the mountain. Storm water can erode the loosely consolidated ashes rapidly. During the 1961 flood in Kenya the motorable track to the base of the mountain became a 9 m (30 ft) deep gulley!

The construction of Mount Longonot by layers of ash and lava which flowed slowly and soon solidified is very similar to the activity which produced the much greater cones of Mount Kilimanjaro, Mount Kenya and Mount Elgon. However, where the lava was of a type which flowed easily, it spread a long way, and a large part of the highlands of East Africa is formed of lava

The heavily glaciated neck of Mt Kenya. Erosion and weathering have been so severe that the shape of the volcano top is much more the result of glaciation and freeze-thaw than of its volcanic origin. Notice the two small glaciers still present; the areas of paler rock recently de-glaciated; arêtes and pyramidal peaks; and the very jagged nature of the peaks, due to freeze-thaw weathering.

An aerial view of Mt Mawenzi, with Kibo (Kilimanjaro) about 12 km (7 miles) beyond it to the right. Mt Meru is in the background.

flows. These built up a succession of beds of lava, forming and cooling on top of one another. The most impressive example of this is the Aberdare Mountains, which rise to over 3 950 m (13 000 ft).

Volcanic activity in East Africa has produced other interesting relief features. In some places, especially parts of Western Uganda, it took the form of explosions of gas, which drilled through the earth's crust producing small explosion craters. These are very numerous on the edge of the western Rift, and in its floor, within the boundary of the Queen Elizabeth National Park.

They are each several hundred yards wide, circular, and some enclose lakes. Their existence adds greatly to the scenic attraction of the park.

All these highland areas have certain things in common, however they were formed. Because of their height, their climate differs from that of the plateaus. Temperatures are lower and the highest mountains (over 4 850 m, 16 000 ft) have ice caps. Most of them also have a high rainfall. The high rainfall produces rivers which have cut deep valleys into the mountain sides. These valleys often have steep slopes and the rivers are costly and hard to bridge. The rapid erosion on steep hillsides with a high rainfall makes the roads and railways expensive to build and maintain in good condition. This is unfortunate as the higher lands are among the most valuable parts of East Africa.

Bismarck Rock, a famous tor in Lake Victoria, near Mwanza. Chemical weathering has acted mainly along joints in the granite to produce this rounded effect typical of tors.

Lakes

Lakes have played an important part in the pattern of East Africa's communications, and it is worthwhile considering the main ways in which they have been formed. Most lakes here are the result of either earth movements or volcanic, glacial and coastal processes. The first agency, described as *tectonic*, has formed most of East Africa's lakes.

35

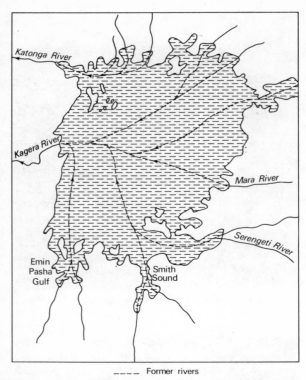

Fig. 31 Lake Victoria, showing the pattern of rivers before the lake basin was formed

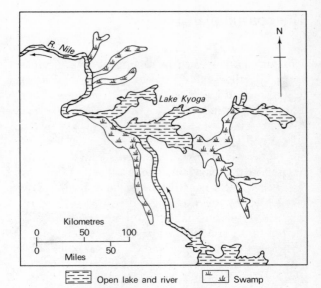

Open lake and river   Swamp

Fig. 32 Lake Kioga and adjacent swamps

Two main types have resulted from these movements. Firstly, there are those formed within the 'parallel' faults of the Rift Valleys. There is a considerable number, in both east and west branches, some extremely shallow, like Lakes Nakuru and Naivasha, while others are very deep, as for example, Lake Tanganyika (655 m, 2 150 ft below sea level).

The second group of lakes results from the warping of the ancient plateau rocks. Lake Victoria (Fig. 31) and Lake Kioga (Fig. 32) were both formed by the warping and tilting of the land. The lower reaches of some river valleys have been raised, so that they flooded, and the direction of the rivers changed. A classic example is the Kagera river. It probably flowed westward to join the headwaters of the river Zaire. Warping has caused it to flow back the other way and it now feeds Lake Victoria.

The river valleys

Rivers and coastal creeks have to be bridged. Some are still crossed by ferries. Many of the rivers vary very much in size with the seasons. Long bridges have to be built so that they will not be carried away in time of flood. In Tanzania, movement by road in the wet season is often interrupted by the washing away of bridges.

A cylindrical pothole drilled out in the wet-season bed of a river near Kapsabet, Kenya. The dry-season river is visible flowing behind and below the level of the pothole. (The paperback book is included to give an approximate scale.)

36

The coastal plain

This forms a very narrow section of land in most cases. Together with the part of the plateau nearest to the coast, it has had a geological history rather different from most of East Africa. While it was covered by the sea, sedimentary rocks were deposited. The whole area was then pushed up out of the water. Recently it has become partly covered by the sea again. The result is that some of the river valleys near the coast have been partly submerged by the sea. These drowned valleys, or rias, are very useful as they form natural harbours such as those of Mombasa and Dar-es-Salaam.

Between the open sea and the green palms and mangroves that fringe the coast there is a line of white where waves break against the edge of the coral reef. Coral reefs are built by small organisms called 'polyps' that live in shallow, warm, clear tropical waters, building the sea bed up towards the surface. Hence the shallow water is a danger to shipping. These fringing reefs are found especially on the east of the great continents where water temperatures average 21°C (70°F). The reefs bar the way inland for all but small craft.

If, however, the water is muddy because it is full of silt brought down by rivers, the coral polyp cannot live, and the reef does not grow. Thus where a river flows into the sea there is a break in the reef and larger craft can sail inland and find safe harbour. When a great harbour has been needed it has usually been possible to find a good site, for example, Mombasa. Although it owes its importance to the drowning of river valleys (or submergence) Mombasa island and the nearby mainland has also undergone recent uplift, or emergence. This uplift has resulted in raised beaches and a coral platform which can be easily identified. The low cliffs which border them persist for hundreds of miles along the east coast. Coral forms a rock which is eroded by the sea in much the same way as other rocks. This means that small cliffs are produced by undercutting, and caves develop which may later become archways. A further stage is the collapse of the arch to form a stack. Wherever coral now stands above sea level along the East African coast these features may be found. The photograph on this page shows some of these features on Mombasa Island.

Coastal erosion on the coral rocks of Mombasa Island has undercut a small cliff 4 m (13 feet) high. Continued undercutting and collapse of the cliff has led to the formation of a wave-cut platform which is exposed at low tide.

2. Economic factors

In general, the relief of East Africa has been a hindrance to the easy development of communications. Movement within both Kenya and Tanzania has been made more difficult by the huge eastern Rift Valley system crossing both countries. There is no doubt that both rail and road transport have been put to a great deal of trouble, expense, and engineering problems in the cutting of gentle slopes (gradients) along the sides of the escarpments. But higher land is often well populated and productive, and communications are needed. Everywhere distances are great, and it is not difficult to understand why roads and railways have been slow to reach many parts of East Africa.

The story of transport is not only a matter of understanding relief, important as this subject is. A system of communications must carry something in order to pay. Without roads or railways little can be exported. Without exports, however, there is not the money with which to build the roads or railway. During the first half of this century East Africa was in this economic vicious circle. In many cases, the building of the road or railway was carried through in a spirit of hope. Lately, however, foreign aid programmes have assisted in the breaking of the circle, usually by lending funds and supplying experienced manpower for construction. New lines have been laid down to reach areas of dense population such as West Nile. Since the mid-1960s there has been a direct connection between

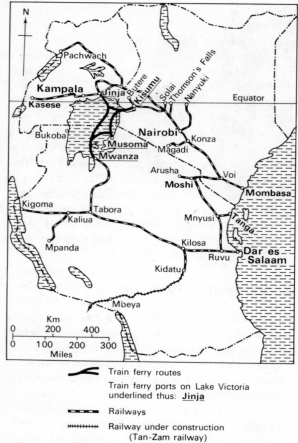

Key:

<u>⌐</u> Train ferry routes

Train ferry ports on Lake Victoria
underlined thus: <u>Jinja</u>

━■━■━ Railways

╫╫╫╫╫ Railway under construction
(Tan-Zam railway)

Fig. 33 Railways and train ferry routes

the Central Line of Tanzania and the Kenya-Uganda network along the Ruvu-Mnyusi branch (see Fig. 33). Now there is the exciting prospect of a railway extension from the Central Line to the Zambian border (see Fig. 33). This will open up a vast area, remote but known to be productive.

It is sad to have to record that some railways (e.g. the line to Mtwara) have not paid, and are no longer used.

The type of transport used

Some forms of transport are cheaper to run than others. Railways require a very expensive outlay at their beginning. Track, rolling stock, stations and signals all need to be provided and maintained in good order. The main advantage is that large quantities of goods can be moved at the same time, and relatively quickly. The initial expense on roads

depends on their quality. They can be progressively improved up to tarmac standard. Road vehicles can join and leave the main routes at many places, and every factory, farm or estate has its own road. The railway cannot compete with this flexibility, but does provide suitable transport for bulky goods such as coffee, cotton and tea. Therefore, probably the best system is one which involves many roads acting as 'feeders' to the main railway line. In this way small quantities of agricultural and industrial produce may be quickly brought to the railway station for onward despatch to the coastal ports or other places.

In the past, time and effort have been spent unloading from one vehicle to another, resulting in increased costs and some delay. Now a revolution in cargo handling is being brought about by the use of containers. *Containerisation* involves the use of large rectangular metal boxes. They are about 16 cubic metres in size, or 4 m long by 2 m wide by 2 m high (13 ft × 6·6 ft × 6·6 ft). They are filled with goods and sealed at the factory. Hooks are fitted on top of the containers so that they can be quickly transferred from a lorry to a railway wagon and from there directly into a ship's hold. This greatly speeds up and reduces the cost of the movement of goods, avoids the need to use costly packing materials and reduces the risk of damage and theft during transport.

Natural water communications have the advantage that only the boats and jetties need to be maintained. For this reason water transport is favoured even though it is the slowest of all forms. Unfortunately, it is only the lakes of East Africa which can profitably be used. Navigable canals are largely out of the question due to the expense in construction and maintenance, and also because the relief is so varied.

Air transport is extremely expensive but has the advantage that it is quick, and can often operate when roads and railways are out of action.

Railways
A study of railways is placed first because they provided the earliest means of opening the interior to economic development.

From Mombasa to Kasese
This railway line illustrates well the difficulties of rail construction and operation in East Africa. The

line was built in 1902 to Kisumu partly to stop the slave trade and to serve the Lake Victoria shore lands. It was extended to Kampala by 1910 and to Kasese by 1913. The original grant of £5 500 000 was never paid back. It was only after twenty-five years that the railway had sufficient income to pay its way.

Operation costs are high.

1. There is an absence of fuel in East Africa, and engines are now oil-fired. All fuel oil has to be imported from overseas.
2. A small pay-load: long stretches of line can earn very little. Between Mombasa and Nairobi, the country is dry and largely unproductive apart from the Teita Hills.
3. Once the highland area is reached, the slopes make operation and maintenance expensive. The two great walls of the Rift Valley also made construction difficult and expensive. Similar problems are met with in the highlands west of the Rift Valley. The railway reaches points higher than any other railway in the Commonwealth (Timboroa 2 743 m, 9 000 ft, Mau Summit 2 536 m, 8 321 ft).

The Central Line of Tanzania

Although relief problems are less serious, the line has found it very difficult to attract paying loads. Vast areas of the plateau have so far produced little of sufficient bulk and weight to justify a railway line. Reference to the Tan-Zam railway is made in chapter 13.

There is a fundamental difference between rail and road transport in East Africa which has led to the East African Railways suffering unavoidable loss of income. The East African Railways Corporation is legally described as 'a common carrier'. The main effect of this is that they are required by law to carry different classes of goods at different rates. This *differential tariff*, as it is called, means that the railways can charge high rates on luxury items. But many commodities, including the primary agricultural and industrial exports *must* be carried at rates so low that they are unprofitable. This was a very good scheme in the period when road competition was nonexistent. It used the profits made on the high-priced goods to subsidise the development of agriculture and industry in East Africa. Indeed it has been said that the railway was a chosen instrument of development. However, many high-tariff goods are now being carried by road, so that the railway can no longer make a profit on these.

In spite of all the difficulties outlined, the East African Railways Corporation is a vast industrial organisation. It is the biggest railway corporation in Africa, being described as a government within a government, and employs 43 000 men.

It is not easy to see what the future holds for the railways. If they are to compete successfully with road transport they will have to be freed from the responsibility of being a 'common carrier'. Two railway lines have already been dismantled because they could not pay their way.

Cattle being loaded at a Central Line station for the journey to a meat factory at Dar es Salaam.

Road construction near Kampala. Note the heavy earth-moving equipment (in this case a scraper)

Roads

For most of East Africa the future undoubtedly lies with road transport. Rail construction requires too much initial expenditure. To make it worth while running a train service there must be hundreds of tonnes of goods to carry all the year round. A lorry, however, pays with only a small load. It is also much more flexible. It can run from door to door, and can change its route as the need arises.

The improvement of roads is one of the main aims of the East African governments. Until recently there were only a few hundred kilometres of road surfaced with bitumen, or tarmac. Now there are nearly 6 400 km (4 000 miles), and many others have been upgraded to 'all-weather' standard. These are surfaced with gravel, or murram, which is a red earth containing lumps of ironstone, or laterite, hard enough to give a firm surface. Elsewhere, however, roads are not good, and a period of rain turns them into slippery bogs in which it is easy to skid or stick. Much depends on the type of material available for road-making, but everywhere the roads which do not have tarmac become rutted and, when dry, make driving slow and exhausting and shorten the life of any vehicle. Expensive grading equipment has to be maintained to smooth out these corrugations.

Since East Africa's economy is overwhelmingly agricultural, much attention is being given to secondary roads. These are interwoven throughout the land, linking individual farms with processing plants and main routes. They have rightly been called 'feeder roads', since they feed both farms and factories and also the main arterial roads and railways. As 'Work for Progress', Uganda's Second Five-Year Plan stated, 'Each has a definite purpose, for example to promote tea development, to assist coffee processing and marketing, to open up potential cotton areas, to help marketing of food crops, to improve access to fish landings'. Milk must be taken to the creamery immediately; tea must be processed the same day it is plucked. This gives a sense of urgency to the transport of produce, and has led to much improvement in the standard of such roads. Roads are expensive to keep in good repair. However, it is also realised that this is as necessary as the maintenance of factory machinery in working order.

A first class road system is a matter of time and means more production and more money for road

The *Bonanza* bringing cattle from Lamu in the north to the K.M.C. meat factory at Mombasa.

building; bad roads discourage economic development and so also the means by which better roads could be built. This vicious circle has been broken by the injection of capital for road works. This will bring about increased efficiency in the production, processing and marketing of basic commodities.

Water transport

Within the boundaries of East Africa the only important waterways are those provided by the lakes. In the case of the Rift Valley lakes, Tanganyika and Nyasa, a steamer service plies regularly but the countryside surrounding the lakes is not sufficiently wealthy to make it worth running more than a limited service.

The case of Lake Victoria is rather different because the lake is really a feeder to the railways. The steamers pick up goods in areas such as Bukoba and Bukakata where there is no railway. The northern and western shores are very productive although there has always been considerable competition from the railways from Kampala eastwards and from Mwanza to the south.

In 1961 the MV Victoria, at that time the largest vessel ever built for service on an inland lake, entered service on Lake Victoria. She provides modern passenger accommodation and can also carry motor vehicles and refrigerated cargo. In 1966 an important step was taken when two new vessels, the MV Umoja, and MV Uhuru, began a wagon ferry service (see photograph opposite). This physically connected the Kenya/Uganda railways with the Central Line in Tanzania. It enabled goods loaded in wagons in Kenya and Uganda to move to Mwanza without trans-shipment and in the shortest possible time.

Specially designed terminals had to be built for

The wagon-ferry terminal at Jinja. An engine is shunting its wagons on to the specially constructed ship for the journey southwards

the ferries, so that the wagons could move directly off the railway and on to the ship. These consist of locks which hold the ship rigid during loading and a connecting bridge which automatically adjusts itself to the varying levels of the ship's deck, and over which the wagons roll on and off the ship. There is a minimum of delay, and a ship can dock and be fully loaded and unloaded in one hour, ready to sail again. Terminals have now been built at Kisumu, Mwanza, Musoma and Jinja, the four principal ports on the lake. Later others may be added.

The two ferries and the terminals cost more than £2 million. The spending of such a large sum clearly indicates the importance attached to Lake Victoria as a routeway across which trade can flow from region to region.

In East Africa transport by river is limited. The Nile has been the only river of major importance, being used for parts of its course from Lake Albert down to the Sudan and between Namasagali and Atura Ferry. Any further use was prevented by the Murchison Falls and the Owen Falls Dam. Now the northern Uganda extension railway to Pachach has replaced the steamer service which for fifty years had moved cotton and other cargoes out of West Nile. All the other rivers are either too

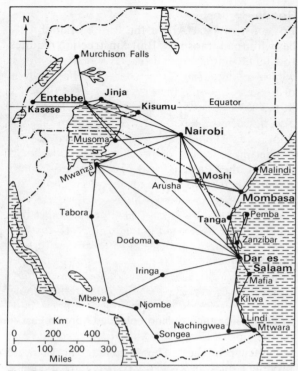

Fig. 34 East African internal air routes

small or suffer such serious changes in level that they are not suitable for navigation.

Air

In East Africa there are at present only four fully equipped international airports, at Nairobi, Dar es Salaam, Entebbe and Mombasa. These have become very important passenger terminals, especially with the development of charter services for tourists. As a direct result of the great increase in tourism in northern Tanzania, Arusha also is soon to have an international airport.

The internal system of air services is very important. East African Airways have regular flights linking many of the smaller towns with the capital cities and each other (Fig. 34). Also, a number of companies have light planes available for charter. There are dozens of landing strips throughout East Africa. In some parts of Tanzania these air services are very valuable indeed as they form the only link between places cut off during the wet season.

In general, however, except for passenger traffic, the cost of air freight is too high to make this a possible line of export for other than the most

Fruit and vegetables being unloaded from an East African Airways VC10 at London Airport.

valuable products. These include horticulture products such as avocado pears, green peppers, strawberries and pineapples, which can command a high price during the European winter, especially in Britain and West Germany. Beef and pork products, coffee samples, game trophies and wood carvings are among the many other goods exported by air. But there is fierce competition from Israel, Ivory Coast and South Africa in the fruit and vegetable trade. Some air companies have offered special freight rates to East African exporters. Even so it is very difficult to offer produce in European markets at a competitive price. It is likely that only small amounts of fruit and vegetables will be moved this way.

Communications in Uganda and in Southern Tanzania

Two studies of transport networks follow. The Uganda study illustrates one of the easier situations. Southern Tanzania is typical of the problems facing railway and road builders in much of Africa.

Uganda

Uganda is fortunate in many respects. It has the advantage that it is small and that all the highest parts of the country are placed round the edges. The central plateau, although it has its swamps, lakes and quite steep valleys, presents no major obstacles to the building of roads and railways. In addition, by East African standards it is a wealthy country, so there has for a long time been a demand for roads and railways, and money with which to build them. An early advantage was the Nile, a waterway flowing right through the heart of the country. Even though the Nile is interrupted at the Owen, Atura and Murchison Falls, it is unique in East Africa as a navigable river. On top of all this, almost everywhere in the country it is possible to get murram with which good earth roads may be built.

A famous politician once described Uganda as 'the land at the top of the beanstalk'. This was a reference to a fable which tells of a wonderful prosperous land at the top of a giant beanstalk. In Uganda's case the beanstalk is the railway which links it to Mombasa. The railway is also the spinal cord of the communications system within the country. The main line runs from the Kenya border via Jinja to Kampala and on to Kasese in the west for the Kilembe copper mines. A major branch runs north to Soroti and then west to Pachwach on the Nile north of Lake Albert, tapping the pro ductive cotton-growing areas of the entire north. All the wealthiest part of Uganda is therefore within reach of a railway.

Uganda developed a unique network of roads centring on Mengo (Kampala) before the railway was built. This arose because the Saza chiefs were required to keep a road to the capital in good repair. As a result Kampala is the centre of a road system rather like a spider's web. The arrival of the railway strengthened this pattern. Roads go out in almost all directions. The one exception is to the north-east, where the combined barriers of Lake Kioga and the Nile hinder travel. The main roads are all tarmac surfaced, for on them traffic is heaviest and murram cannot stand up to the wear and tear. Over 1 280 km (800 miles) have now been bitumenised.

Southern Tanzania

The story is very different in that half of Tanzania which lies to the south of the Central Line. This area is nearly three times the size of Uganda. Distances are therefore very much greater. Enormous stretches are covered with tsetse fly infested woodland, still largely uninhabited. The most valuable areas are the Southern Highlands but these are far from railways. The relief of the Southern Highlands makes road and rail building difficult. Economic development has been held back by the lack of good communications.

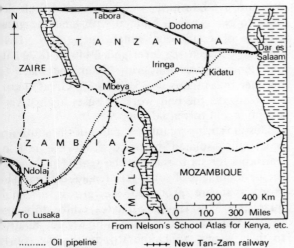

From Nelson's School Atlas for Kenya, etc.

.... Oil pipeline   +++++ New Tan-Zam railway

═══ Existing railway   _._._ International boundary

Fig. 35 The Tazama pipeline and the Tan-Zam railway

Heavy earth-moving equipment clearing the site for the new wagon-marshalling yards at Yombo outside Dar es Salaam where the Tan-Zam railway begins.

For a long time it was felt that the building of a rail link to Zambia was not feasible. It was argued that for many years there would be insufficient trade to make the railway pay. The changing political situation in southern Africa in the 1960s caused Zambia to turn northwards in search of outlets for her exports and routes for imports. In particular, Rhodesia's unilateral declaration of independence in 1966 cut off Zambia's supply of petroleum. At first supplies were flown in from Nairobi and Dar es Salaam, but soon a less costly road service was begun. This route was through Iringa, Mbeya, and Tunduma to Ndola, Kitwe and Lusaka.

It was quickly realised that the road could not support the traffic of fifteen-tonne oil tankers. Steep slopes and sharp corners caused many accidents, while the surface of the road itself broke down very rapidly. During the wet seasons which followed bridges were washed away and thick mud bogged down trucks, closing the road for weeks. The road was usually in such bad condition that it was nicknamed 'The Hell Run'.

This intolerable situation led to the building of the 'Tazama' pipeline. It was completed in thirteen months and ready to carry petroleum products 1 696 km (1 060 miles) from the refinery at Dar es Salaam to Bwana Mkubwa in the Zambian Copperbelt (Fig. 35). 'Spear' magazine gives a vivid impression of the difficulties which hampered the work: 'Apart from crossing three railways in

43

Men of three nations, Chinese, Tanzanians and Zambians, working together to construct the Tan-Zam railway. The train in the background brings the workers and their equipment to the construction point each day.

Tanzania and one in Zambia, traversing more than 20 rivers, winding over mountainous and heavily forested terrain to altitudes as high as 2 000 m (6 500 ft) above sea level, the pipelaying job also faced the most inclement weather. During the winter of 1967 all local rainfall records were broken with precipitation running as high as 310 mm (12·2 ins) in 48 hours. Bridges were washed out, hundreds of vehicles were blocked for days. On one occasion there were some 600 vehicles stranded in the mud.' (Quoted from *Spear* magazine, published by E.A.R. & H.) Here we have some idea of the great feat accomplished in the construction of the longest pipeline in Africa at a rate of over 5 km (3 miles) a day! However, obviously the pipeline can only carry liquids. What of Zambia's copper and other exports?

The main north-east south-west road will be tarred, and a railway built from the present railhead at Kidatu in the Kilombero valley through to Zambia (Fig. 35). Not only will this railway link Zambia with the sea, but it will also open up great prospects for the Southern Highlands of Tanzania. But at present local movement is still very difficult,

particularly in the wet season.

East African Railways operate a road service consisting of trucks, tankers and buses, over 3 220 km (2 000 miles) of roads. Only 512 (320) of these have a tarmac surface, the rest consisting of murram, sand, or in the wet season, mud. Vehicles need to be very well built to withstand the great variety of conditions which they meet. They operate between sea level and 2 440 m (8 000 ft) and temperatures may vary from one place to another by as many as 35°C (64°F). Great care is taken to seal the bodywork of buses against very fine dust and torrential rain.

Despite such precautions, parts of the south are practically isolated by road from the rest of Tanzania for six months of the year. This hinders the development of some very fertile sections. The crops that are produced are grown in small quantities. Most of them, like tea, coffee, tobacco, cashew nuts and wattle, have a high value relative to their weight. Only the Rondo Plateau, fairly close to the coast, can export as heavy a commodity as timber.

Part two: Regional studies

Introduction

The previous five chapters have dealt with situations rooted in the physical environment of East Africa. The conditions discussed have been those that affected the economic development of the area. The problems must be recognised if they are to be solved. Other countries have overcome the same difficulties. Canada, the U.S.A. and the U.S.S.R. have conquered far greater distances. Soil erosion can be controlled. In the past a tropical climate did not prevent the Maya of Central America from developing a civilisation. The Aztecs of Mexico and the Incas of Peru founded civilisations in mountain regions in tropical latitudes. Denmark and Switzerland have shown that relatively poor countries can achieve great things.

The conclusion to be drawn is that people with ideas and energy can make a success even of a difficult environment. A great effort on the part of all people can make Uganda, Kenya and Tanzania into progressive countries with a higher standard of living. The peoples and environments are varied and the studies that follow show the different ways in which the peoples of East Africa have used their environment. Much depends on the ability of people to work together and cooperate.

Some peoples have been content to live as their ancestors lived, and there is much of value in traditional ways. Others have found that new ideas and new methods have brought rewards. East Africans are living in a period of great change.

Case studies in a regional setting

In the following chapters we have chosen for study several interesting examples of the ways in which people are changing the landscape. A book of this kind cannot describe every project for developing agriculture, every irrigation scheme, every factory, or every town. Instead, the writers have selected crops, farms, companies, industries and towns which provide examples* of the general East

shown on the maps (Figs. 36 and 37) and list page 49.

African patterns. We have given greater attention to areas that are particularly important either because of the high density of population or for economic reasons. Focussing on case-studies is a useful method of study provided that it is remembered that they have been chosen to represent a wider area, and other examples which cannot be described in detail. Most important of all, a few *general* points or 'truths' which apply to the larger area or group, should be drawn from each case study.

'Self-help' schemes are playing a very important part in the improvement of life in the countryside. Many studies which follow concentrate on the ways in which 'self-help' can combine with technical assistance and advice from the government to develop resources in rural areas. Also emphasised are the kinds of project based on cooperative and community action such as, for example, *group farms* in Uganda and *ujamaa villages* in Tanzania.

East Africa can be divided into three types of physical region: coast, plateau and highland.

The coast
The coast region forms only a narrow belt. It differs from the neighbouring plateau in altitude, in its long history of Arab trade and settlement, and in its climate. High temperatures, humidity and rainfall are found through almost its whole length.

The plateaus
The rest of East Africa is plateau. This very large area contains many contrasting landscapes. These result mainly from differences in rainfall.

The highlands
These include all the land over approximately 1 500 m (4 921 ft) above sea-level. These areas also have high rainfalls. Because of their altitude the temperatures are much lower than on the coast.

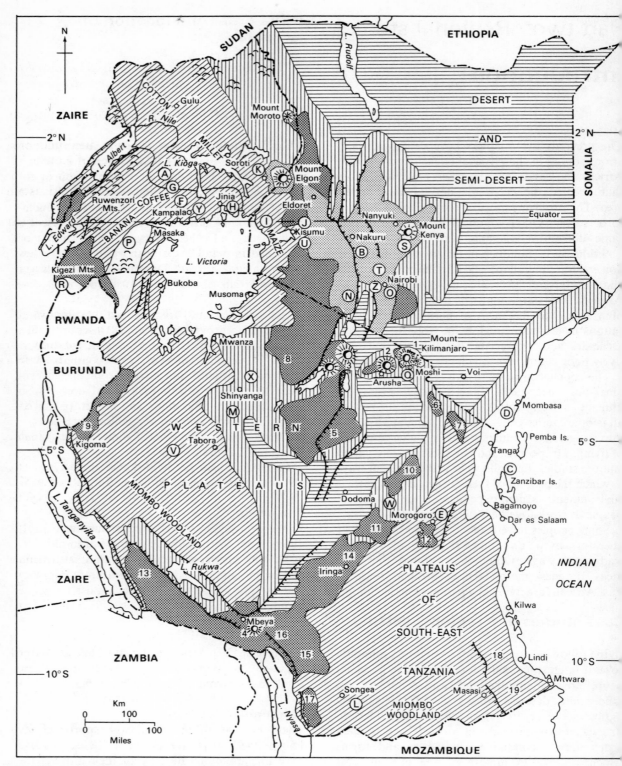

Fig. 36 Landscapes and regions of East Africa

46

Highlands

▨ (shaded pattern)

▦ Volcanic

☀ **Volcanic Cones**

1. Mount Kilimanjaro
2. Mount Meru
3. Ngorogoro and Loolmalasin
4. Mount Rungwe

High Plateaus

5. Kondoa
8. Serengeti "Plains"
10. Nguru
11. Rubeho
13. Ufipa
14. Iringa
15. Njombe

Mountains

6. Para
7. Usambara
9. Kasulu
12. Uluguru
16. Livingstone
17. Matengo

Plateaus

▨ Wet

▥ Dry

▤ Very dry

18. Rondo
19. Makonde

▢ Coast

Ⓑ Study

⊓⊓⊓ Escarpments

⊔⊔⊔ Rift valleys

The order and location of case-studies

The position of the case-studies is shown by a letter in a circle thus: Ⓒ *on opposite page*

Part I   A   Tsetse fly control in Bunyoro, Uganda

         B   Volcanic features in a small area in the Rift Valley of Kenya

Part II   C   Clove growing and land use in Zanzibar and Pemba

         D   A coast market garden near Mombasa

         E   Sisal estates

         F   A smallholding in Buganda

         G   A dairy farm in Bunyoro

         H   A Busoga sugar estate

         I   Farming in Nyanza, Kenya

         J   Ahero pilot scheme

         K   Cotton growing in Uganda

         L   Miombo woodland, Tanzania

         M   Sukumaland

         N   Masai studies

         O   The Kaputiei ranching scheme

         P   Ankole Ranching

         Q   Wachagga kihamba near Moshi, Tanzania

         R   Kigezi, Uganda

         S   Resettlement in Kenya: Mr. Kamunyu's holding, Nyeri, Kenya

         T   Lari settlement scheme

         U   Kericho tea estate

Part III   V   Tobacco growing in Tanzania

         W   Ujamaa villages near Mpwampwa, Tanzania

         X   Mwadui diamond mine, Tanzania

         Y   Kampala: planning a town

         Z   Nairobi: shaping the growth of a town

Case-studies related to countries:
Letters
Kenya: B D I J N O S T U Z

Tanzania: C E L M Q V W X

Uganda: A F G H K P R Y

Chapter 6: The coast of East Africa

The coastlands have a different appearance from the rest of East Africa. There are many ways in which they contrast with the plateaus and mountain lands. They are lower areas, although there is little true plain; because of lower altitude and nearness to the sea temperatures are high and equable; the air is very moist.

A coastal position has influenced things other than climate. Trade has brought many peoples to the Coast, especially from the Middle East and other parts of Asia. Those who have settled have brought their religion, their customs, their own way of life. There is a strong historic tradition on the Coast: trade flourished and towns grew. They were the most important towns in East Africa before the European building of the twentieth century. These things and the character of the people themselves make the coast a very different place from the rest of East Africa.

Early exploration

Many of the first explorers and traders on the coast of East Africa came from the ports along the northern shores of the Indian Ocean. The monsoon winds, changing with the seasons, gave direct passage to East Africa from December to March and home again from April onwards.

For 200 years after da Gama's first voyage there was a struggle for power between the Portuguese and the settled peoples. In 1592 the Portuguese began to build the Fort of Jesus at the entry to the old port of Mombasa; a hundred years later they lost it to the Arabs after a long siege.

The British and the Germans had little to do with the east coast of Africa until the middle of the nineteenth century, when European countries were seeking land for development and trade.

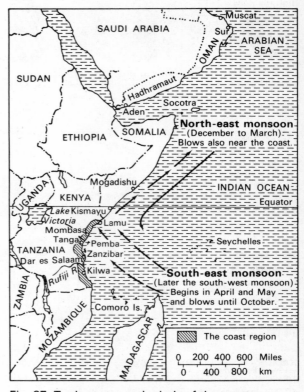

Fig. 37 Trade routes and winds of the coast

The dhow trade of the Indian Ocean (Fig. 37)

First written in 1956, the following remarks about the dhows are no longer entirely true. They are included to show the changes taking place.

'As the days of December pass in Zanzibar the weather gets very hot. There is little wind except that which comes in from the sea as night falls.

'Then, while the north-east monsoon blows, the dhows sail into harbour. They bring dried fish, dates, salt, matting and basketry, saris and henna dye from Oman and the Hadhramaut; figs, dried fruits, nuts, perfume and fine carpets from Persia;

Unloading provisions from a dhow at Lamu waterfront. There is no quay, and all goods must be manhandled from ship to shore.

dates and clay pots from Iraq; tiles from Mangalore in southern India*; ghee (clarified butter) from Socotra; cattle and goats from Somalia.

'After several months of blazing sun and airless heat rain storms clear the air and it becomes a little cooler. The wind begins to blow first from the south-east, then from the south-west. From April onwards, the dhows travel back home to Asia on the south-west monsoon. With them they take mangrove poles from the Rufiji Delta. Mangrove timber is especially valued because of its long life and because it resists the attacks of insects that bore into wood and destroy it.

'Some traders come regularly, year after year; others have made the coast their home. They trade in agricultural products, open shops in the countryside, or stay in towns making baskets, mats and reed bags. Some of them sell coffee and run eating houses called *mikahawa* or *hoteli*.

'The early traders came to buy slaves and ivory.

'In the past as many as four hundred dhows came to Zanzibar during the monsoon. Recently the number has been less because they can find more trade at home because of development of oil and petroleum in the Persian Gulf.

'The Shirazi and Arab colonists made Zanzibar their headquarters and intermarried with the Africans; their descendants are the Swahili. In this way the culture and civilisation of the Arabs came to the east coast of Africa. Many people on the coast adopted Islam as their religion and Swahili as their language, with Arabic as their

*Mangalore tiles are now being made at the Pugu Brick and Tile Works in Tanzania.

second tongue'.

There is little doubt that the changing monsoon winds made movement easy, out at one season and home at another. Secondly, the many small creeks and inlets give harbours where small ships can shelter. Thirdly, the lands at each end of the route are very different. Each produces its own special goods which are wanted by the other. Thus trade benefits both places.

Studies from the coast

The people of the coast share a common cultural tradition. Hence there is a certain similarity in the way of life throughout the area although there is a sharp contrast between the countryside and the towns.

What is written about the climate of Zanzibar and Pemba is true of much of the coast, although the amount of rain that falls is variable.

The following topics are studied:

Farming in Zanzibar and Pemba
State farms in Zanzibar
Zanzibar town
A coast market garden
Sisal estates
Mombasa: the port and industrial development
Dar es Salaam

Zanzibar and Pemba

The weather and the use of the land
The pattern of weather and climate that brought traders to the coast of East Africa also influences farming. The changing weather through the year is well described by F. D. Ommanney in his book *Isle of Cloves*:

'It is very hot and damp from about November to May*. During these months the north-east Monsoon blows from the Equator. The temperature seldom reaches 90°F (32°C) . . . The humidity however is very high so that one lives in a state of unbecoming dampness and nothing seems to dry.

'In about May a welcome change takes place; it begins to rain. Heavy black clouds build up over the island and spill their contents in crashing downpours which become more and more

*The months named here differ slightly from those shown in Fig. 38 which represents the average. The *masika* begins in mid-April.

frequent until they form into a steady continuous downpour which lasts through the month of May.

'Roads become impassable. The narrow streets are racing rivers of muddy water. Water spouts solidly with a ceaseless chatter from every pipe and gutter. Broad lakes pocked by the pitiless falling pencils of rain cover every square yard of flat ground. The people paddle about under umbrellas, holding up their white robes about their knees. The mosquitoes and every other insect imaginable, rejoice and arise in clouds, singing. Then quite suddenly the rain stops and the sun shines again.

'The 'Masika' brings a miraculous change in the climate. For as the rain belt moves north the south-east monsoon comes in behind it. It blows hard at first . . . but after about three weeks the wind slackens. Then for five months the green islands and their crowded capital enjoy a paradisal climate, cool and bright and rainless.

'The landscape which had burst into a riot of heavy green during the 'Masika' soon takes on a thirsty look. The north-east monsoon comes like a fierce hot damp breath, covering the surface of the straits between the island and the mainland with white horses and dark squalls'.

(*Simplified extract*)

Here, as everywhere, work on the land is tied to the seasons. The diagram (Fig. 38) shows this very clearly.

Use the description and Fig. 38 to answer the following questions.

1. How many rainy seasons and how many dry seasons are there? Which winds relate to each?
2. What is the average temperature of the longest dry period?
3. The period of heaviest rain usually comes just *after* the passing of the overhead sun. Does the diagram show this?
4. Work out the times of planting and harvesting of different crops in relation to the wet and dry seasons.

The months of *very* heavy rainfall (April and May) are those following on the months of *greatest* heat in East Africa when the monsoon winds are drawn inland away from their normal course. This rain might almost be thought of as a combination of monsoon rain and of convectional rain. But the heaviest storms of all often occur just before dawn (see chapter 2).

Farming in Zanzibar and Pemba

Both the map and the section (Figs. 39a and b) show that there are two main farming regions in Zanzibar and Pemba. On the western sides of both islands the land is hillier and the soils deep and fertile. It is on these more fertile soils that the clove gardens and most of the villages are found. In the eastern parts of both islands, thin soils cover a coral plain. This area is known as the *Wanda*. In both Pemba and Zanzibar the 'clove landscape' is quite different from the 'coral landscape'. Villages are more evenly scattered in Pemba than on Zanzibar Island.

The villages of the coral wanda

The *wanda* often seems an empty land, because so few people live there. The surface of the coral rock is fairly level, banked up along the shore with white coral sand. The soil is thin, even absent, so that very tall trees cannot grow. Where the soil is deeper it is covered by dense coral bush, almost unused except for an occasional village with its coconut palms and mango trees. Elsewhere there are open grassy plains.

Most people live near the sea. The fisherman is also a farmer who grows a great variety of crops. The boats, carved out of a single trunk, skim over the shallow water of the lagoon balanced by outriggers. Cassava grows under widely spaced palms; pits and ridges bear bananas, yams and sweet potatoes; a marshy clearing is used as a rice paddy field during the rains; millet, sorghum, maize, beans and other vegetables in their turn come to harvest through the year. Nearly everything that a family needs can be provided within the community. Even in the tiny villages there is a mosque, a school, and a shop or two.

The coconut and its uses

The coconut palm is a great provider. It grows along the coasts and scattered through the better parts of the *wanda* and the clove areas. The houses are built of coral rock or of a mixture of coral and clay worked into a cement. The roofs of many homes are heavily thatched with palm leaves—*makuti*—and screens and fences are made of skilfully woven rattan palm fronds. The leaves are also used for baskets. The nut provides food

Winds and dhows	Month	Rainfall				Work on the land		
		Zanzibar	Pemba	Temp.	Season	Sow	Harvest	General
South-west monsoon. Blows hard at first, then slackens	June	1½″ [38 mm]	4″ [102 mm]	78° F [26° C]	Cool Dry		Rice, sweet potato	
	July	1″ [25 mm]	2½″ [64 mm]	77° F [25° C]		Sweet potatoes, pulses, etc	Mwaka clove crop (main crop)	
	Aug.	1″ [25 mm]	2″ [51 mm]	77° F [25° C]				Weeding round clove trees. Beginning of new year for local people
	Sept.	2″ [51 mm]	2″ [51 mm]	78 F [26° C]				
South-west monsoon begins to drop: winds variable	Oct.	3″ [76 mm]	4″ [102 mm]	79° F [26·5° C]	Mvuli Short Rains			
	Nov.	6″ [151 mm]	9″ [229 mm]	81° F [27·5° C]		Cereals, maize, millet, pulses	Mvuli later harvest of food crops, cloves	Drying cloves
Dhows begin to arrive: 10 days earlier at Mombasa	Dec.	4¼″ [108 mm]	4″ [102 mm]	82° F [28° C]				
North-east monsoon	Jan.	2½″ [64 mm]	2½″ [64 mm]	83° F [28·5° C]	Hot Dry	Rice any shower in Jan. or Feb.'		Hoeing under clove trees. Preparing ground for food crops (hot sun kills weeds)
	Feb.	1½″ [38 mm]	2″ [51 mm]	84° F [29° C]				
Winds changing. Dhows return Apr. 26th at latest. Dislike leaving before winds change but get away before heavy rains	Mar.	7″ [177 mm]	5¼″ [133 mm]	[29° C]	Masika Heavy Rains	Mwaka food crops (sweet potatoes)		
	April	14½″ [368 mm]	17½″ [444 mm]	81° F [27·5° C]		Too wet for planting		Scaring birds from rice. Transplanting seedling trees
	May	11½″ [292 mm]	23″ [584 mm]	79° F [26·5° C]				

Fig. 38 Zanzibar and Pemba: seasonal work on the land

and the husk can be woven into rope.

The nuts are cut every three months for copra (dried coconut). They lie in a heap to mature and then are split and the kernel removed. It is then placed on platforms and dried in the sun; this takes a very long time on its own (about three months) so the nuts are dried by smoking in the open or in kilns. Zanzibar produces much more copra than Pemba (about four-fifths of the combined annual total), while Pemba is the main clove island.

The shell or husk of the nut is processed and the *coir* or fibre used for rope and mats. In Zanzibar the husks are buried below high tide level for nearly eight months to 'cure' before being used. The Zanzibari women are the chief makers of coir.

Clove growing

As one flies low over the landscapes of Pemba and Zanzibar the regular lines of clove trees make a different pattern from the mixed farming villages. The clove trees cover almost one-tenth of the area of the islands and there are over 6 million of them.

At one time cloves, which were greatly prized, were grown only in the East Indies; Vasco da Gama took a cargo back to Portugal after his first voyage. Later the French planted cloves on Mauritius and they were introduced into Zanzibar by the first Arab Sultan. At that time all the work was done by slaves, and Arab clove estates were dotted over the islands. When slaves were freed and labour had to be paid, some plantations declined. Arab owners left their estates in the hands of a manager and went to live in town. But the crop introduced by Seyyid Said has established Zanzibar in the markets of the world. For a century most of the world's clove production has centred on Pemba and Zanzibar.

Production

Cloves are the unopened flower buds of the tree. They grow in dense clusters and the sprays are picked when the buds are full but not opened. In the evenings the pickers sit around the great piles and take off the buds, chatting as they work.

The buds are spread on mats of woven palm leaves for about five days to dry. The very best days for this are those of January and February when the sun beats down out of a cloudless sky. A second picking season comes in the cooler months of July, August and September when there is also less rain. The buds are turned over from time to time so that they dry evenly. The quicker they dry the better the product.

A clove plantation on Zanzibar Island. Notice the coconut palms, especially around the clove drying ground in the centre.

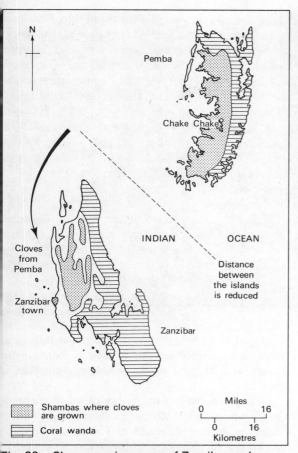

Fig. 39a Clove growing areas of Zanzibar and Pemba

Pickers often come from the villages or even from the mainland, at picking time, for it fits easily in between the work on their own plots.

A spray of fresh cloves.

They build temporary homes on the estates and the whole family moves in to earn as much as it can. The women and children pick the lower branches; men climb the main branches or use ladders to break off the high sprays. Some of the older trees are 15–24 m (50–80 ft) high. The sprays have to be gathered up and carried into a pile ready for the bud-picking in the evening. The stems are not wasted, for they too can be sold.

The pickers are paid according to the weight of buds. A good man may pick 54 kg (120 lbs) of green buds a day but most people cannot work as quickly as this. The buds dry to only a third of their green weight.

Marketing cloves

At one time Zanzibar Island had by far the greater number of clove trees. Then, in 1872 a great hurricane tore most of them up. Although many

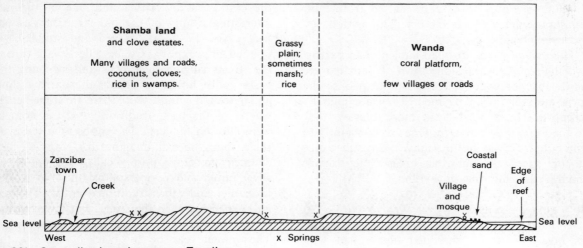

Fig. 39b Generalised section across Zanzibar

Cloves being spread out to dry in the sun.

have been replanted, Pemba has, since that date, always been the larger producer. Today four-fifths of the combined clove crop comes from Pemba. But Zanzibar Town is still the chief selling and exporting centre, so that all Pemba cloves are first brought to Zanzibar. The cost of transport usually means that Pemba growers are paid a little less than Zanzibar growers.

Zanzibar town smells of cloves! The cloves are brought in from the countryside (or over from Pemba by boat) and are stored in 'go-downs'. Distillation of the oil of cloves takes place in the factory on the water front near the main harbour, so that the sacks have to be shifted from their temporary sheds to the factory. This is done by the *hamali* teams.

The *hamali* carts are man-hauled. The narrow twisting streets of the stone town of Zanzibar are impossible for wider trucks or ox-teams; so the carts are still pulled by men. They are paid by piece-work rates, so that the more journeys they do the more they can earn. One has constantly to leap out of the way of the *hamali* carts as they race at top speed through the streets, their teams chanting and shouting in rhythm.

How cloves are used

Cloves and oil of cloves are sent all over the world. In Java cloves are shredded and rolled with tobacco to make cigarettes. Throughout India and South-East Asia the spice is used in curries and sauces and as part of the betel mixture that is chewed.

Perhaps the widest use today of oil of cloves is in the preparation of vanilla flavouring. This is added to chocolate, sweets and cakes all over the world. Oil of cloves in different forms is used in perfume, soap, medicine and by dentists.

Zanzibar town (population 68 380 in 1967) (Fig. 40)

Zanzibar town is one of the oldest settlements on the east coast of Africa and one of the most interesting. Many of the old Arab houses have heavy wooden doors, carved and studded with pointed brass knobs. Coffee sellers walk through the streets ringing their bells and swinging their brass coffee holders. Outside the narrow shops, and indeed, the houses too, there are stone benches where, in the past, tradition says, the homeless were allowed to sleep. The shops now sell everything that one can imagine, for ships of many countries make it a port of call; but there are still silversmiths and coppersmiths and the workers in leather and other traditional crafts. There are many men about in the streets but fewer women, as one would expect in a Moslem community. The women wear the thin black *bui-bui* over their gay cotton dresses and high-heeled sandals.

Nearly all the buildings in Zanzibar town are painted white. The shops and homes are closely packed, with narrow lanes between. Beyond the Arab town there is a change to the thatched roofs of the country homes. One can also see the broad sweep of the white beaches, and three or four large vessels anchored and unloading goods. The old Portuguese Fort, the administrative centres and the former palace, line the bay.

In the past, Zanzibar town was almost separated from the main island by the creek to the east. Now the creek is nearly empty of water and parts are being filled in. Already there are playgrounds and a hockey pitch on the open land. In the cool of the evening crowds of people stroll here and along the water front. A little to the west there was once a slave market but the Anglican Cathedral is now built on the site. Because most of the people are Moslems there are many mosques.

State farms in Zanzibar

Since Independence there has been a very powerful drive to reduce imports. Three large state farms have started to produce basic foods such as rice,

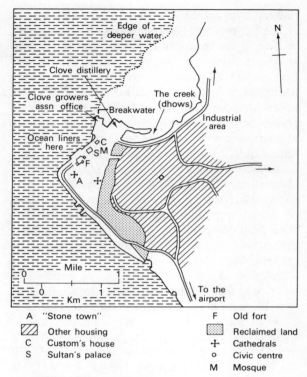

A   "Stone town"   F   Old fort

Other housing   Reclaimed land

C   Custom's house   Cathedrals

S   Sultan's palace   o   Civic centre

M   Mosque

Fig. 40 Zanzibar town

Zanzibar town. Study this aerial photograph together with Fig. 40. In which direction was the camera pointing? Try to find the buildings named on the map.

poultry, eggs and milk.

The 522 hectare (1 300 acre) Upenja farm, begun in 1966, is the largest of the three, and work there is concentrated on rice production. About 400 hectares (1 000 acres) will eventually come under paddy, as growing rice is called. Rice production needs abundant labour and the farm has been greatly helped by large numbers of school students at planting time in January, and during the Easter school holidays when weeding is done. They work for at least a month a year as part of the country's 'Education for Self-Reliance' programme. The paddy is harvested in July and sold by the Ministry of Agriculture and Land Reform through the Rice Mill Corporation. Experiments have been carried out to see if two crops a year could be grown using irrigation.

In 1968 33 385 kg (73 600 lbs) of paddy rice were produced by Upenja Farm. In addition to rice, the farm has a poultry unit of 3 000 chickens, 2 000 of them laying eggs. Work on the farm is divided into various sections. In one group people are training to become skilled drivers. They will operate the seven tractors (which do all field operations such as ploughing, harrowing, planting and weeding) and three combine harvesters. Others are training to be mechanics and electricians. Carpenters, masons and painters belong to a building and carpentry section, and the poultry section has fifty-six labourers. Having begun under the management of expatriate agricultural experts, the farm is now run by Tanzanians.

The Mtoni poultry farm has an area of 6 hectares (14 acres) and is devoted to the raising of about 4 500 poultry. Zanzibar is now self-sufficient in eggs as a result of increased production from this and other farms.

The Mtoni Jersey cattle farm aims mainly at supplying all the fresh milk needed by the islanders, and it is hoped that eventually they will make Zanzibar self-sufficient in beef also. It has at present about eighty cows and bulls, some of which came from Kenya, as well as 150 cattle for cross-breeding purposes. The grassy plains of the parts with thin soil may well support herds of cattle in future.

Agriculture in the east coast region

What has been written so far about countryside and town in Zanzibar and Pemba is, in general, true for the whole of the coast region.

Two landscapes dominate the country areas of the coastlands of East Africa. Along much of their length the coastlands are formed of coral rock covered with coconut woodland or bush. Secondly, mangrove swamps line the coastal creeks and river valleys. Only occasionally is forest as dense as tropical rain forest found.

The coastal towns and villages on the mainland have less rain than Zanzibar and Pemba; often there is little more than 760 mm (30 ins). Lamu and Lindi have 915–940 mm (36–37 ins), Dar es Salaam about 1 040 mm (41 ins) and Mombasa nearly 1 270 mm (50 ins). Between Lamu and Kilwa the pattern of the rain falling in the different months always shows the effect of the monsoon. North of Lamu the total rainfall becomes lower until the desert conditions of Somaliland are

Mr Patel examining the fine crop of okra on his market garden near Mombasa.

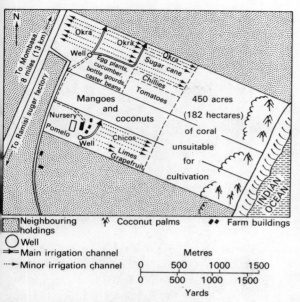

Fig. 41 A large coast market garden

Bottle gourds.

Mature sugar-cane near Ramisi on the Kenya coast. Compare its height with the tall schoolboy in the foreground.

Freshly cut sugar cane being brought into the Ramisi sugar factory by light railway. It will soon be crushed and the juice processed to produce fine white sugar.

reached. South of Kilwa the pattern of rainfall is similar to that of the interior of Tanzania with one wet and one dry season.

It is not surprising, then, to find that the agriculture carried on along the Coast is similar to the mixed coconut farming of parts of Zanzibar, less rich where the rain is less. In some places cash crops are grown. Instead of cloves, other crops become the chief crops of commerce. Sisal is an important crop in the drier areas. Sometimes there are coconut, sugar and kapok estates. An interesting development near the towns is the growing of fruit and vegetables with the help of irrigation. This is illustrated by the coast market garden.

A coast market garden (Fig. 41)

The map (Fig. 41) shows the layout of the large market garden which Mr. Kurji Patel manages 13 km (8 miles) south of Mombasa Island. The emphasis is on the growing of three types of crop: vegetables used in Indian cooking, the chief one being 'okra', or 'lady fingers' used in pickles and soups, secondly sugar cane, and thirdly citrus and other fruits.

Water from one of two wells is used to irrigate 8 hectares (20 acres) of the okra crop and also about 6 hectares (15 acres) of caster beans, chilis, aubergines (egg plants), cucumbers and bottle gourds. The water, pumped up to the surface,

flows along shallow furrows in the soil, and then is allowed to spread out between the plants. Although the weather is dry enough for irrigation

57

During the dry season a crop of rice is grown on the damp bed of the Lower Tana river. In the background is the natural levee, built up by mud deposited during repeated flooding. What food crops are growing there?

to be necessary in the early stages of growth, there is a very real danger of soil erosion when the long rains arrive. To prevent this earthen banks have been built up around the plots. When the rains come, about 16 hectares (40 acres) of tomatoes are transplanted out of the nursery. At this time there is enough work for forty farm labourers, though in the dry season only about twenty-five people are employed. In this irrigated northern part of the farm there are 12 hectares (30 acres) of sugar cane, which is harvested in October and November and taken to Ramisi Sugar Factory for processing.

Over half of the farm is given over to various fruit trees, mangoes, coconuts, limes, grapefruits, oranges, chicos and pomelos. This last one is like a large grapefruit with red 'meat' inside. The farm lorry delivers loads of fresh vegetables and fruits to Mombasa market regularly and occasionally to Nairobi. A small quantity is sometimes air freighted to London.

This market garden is much too large to be typical of coast smallholdings. Most are much smaller, and grow a variety of subsistence crops, especially bananas, maize and coconuts. The coconuts provide some cash return, along with cashew nuts, mangoes, kapok and citrus fruits.

Rice production may well expand and become the chief crop in the alluvial parts of the coast. It is especially important in the Rufiji and Ruvu (Pangani) river valleys of Tanzania. The rice is grown on peasant holdings (0·4 to 1·2 hectare, 1–3 acres of rice), taking advantage of flooding in the rains. The rainfall of the region is only about 890 mm (35 ins), but the rivers draw their supplies

A large sisal estate near Mt Kilimanjaro. Two of the plants have produced the long poles on which bulbils develop—the first stage in the production of new sisal plants.

Sisal plants at the experimental station near Thika, Kenya. The plant in the foreground has been cropped.

At the end of a day's cutting, a train arrives to take the sisal leaves (seen piled on either side of the track) to the factory.

After the fibres have been separated from the sisal leaves, young workers lay them over wires to dry in the sun.

from the distant mountains. Yields can be increased when irrigation water is provided by flood control. Other help is planned through the mechanical ploughing of smallholdings with the aid of the Ministry of Agriculture.

Sisal estates (Fig. 42)

One of the plantation crops on the coastal belt is sisal. Sisal is important in East Africa because for a long time it was Tanzania's main export. As recently as 1963 as much as one-third of the country's export income was from sisal. Since then, however, there has been a serious decline in the value of sisal on the world market, and it has dropped to third place after coffee and cotton.

Sisal is especially important because it resists drought and survives a long dry season. It is grown in different regions because it has the unusual quality of being able to grow both in dry and in wetter areas.

Sisal is a form of coarse white fibre which is obtained from the long hard leaves of the sisal plant. The main uses for sisal are in the making of string, ropes, sackcloth and matting. The fibre is tough and strong but not very easy to spin as it is of equal thickness all the way along.

Growing sisal

If a sisal plant is allowed to flower it grows a long pole with sprays of flowers at the end. As these bear fruit, a 'bulbil' is formed. These are

59

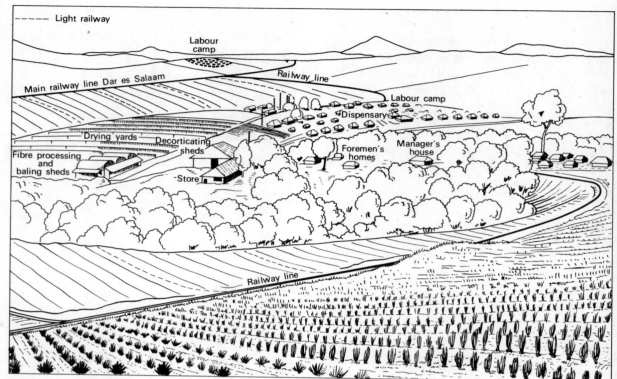

Fig. 42 A sisal estate

planted in a nursery and transplanted after about nine months. The first bulbils came from Central America.

Cutting takes place all the year round on different parts of the estate so that there is a constant supply to the factory. The leaves first have their very sharp tips cut off. They are then cut from the plant very near to their base and loaded on to trucks. Bundling and carrying to the trucks of the small track railways that serve every part of the estate is very heavy work.

Processing sisal

On reaching the factory, three things are needed to get the sisal fibre ready for market. It needs to have the fibre exposed by stripping off the fleshy part of the leaf. This is done by putting the leaves through a machine called a decorticator. Then the fibre is washed and put out to dry over wires. This helps to bleach it to a pure white. Lastly, the sisal is brushed, graded and put into bales for export. The drawing (Fig. 42) shows where these processes take place.

The area where soils and rainfall are most favourable for sisal is near Tanga. This area extends for 130 km (80 miles) along the coast and for a similar distance inland. Another important area is found inland near the central line railway near Morogoro and Kilosa. Smaller areas are found to the east of Nairobi, near Lindi and north of Mombasa. There are a few plantations inland in the Lake Victoria Region of Tanzania and near Kitale in Kenya.

Synthetic or artificially produced fibres have been responsible for sisal's downfall. The increase in the use of synthetic materials, in particular nylon for ropes, has resulted in a greatly reduced demand for sisal, and a considerable lowering of its value.

Many sisal estates have been converted to other uses. Up to 162 000 hectares (400 000 acres) of sisal estates may become cattle ranches. Already several are maintaining large herds of beef cattle. Near towns and cities dairy herds are being introduced to supply fresh milk to the towns-people. On some estates other crops, such as cashew nuts, rice and other cereals are being grown.

However, it is not likely that sisal will be

completely replaced as a raw material for agricultural twine. Therefore many estates are still growing the crop. They are the farms which are most efficient, or which grow sisal best, and are most likely to make some profit even while prices are low. Also, new uses for sisal have been found. At Moshi, the Tanzania Bag Corporation factory is producing nearly 3 million sisal bags for coffee each year. A pulp and paper factory at Tanga will soon be producing paper and paper products both for export and for use within Tanzania. No doubt other uses for sisal will be found. One experimental use for the juice squeezed from the plant is the production of a pain-killing drug, cortisone. These new developments will ensure that the best sisal estates will continue to produce for some time to come.

The ability of sisal to grow where the rainfall is varied is shown by the three sets of figures that follow. Amboni is shown on Fig. 45 (Tanga). Morogoro and Kilosa are further from the sea.

Table 2: Monthly rainfall in mm (inches)

Jan.	Feb.	March	April	May	June	Year: Total
Amboni (60 m, 200 ft above sea-level)						
20	31	107	204	292	56	
(0·8″)	(1·2″)	(4·2″)	(8·0″)	(11·5″)	(2·2″)	
Kilosa (450 m, 1 500 ft above sea-level)						
150	122	183	193	81	8	
(5·9″)	(4·8″)	(7·2″)	(7·6″)	(3·2″)	(0·3″)	
Morogoro (570 m, 1 900 ft above sea-level)						
99	97	173	203	99	25	
(3·9″)	(3·8″)	(6·8″)	(8·0″)	(3·9″)	(1·0″)	

July	Aug.	Sept.	Oct.	Nov.	Dec.	Year: Total
Amboni (60 m, 200 ft above sea-level)						
51	69	86	125	119	76	1 240
(2·0″)	(2·7″)	(3·4″)	(4·9″)	(4·7″)	(3·0″)	(48·8″)
Kilosa (450 m, 1 500 ft above sea-level)						
8	16	19	33	76	125	1 021
(0·3″)	(0·6″)	(0·7″)	(1·3″)	(3·0″)	(5·3″)	(40·2″)
Morogoro (570 m, 1 900 ft above sea-level)						
15	10	15	25	51	71	884
(0·6″)	(0·4″)	(0·6″)	(1·0″)	(2·0″)	(2·8″)	(34·8″)

Cities of the coast

Until recent years, the only modern cities in East Africa were those of the coast. It is only here that there is a long tradition of town life brought by the Arabs. Kilwa, Sofala, Malindi, Mombasa, Lamu, Tanga and others existed long before they were visited by Vasco da Gama and other explorers. Dar es Salaam is an example of a 'new' town for

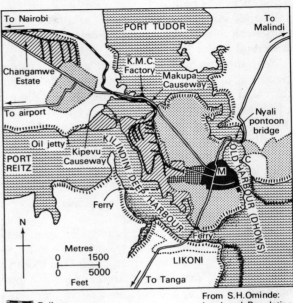

From S.H. Ominde: Land and Population Movements in Kenya

—⊢⊢— Railway

■ Old Mombasa

Main residential areas

Main industrial and port areas

Main commercial area

■ Fort Jesus

⑄ Cliff

〰〰 Edge of coral reef

M Market

C Cement wharf

Fig. 43 The port and town of Mombasa

An aerial view of Kilindi harbour and part of Mombasa: the mainland is in the foreground. Compare this photograph with the map, Fig. 43. In which direction was the camera pointing?

61

Seyyid Majid, Sultan of Zanzibar, decided to build a town there in 1862 to replace Bagamoyo: it became the centre of government in 1891. The Port of Mtwara is newer still and its first deepwater quay was built in 1952.

The old Arab cities were nearly all ports. Their sites were chosen with an eye to defence, and the trade and slave routes inland.

With the coming of railways the natural starting point was one of the coastal towns; this gave them increased importance so that they have become much bigger than the other towns. This is true of Tanga and Dar es Salaam and especially of Mombasa. The section that follows shows the stages of its growth from a dhow harbour to a major port, and how industries developed.

The port of Mombasa (population 236 000 in 1969) (Fig. 43)

Mombasa grew up on an island site good for defence. North and west of Mombasa two deepwater creeks join as they enter the Indian Ocean. The island of Mombasa separates the old dhow harbour on the east from the western harbour, Kilindini (meaning 'deep water'). Kilindini has become the modern port and part of the industrial area. Now only the dhows and local fishing and coastal ships use the old harbour near Fort Jesus.

Although coral reefs guard the entry and the whole coast is formed of coral rock, the river silt keeps the two creeks clear of growing coral (see page 37). The entry to the western channel is 36·5 m (20 fathoms) deep and it can take large ships; the tidal range is never more than 3·7 m (12 ft), so that enclosed docks are not needed, except for repair work.

Kilindini is a safe and well-equipped modern port able to cater for special cargoes. There are now thirteen deep-water berths at which ships can discharge and take on cargoes directly, and also anchorages and moorings for nearly twenty more vessels. In addition, the oil terminal can accommodate tankers of up to 65 000 tonnes (63 950 tons). From there, crude oil is discharged into shore storage tanks and then is pumped to the East African Oil Refinery 3 km (2 miles) away at Changamwe.

There is little doubt that Mombasa owes much of its importance to the fact that until 1963 (when the Mnyusi to Ruvu line linked the Moshi and

Arusha areas to the Tanzania central line) it was the only outlet by railway for almost the whole exportable produce of Uganda, Kenya and Northern Tanzania. This hinterland rails large tonnages of varied commodities to Mombasa (see Fig. 83).

Fig. 44 *Mombasa: volume of principal commodities exported 1967*

Commodity	Harbour Tons
Coffee	258 888
Cement	246 078
Cotton	175 141
Maize	140 644
Soda ash	98 141
Oil seed and cake	82 761
Tea	70 212
Sisal	60 594
Molasses	42 505
Wattle bark and extract	18 419
Copper	13 701

Mombasa now ranks among the most modern ports. Modern methods of cargo handling have been introduced which may radically alter the system of loading and unloading in the port. The first, *containerisation*, has been described in chapter five. The second method *palletisation*, consists of stacking cargo on to small wooden platforms, or *pallets*, made so that cranes and fork-lift trucks can lift the load easily and transfer it to the ship's hold as a unit.

Other improvements are constantly being made to deal with special cargoes. Overhead conveyor belts deliver bagged soda ash direct to the ships; compressed air is used to boost the movement of bulk molasses (syrup or treacle) from large storage tanks to ships holds; bulk road tankers bring 24 tonne loads of cement from Bamburi to large silos at English Point, from which specially designed ships like the 'Southern Baobab' are loaded at a rate of 2 000 tonnes in five hours.

Formerly ships called at Mbaraki wharf for coal supplies, but now this area is being redesigned. Cement silos and a packing plant will be erected to bag cement for export. Maize, vegetable oil and other bulk products may also use this wharf to relieve pressure on the Kilindini deep water berths.

With the closure of the Suez Canal in June 1967, many more vessels have had to take the much

Zambian copper being loaded at the quayside, Dar es Salaam

longer route around southern Africa. Much more shipping has been entering Kilindini than formerly as Mombasa is now very well placed to fill the ships' fuel and water tanks, or 'bunkers' as they are called. It was for bunkering that the largest ship ever to enter the harbour, the 80 083 tonnes oil-tanker Santiago, arrived in late 1967. Since the Santiago was carrying no cargo, it was floating high enough in the water to enter safely.

Industry in Mombasa

Although the chief modern function of Mombasa has been that of a port, important industries have been established, partly owing to its situation as one of the main gateways to eastern Africa. A good example is the refining of crude oil, which is imported in bulk. It is then converted into a variety of fuels for cars, trucks, trains, ships, aircraft and for domestic uses. Most of this is distributed 'up-country' by road and rail, though some is re-exported.

A fertiliser factory being built at Kwa Jomvu overlooking the Kipevu oil jetty will produce 110 000 tonnes of calcium ammonium nitrate per year. Liquid ammonia, one of the raw materials, will be imported in special tankers at −35°C (−30°F), discharged at the oil jetty, and then pumped to the factory by way of a hill top storage tank.

There are also many small factories preparing and packing foods, making soap, all kinds of aluminium goods, bottles and furniture. Engineering and repair shops have been established for many years.

The tourist boom has affected Mombasa. The combination of sea, sun and history in old Mombasa has attracted growing numbers of tourists. Existing hotels have been extended and many new ones have been built to the north and south of Mombasa Island. The island itself is now almost totally built over, and new residential areas are developing at Likoni to the south and Nyali to the north.

Dar es Salaam (population 272 515 in 1967) (Fig. 46)

Dar es Salaam has not the long Arab tradition of many of the other east coast cities. It was only a fishing village when the Sultan decided to build a town there in 1862. It became the centre of German administration in 1891 instead of the old capital, Bagamoyo. At one time Tanga was more important because the first railway inland in Tanganyika used that port. But once the railway to Kigoma on Lake Tanganyika was finished in 1914, Dar es Salaam – 'Haven of Peace' – was able to serve a very much larger hinterland than Tanga, and it now carries more than two-thirds of mainland

Part of the oil refinery at Dar es Salaam

The cement factory at Wazo Hill near Dar es Salaam, during construction.

In addition to the Tanzania hinterland, Dar es Salaam has, since 1965, served a much larger area including Zambia, Rwanda, Burundi and Zaire. Because of Zambia's contribution especially, the amount of trade passing through Dar es Salaam has been greatly increased (see section on communications, chapter 5, page 43). Zambian exports, mainly copper, are taken direct to the harbour. But in order to handle imports more efficiently an entirely new transit shed, the largest of its kind in Africa, has been constructed at Ubungo. It is 10 km (6 miles) west of the port, to which it is connected by both road and rail. As a result of its increased hinterland, and of the rapidly developing economy of Tanzania, tonnages of imports and exports of dry cargo (that is, excluding crude oil) more than doubled between 1964 and 1968.

This expansion is especially creditable and fortunate in view of Tanzania's loss through the changed value of sisal on the international market.

Since Tanganyika's Independence in 1961, Dar es Salaam has grown at a remarkable rate due to its position as the capital city. This is true of its population and industry. One of the most obvious increases has been in the numbers of diplomatic staff, now representing over forty countries compared with nine in 1960. The number of government ministries has also increased, and the siting here of their headquarters has encouraged the development of a truly national capital, with people representing all parts of the country.

trade (see Fig. 83). A branch line from Tabora to Mwanza serves the very productive southern shore of Lake Victoria, and the port is now linked through Ruvu and Mnyusi with the rich Kilimanjaro-Meru area. Until 1956 all goods had to be loaded and unloaded by lighters, so it is a truly remarkable growth.

The Tanzanian government has encouraged industrial expansion, both by exempting most industrial equipment from customs duty and by providing information on suitable sites and sources of power, labour and raw materials. In response to this and to the development needs of the country, large and small enterprises have been established. Among the larger the £5 million TIPER oil refinery is capable of producing 600 000 tonnes of petroleum products annually. This is fortunately more than Tanzania's needs at present, for since it first came 'on stream' in 1966, Zambia has also relied on this supply. This was made possible by the construction of the 1 696 km (1 060 mile) long 'Tazama' pipeline from the refinery to Ndola in the Zambian copperbelt. The equivalent of 9 000 barrels of petroleum a day can be passed along it, see pages 43–44.

It has been said that the rate of a country's modern development can be gauged by the increased use of cement. Some 26 km (16 miles) north of Dar es Salaam, on Wazo Hill, a factory is producing over 50 000 tonnes of cement per year, the bulk of which goes to Ubungo to be bagged and railed out to construction sites all over the country.

The establishment of the university just outside the city has caused an increased demand for goods and services. Dar es Salaam is also attracting growing numbers of tourists.

Tanga (population 60 935 in 1967) (Fig. 45)

Tanga is another old city that has profited from the building of a railway inland along the Pangani river, called Ruvu near its mouth, and also a line between the Ruvu and Mnyusi. It serves the sisal area of Korogwe and the agricultural districts of the Usambara Mountains, Mount Kilimanjaro and Mount Meru.

Tanga stands on a low coral platform, protected from the open ocean by a headland that almost encloses the harbour. The diagram shows how it is sited on the relatively small part of the coast that is free from coral reef and from mangrove. Ships lie off-shore and cargo is unloaded by lighters. It has lost some of its importance because the inland towns of Moshi and Arusha have a railway line direct to the better equipped port of Mombasa.

Tanga is important as an exporting centre, but it is developing industries, especially milling oil

seeds and wood-working. Electrical power is supplied from the falls on the Pangani river 56 km (35 miles) to the west. Exports include sisal and copra from the coast and some coffee and other crops from further inland.

This rapid growth of towns is now to be found all over East Africa. (Consult the index for other town studies.)

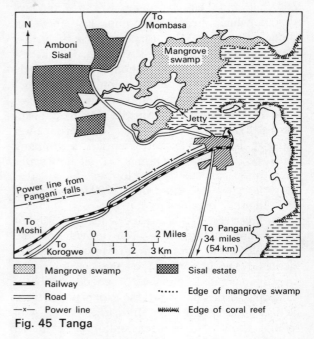

Fig. 45 Tanga

Fishing at the coast

At present at least ten times as much fish is harvested from the lakes and rivers of the three East African countries as from the sea. An important reason for this is that it is easier to fish in shallow water than in deep, but unfortunately the area of shallow water off the East African coast is very small. Indeed this section of the continental shelf is only 5–6·5 km (3–4 miles) wide and is probably only a sixth of the area of Lake Victoria. But there is great potential for sea fishing as more East Africans include fish in their diet, and as better transport and marketing facilities develop. Also, Kenya and Tanzania are well placed to serve the increasing protein needs of land-locked Zambia and eastern Zaire.

Russian and Japanese fishing boats are already

65

exploiting the western Indian Ocean, and their very successful fishing technique of 'longlining' could be used to harvest a large quantity of such fish as tuna and marlin (a type of 'swordfish') for East Africa. This method involves the use of a line 19–24 km (12–15 miles) long baited with 300–400 hooks, designed to sink to a depth of about 122 m (400 ft) before being raised again. Another method already operated on a small scale off Zanzibar and Dar es Salaam is the 'Lampara' system, which uses bright lamps just above or under the surface. The fish, mainly sardines, are attracted to the light and easily netted. The success of both these and other methods depends greatly on the availability of refrigeration, since without it fish deteriorate very rapidly in the tropics. An important advance has been the recent establishment at Lamu of a cold storage and ice production plant by the Kenya Inshore Fisheries, a company which is rapidly expanding its shallow-water operations, particularly for lobster. Its sales in 1967–68 brought a return of £225 000, three times more than the previous year.

The coast zone has been experiencing a period of rapid economic growth. The growth of the economies of all three East African countries has increased the importance of the coastal ports. Greatly increased tonnages of goods are being handled and this has led to the expanison of dock facilities and employment. Industries, such as oil refining, have also been expanding close to the harbours.

Much of the demand for tourist facilities, such as hotels, boating and fishing, has been concentrated along the coast. However, the tourist facilities are situated near the sea and some areas only a few kilometres inland have had little direct benefit.

* * *

Each of the studies included in this section is important because it shows the *kind* of development going on in the coastal areas of East Africa. It is important to understand the *process*, that is, the sequence of actions or interactions by which change takes place.

Work to do

1. Make sure that you know:
   What is meant by 'monsoon'.

   The times of the year when particular winds blow, and the direction.
   How a coral reef is formed.

2. Make a plan of the *clove plantation*, using the photograph on page 52.

   Show the buildings and the clearing round them.
   Show the area covered by clove trees (in rows).
   Show the area covered by coconut palms.
   Show the clearing where rice might be grown.

3. (a) Make a list of the crops grown by the coast market garden (Fig. 41).

   (b) The rainfall (mm) and temperature (°C) figures for Mombasa are:

Table 3: Rainfall for Mombasa in mm (inches)

Jan.	Feb.	March	April	May	June	
25	15	61	198	323	107	
(1·0″)	(0·6″)	(2·4″)	(7·8″)	(12·7″)	(4·2″)	
July	August	Oct.	Nov.	Nov.	Dec.	Total
89	69	64	86	94	61	1 191
(3·5″)	(2·7″)	(2·5″)	(3·4″)	(3·7″)	(2·4″)	(46·9″)

Table 4: Temperatures for Mombasa in °C (°F)

Jan.	Feb.	March	April	May	June
28	28·5	29	28	26	25·5
(82°F)	(83°F)	(84°F)	(82°F)	(79°F)	(78°F)
July	August	Sept.	Oct.	Nov.	Dec.
24·5	24·5	25	26	27	28
(76·5°F)	(76·5°F)	(77°F)	(79°F)	(81°F)	

   (i) How are these figures related to the monsoon winds?

   (ii) Are they also related to the movements of the sun?

   (iii) in which months is irrigation most needed?

   (iv) Can you work out the main planting and harvesting times for different crops?

   (c) If your home is on the coast in the Mombasa area, make a chart of the work that might be done in the different months (like those on page 51 or page 84).

4. Study the maps of Mombasa and find the following things.

   (*a*) The island of Mombasa.
   (*b*) Port Reitz and Port Tudor.

Part of the harbour and town of Dar es Salaam: the deep-water berths are centre left.

(c) Kilindini.
(d) The edge of the reef.
(e) Old Town.
(f) Dhow harbour.
(g) Bridges to the mainland.
Copy the map into your exercise book and name these things.

5. Compare the photograph of Dar es Salaam with Fig. 46.
    (a) In which direction was the photograph taken?
    (b) Find the Town Quays on the photograph.
    (c) Why do the ships not tie up on-shore by the Town Quays?
    (d) Locate new docks on the photograph.
    (e) How does the picture tell us that Dar es Salaam is a fairly new town?

6. Find out what a 'lighter' is.

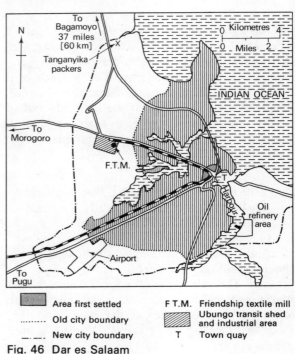

Fig. 46 Dar es Salaam

Chapter 7: The wet plateaus

Most of East Africa is plateau country. Over such a vast area there are many local variations. These fall into two broad groups related to differences in the amount of rainfall that each area receives:

1. The wet plateaus.
2. The dry plateaus.

In the wet plateaus at least 500 mm (20 ins) of rainfall a year is certain. In many places the total is much greater, going up to 2 000–2 500 mm (80–100 ins) in the Sese Islands in Lake Victoria. This means that there is always enough rain for agriculture.

Within this large area there are *three sub-regions*:

A. The country to the north and west of Lake Victoria (banana—coffee belt)

All this area is certain of over 760 mm (30 ins) of rain. Most of it has over 1 000 mm (40 ins) well distributed through the year. The original vegetation was therefore rain forest. Today much of it is cleared for the growing of bananas and coffee. Elephant grass grows when the land falls out of use. (Studies: a smallholding in Buganda; a small township in Buganda; Busoga sugar plantation; a dairy farm in Bunyoro.)

B. The eastern coast of Lake Victoria and north-central Uganda (maize—cotton—millet belt)

Rainfall totals may be similar to those in A but the distribution is different, giving longer dry seasons. The rainfall is also less reliable. Hence maize and millet replace bananas, and cotton takes the place of coffee as the chief cash crop. (Studies: farming in Nyanza, Kenya; cotton growers of Uganda.)

C. The miombo woodland of west and south Tanzania

Some authorities regard the miombo country as being more like the dry plateaus than the wet plateaus. The total rainfall is less than in A and B, and in most places the rain falls in one season. There is therefore a long dry season during which the trees lose their leaves. At this time of the year it looks very dry indeed.

But the rainfall is higher and more certain than in the dry plateaus and there is a better chance of the miombo area being used for growing crops. The rainfall figures for Songea and Seke (pages 85 and 86) show the difference. This is so even in the plateaus of western Tanzania which are drier than those to the south. This is the least important of the three sub-regions because it is infested by tsetse fly. Hence few people live there.

We have again chosen several case studies for each of these three very large regions.

A. The country to the north and west of Lake Victoria (banana—coffee belt)

Four studies have been chosen to represent life in this region. They are: a smallholding; a small township; Busoga sugar estate; a dairy farm in Bunyoro.

Farming in Buganda

The average size of a holding in Buganda is about 2·5 hectares (6 acres). Although this is not very large, careful farming makes it produce food for a whole family and also crops to sell. So most Buganda live well and have money in their pockets.

Anyone who does not know Buganda can learn much by looking at the plan of the farm. One

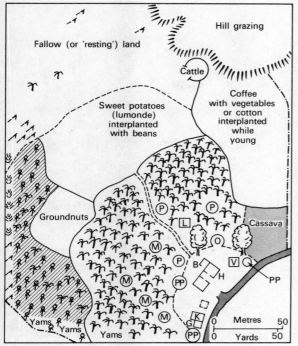

Crops

⫙	Matoke bananas–grown as vegetable also for beer Some young matoke among cotton
⫼	Yellow bananas–for fruit
⫽	Cotton and young bananas
⋀	Sugar cane

Ⓜ	Marrow or melon		
Ⓟ	Pineapple		
ⓅⓅ	Pawpaw trees		

Homestead

H Dwelling house for family

B Bathroom

V House for grandmother or for married children home on a visit

K Kitchen

O Store

⌷⌷ Table for washing up, drying china

G Goat or hen house

L Pit latrine

Ⓢ Mituba tree (for shade and bark cloth)

Fig. 47 A smallholding in Buganda

might ask, 'How closely is the land farmed; how many crops can it grow?' It is possible to find out how big it is, how much of the land is given to each crop and to say something about where each crop is grown (Fig. 47).

The banana supplies many needs. The green *matoke* bananas are steamed and eaten as a vegetable; others are used for making beer – *pombe*; and bananas are also eaten as fruit. The *matoke* is the most important because it is the

basic food. It is what bread and potatoes are to the people of Europe and rice to the people of China and Japan. Matoke bananas are picked while they are still hard, skinned, wrapped in banana leaves, steamed over water and mashed. They are slightly sweet. Matoke can be eaten on its own or with meat stew, or mixed with curry powder or sauces. There are also other kinds of bananas for cooking and many for fruit, as well as the beer bananas.

The Buganda can pick bananas all through the year. They also grow sweet potatoes (*lumonde*) and cassava (another long thick root) which can be

Seasonal work in Buganda					
Month	Temp.	Rain	Season	Planting and other work	Harvesting
Jan.	72° F [22° C]	2·6" [66 mm]	Dry season		Coffee Cotton Matoke
Feb.	72° F [22° C]	3·6" [91 mm]	Dry season		Millet
Mar.	72° F [22° C]	6·3" [160 mm]	The rains	Sweet potatoes Maize Groundnuts Beans	
Apr.	72° F [22° C]	10" [254 mm]	The rains		
May	71° F [21·5°C]	9·6" [244 mm]	The rains		Beans
June	70° F [21° C]	4·8" [122 mm]	The rains	Cotton Beans	
July	69° F [20·5°C]	3·0" [76 mm]	Dry season	Millet	Maize Groundnuts Sweet potatoes
Aug.	70° F [21° C]	3·0" [76 mm]	Dry season	Cassava (Some cotton)	
Sept.	70° F [21° C]	3·0" [76 mm]	Dry season	Sweet potatoes Beans (Some maize)	
Oct.	71° F [21·5°C]	3·7" [94 mm]	Dry season	Maize Beans	
Nov.	71° F [21·5°C]	5·2" [132 mm]	Little rains		Coffee
Dec.	71° F [21·5°C]	4·6" [117 mm]	Little rains		Beans Cotton Millet

Fig. 48 Seasonal work in Buganda

Coffee, maize and bananas grown together on a shamba near Kampala.

dried and stored. There are many other kinds of roots, often called yams, which make good vegetables. Their leaves are used as spinach. Sweet potatoes are grown in the same way as European potatoes; pieces of the root are planted into the tops of earthed-up mounds so that the root tubers can grow under the ground. There are many vegetables too: beans, groundnuts, onions, marrow and sometimes tomatoes. Here and there are pineapples and pawpaw trees and sometimes a mango tree; there are long stems of sugar cane and maize. From time to time the owner has to make a new banana garden because each shoot or trunk of the tree only produces one stem of bananas and when this is picked the tree is cut down. The old tree is split through and the pieces placed on the ground in the banana plantation to rot, to give back the goodness to the soil. This serves as a mulch to protect the soil. Young shoots taken from the base of old trees are planted as cuttings and they soon grow into a new banana garden. While the young bananas are growing, cotton or beans can be grown on the same ground, so the land is not idle.

Vegetables or cotton are sometimes grown between the rows of very young coffee bushes and there is nearly always a separate patch of cotton. Coffee and cotton are the chief cash crops of the Baganda smallholders. The value of the coffee grown in Uganda is now more than the value of the cotton. Cotton is an annual crop, so the grower can sell and have his money back every year. Coffee trees do not start to bear until the fourth or fifth year, so the farmer has to wait several years before he sees any money for his work. So most people grow some of both. Some farmers think that coffee is easier to grow than cotton. It does not have to be planted every year, so there is less work to be done. The Baganda are fortunate in being able to grow either crop, although not every part of the region is equally suited to both.

Smallholding coffee production

Two types of coffee are grown in East Africa, Arabica and Robusta. Arabica grows best at higher levels. Robusta coffee, which once grew wild in Uganda, is now cultivated on the lower plateaus of that country. It needs about 1 000 mm (40 ins) of rain a year.

Coffee seeds are first planted in a nursery bed under a thatch shelter. They begin to shoot in a few weeks and are ready for planting out when 20

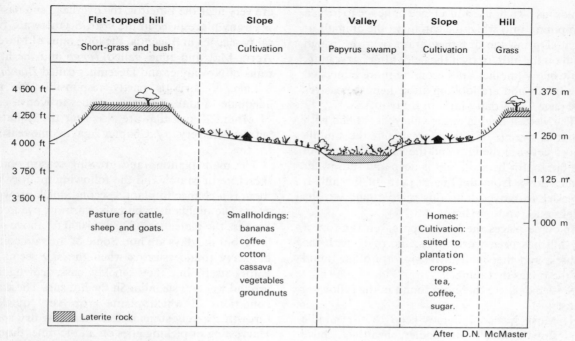

Flat-topped hill	Slope	Valley	Slope	Hill
Short-grass and bush	Cultivation	Papyrus swamp	Cultivation	Grass

4 500 ft — 1 375 m
4 250 ft
4 000 ft — 1 250 m
3 750 ft — 1 125 m
3 500 ft

				1 000 m
Pasture for cattle, sheep and goats.	Smallholdings: bananas coffee cotton cassava vegetables groundnuts		Homes: Cultivation: suited to plantation crops- tea, coffee, sugar.	

▨ Laterite rock

After   D.N. McMaster

Fig. 49 Section across a hillside in Buganda

or 23 cm (8 or 9 ins) high. The seedlings are planted in their final home with great care and they are protected from the sun by palm leaves. Sometimes 'shade trees' are planted so that the ground will not get too hot and damage the roots, for coffee is really a shrub from the shady forests.

The beautiful sprays of white flowers form in January or February and die very quickly. Ten months later the berries turn red and are ripe for picking (see chapter 9).

Landscapes and settlements in Buganda

Almost everywhere in southern Buganda one sees hills with flat tops; in the valleys cut into the plateau lie the swamps of papyrus. For this reason it is quite hard to find a river in some parts of Buganda. This is the landscape of the northern shores of Lake Victoria, just as the great granite rocks rising from the plateau to the south of the lake are the landscape of Mwanza and Sukumaland in Tanzania.

Very few Baganda live in villages. They prefer to build homes in the middle of their own land. The plan (Fig. 47) and the section (Fig. 49) show the location of the homes. The larger building often has several rooms. First the shape of the house is marked out on the ground. A trench is dug along these lines and strong thick poles are sunk into the ground. Then a double row of elephant grass canes is tied to the main framework so that there is a space between, which can be filled with clay to make the walls. The walls are plastered with mud inside and out, to make them smooth, and they can be finished with a coat of whitewash or lime to make them light and clean. The windows have shutters and the roof is thatched or covered with corrugated iron or aluminium. There is usually a separate building for the kitchen. *Note the other things that make up a homestead.*

At the back of the holding, away from the road, the land rises steeply and the hilltops are often covered with a hard, rock-like material called laterite. Few trees grow but the grass is long. Sometimes this land is used for pasturing animals. Although the Baganda are not as interested in cattle as in growing crops, they are quick to see that milk and meat can help to vary and balance their diet. *Matoke*, cassava and sweet potato have only about one per cent protein. Sometimes several families share the services of an Ankole herdsman from the west of Uganda in looking after their cattle, for he understands and loves animals. He

71

builds his own house and a fence or hedge to form a compound into which he can drive the animals at night. During the day they graze over the rough bush on the hills, or over the fields after harvesting. Now many families are becoming more interested in animals and are looking after them themselves (see page 74: A dairy farm in Bunyoro).

The wettest land is in the valley; it is filled with papyrus swamp or thick forest. On the middle slopes between the hills and the valleys lie most of the farms, for here the soil is deep and rain water comes down from the higher parts of the hill. It is easier to move along this middle land, so the tracks and roads are here.

In some places the hard capping on the top of the hill has been worn away; the road, with the houses, and the small townships are often found on the ridges that remain.

Settlements are therefore found in the following places:
1. Most scattered homes keep to the middle slopes, which are cooler, healthier, have better soils, easier slopes to cultivate and easier communications.
2. There are few homes in valley bottoms because they are unhealthy, hot, humid and occupied by swamp or forest.
3. Medium hills have villages or townships; sometimes schools, missions, hospitals or Government headquarters.
4. The highest hills are unused.

The work on the land through the year

The land of this part of the plateaus seldom rests. There are things to be done the whole year round. Nevertheless, there is a pattern to planting and harvesting which fits into the seasons of heavier and lighter rain.

Fig. 48 gives the climatic figures for Entebbe. The total rain for the year is about 1 520 mm (60 ins), that is an average of about 120 mm (5 ins) every month. The rainy months are therefore those with 120 mm or over and the 'dry' months those which do not have as much as 120 mm. But there is no month without rain. This is one of the reasons why Buganda and the wet shorelands of Lake Victoria can produce so much.

Because the northern shores of Lake Victoria

are very near the Equator, the overhead sun passes over any place *twice* in the year. So there are two rainy seasons in Buganda, the long rains of March, April, May and June, called *Toggo* and the little rains of November and December called *Dumbi*.

Lake Victoria is partly responsible for the adequate rainfall. There are places in Kenya east of Mount Kenya that are also near the Equator, yet they are very dry. Chapter 2 gave some reasons for this.

The main planting and growing season comes therefore in March and the following months but there is a chance to plant a second quick-growing crop. The nights may be only warm or even cool because the plateau is 1 220 m (4 000 ft) above sea-level, but the days are hot. Some of the rain comes in heavy thunderstorms when the sky seems to empty itself, but they quickly pass, leaving the ground wet and steaming in the hot sun. These are conditions in which plants grow very quickly. Growth scarcely stops unless there is a dry spell. Harvesting or picking goes on all the time, though there are main picking seasons which correspond to the main planting times.

A small township in Buganda— Kasangati (Fig. 50)

Although most people live in the countryside there are also small markets, villages and duka towns scattered at intervals. They are usually found at crossroads where people can easily meet. There may be little more than two or three shops and a bicycle repairer or they may be quite large like the one shown. The roads are built along the tops of the gentle hills and homes and farmland fill the slopes of the valleys. In the valley bottom there is swamp and there are places where it is easy to get water. The groups of shops (or dukas) are usually found where roads meet. They are of every kind. There are butchers, grocers selling all kinds of packet food, tea, flour, toothpaste, ink, books, etc., a hardware shop selling bowls, tins, pots, charcoal stoves, ropes, etc., another selling shirts and dress materials and another where the tailor machines shirts and dresses for customers. There are small cafés or bars, garages, a bakery and a post office. Some of the shops in Uganda, indeed in many parts of East Africa, are owned by Asians, but now the number of African shop-

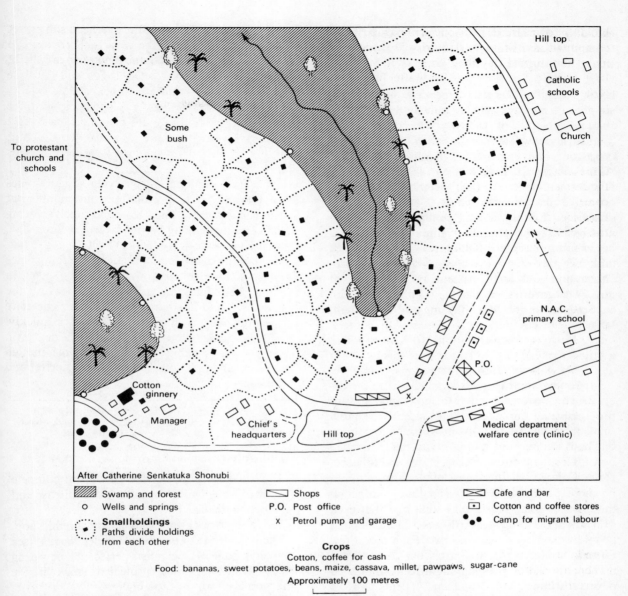

Fig. 50 Kasangati (N.B. This map was drawn some years ago. Those of you who live near Kasangati may like to bring it up to date.)

keepers is growing, and this is so in Kasangati. Those who know the country will be able to write a lot about the work of such a small township and the district that it serves. Those who do not can still find out a lot more from the map.

In any place of this size there are usually four or five stores where people can sell their cotton or coffee crop as they pick it. These offices look like shops, but are shut most of the year. As the picking season begins they open up and put a list of the market buying and selling prices outside. As bags of coffee are brought in, the crop is weighed and the owner paid. Different co-operatives compete for the crop. When the buyer has enough to make a load it is taken by lorry to coffee hulleries and to cotton ginneries.

A dairy farm in Bunyoro: An example of a small enterprise that grew into a co-operative (Fig. 51)

Until recently Uganda depended heavily on supplies of milk brought by railway from Kenya. In 1967 the Dairy Industry Corporation was founded and it will eventually control all collection, processing and distribution of milk in Uganda. At present the situation is one of transition: some farmers sell direct to their neighbours, but co-operative dairies with coolers are also being established throughout the Republic. Already there are over fifty coolers. In Kampala a plant has been built to handle 136 400 litres (30 000 galls) of milk per day, to make cheese, butter and ice-cream, and pack fresh, pasteurised, homogenised milk. The government is assisting producers with subsidies on sprays, dips, fencing and equipment. It helps the co-operative societies with coolers, loans, transport of surplus milk to Kampala and a brand name (D.I.C.). To see how this works in detail, we will look at the efforts of one man.

Mr John Habyirimana is an official with the co-operative movement in Masindi and a very progressive farmer indeed. Until recently he had a small farm on the road from Masindi to Hoima but bad weather and falling prices made him fed up with his main crops, cotton, coffee and tobacco. He considered whether some other venture might be more profitable. He noticed that in Masindi there was a great shortage of milk and that even 213 km (133 miles) north-west of Kampala, people were buying Kenya milk. Each day a few farmers brought milk in churns, but this was not nearly enough and people bought Kenyan or used poor substitutes. Milk was from 70 cents to 1/– a pint. Yet, in that district the diet of the people was very poor, being based on cassava and plantains and lacking protein. He thought about developing a dairy farm but then realised the problems:

1. The Masindi area suffers from the tsetse fly and local cattle develop *trypanosomiasis*.
2. Exotic cattle, that is, European stock brought in, would surely die from this disease and they were very costly.
3. If he had a lot of milk to sell how would he keep it fresh until everyone had bought it — for in the heat of Bunyoro milk is sour by 12 noon?

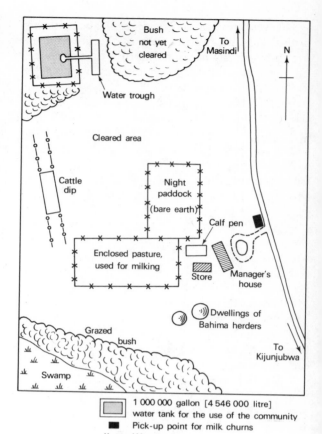

Fig. 51 A dairy farm in Bunyoro

4. Would his milk be safe enough to compete with Kenya milk, for milk carries disease and people realise this?
5. He could not afford a cooler and a retail shop.

Then in 1951 tsetse fly clearance began (see chapter 4, page 24). Scientists perfected a new drug called *Ethidium* which protected stock if the infection level was not too high.

Mr Habyirimana decided to invest in a dairy farm but first he had to overcome the problems of a cooler and a shop. With some of his friends and other businessmen and farmers of the area they formed a co-operative and this opened a shop in Masindi. The U.S.A.I.D. gave them a 682 litre (150 gall) cooler and now he could begin. Mr Habyirimana developed his farm in part of the cleared area where there was plenty of land with good grass, and water from the Kizii swamp. The farm began with a small herd of local animals and milk was taken each morning on a bicycle to Masindi.

The venture was very successful and with his profits, savings and the help of the government Mr Habyirimana began to improve the enterprise. First he had a subsidy to build a dip: into this dip disinfectant is poured, and then the cattle are pushed in, one after the other, to rid them of the ticks which carry East Coast fever and other killer diseases. Next, with a government subsidy he built a little fenced area for a night paddock where cattle could be herded after dark to protect them from theft and wild animals. To look after the stock Mr Habyirimana hired some Bahima, the traditional cattle people of the west.

Gradually the profits grew and Mr Habyirimana was faced with a problem of getting the milk to Masindi each day for the quantity was growing and bicycles were proving inadequate. Yet Mr Habyirimana was not in a position to buy a van. Mentioning this to his friends, also dairy farmers, he found that they were in the same position, and realising the benefits of co-operation they grouped together to hire a van which collected the milk each morning.

After two years Mr Habyirimana had saved enough money to buy some exotic cattle to cross breed with his own and these he decided should be crossed with Friesian, a breed originally from the Netherlands. Why? Because these cattle yield six to eight times the usual amount of milk from the Nyoro Zebu. Guernseys, producing very rich creamy milk, were not a match for the Friesians as regards quantity, and that was what counted. Many of Mr Habyirimana's friends bought exotic cattle too, so that there were 800 in the district by 1969 and there was now more milk than Masindi could absorb. So with government help the surplus was taken to Kampala. A 1 820 litre (400 gall) cooler replaced the earlier one which was now inadequate.

As yet milk is not sent around Bunyoro from Masindi because there is not the means of transporting it and there is a reliable market in Kampala, but this will have to change if the diet in the rural areas of Bunyoro is to improve. At the moment the small farmers far from Masindi still sell direct to their neighbours.

The government helped Mr Habyirimana once more in 1968. The water of the swamp contained parasites which are very harmful to sensitive animals, and Mr Habyirimana felt that he could no longer rely on the swamp for watering the exotic stock. The government realised the problem and provided a bore and a 4 500 000 litre (1 000 000 gall) tank for Mr Habyirimana and all the people in the nearby area. This tank had a trough and constant fresh, pure water. The government is distributing Chloris grass, which is well suited to the wet Bunyoro hills; it will improve the pasture and milk yield of the stock in the area.

The main problem remains the bush. There is much to be cut down as the dairy farm is enlarged, and as this is done each part must be enclosed and rotated to keep the grass short, fresh and nutritious. But cutting bush is difficult work and in this humid area it grows again twice as thickly if cattle are not grazed on the pasture at once. So the expansion of the farm is gradual, going only as fast as Mr Habyirimana's ability to settle new cattle. He now has 300 head of cattle of which thirty are exotic, a semi-skilled manager, a dip, a night paddock, one fenced paddock and access to fresh water (Fig. 51).

Masindi has been transformed from a town importing its milk to one with a healthy export.

A Busoga sugar estate (Fig. 52)

In many parts of East Africa some of the crops grown on smallholdings are now being grown on a large scale on plantations. This is true of the wet plateaus.

Our first study showed small-farm cultivation in Buganda; a sugar plantation in Busoga is chosen as an example of the plantations found in some parts of the wet plateaus. These include tea and coffee estates.

The Madhvani Sugar Works Ltd (Fig. 52)
The Madhvani Estate is situated near the shores of Lake Victoria a few miles from Jinja. As in Buganda the landscape is one of flat-topped hills, but they are higher and set farther apart. Between the hills are large stretches of rolling country flat enough for machines to work. This is important because although the cane is cut by hand, mechanisation of ploughing and transport cuts costs. About 1 400 mm (55 ins) of rain falls each year and the humidity is very high.

The diagram (Fig. 52) shows only one very small part of the plantation, which covers 22 000 hectares (54 340 acres). From it one can discover

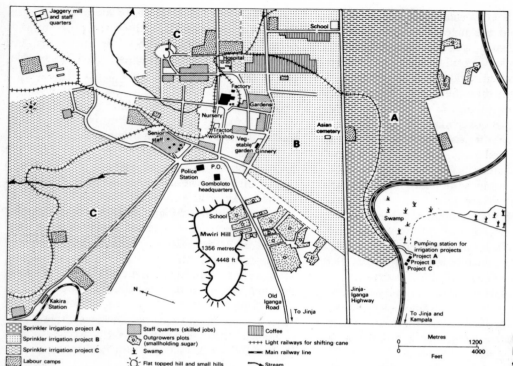

Fig. 52
Madhvani
sugar estate

Map legend:
- Sprinkler irrigation project A
- Sprinkler irrigation project B
- Sprinkler irrigation project C
- Labour camps
- Staff quarters (skilled jobs)
- Outgrowers plots (smallholding sugar)
- Swamp
- Flat topped hill and small hills
- Coffee
- Light railways for shifting cane
- Main railway line
- Stream

Metres 0 — 1200
Feet 0 — 4000

many of the usual features of such an estate.

Work centres round the sugar factory and must never stop if it is to produce most cheaply. All day and all night work goes on. Men work in three shifts of eight hours each. The factory capacity is about 150 000 tonnes a year, though production is lower than this. About ten per cent of the total is refined sugar.

The rain of Busoga is spread fairly evenly through the year, and with added irrigation water it is possible to plant and cut cane all the year round. The big step forward has been the introduction of large-scale overhead irrigation sprinklers for 2 834 hectares (7 000 acres). This is one of the largest single irrigation units in the world.

The fields are planted at different times so that there is always cane ready for cutting. The total cycle is sixty-five months. It takes twenty months for newly planted cane to come to harvest. When it has been cut it takes another eighteen months for it to grow again. After the third cutting the ground is cleared of sugar and given about eight months' rest. A crop of hemp is planted and ploughed in to replace some of the nitrogen in the soil that the sugar has taken away. Once the cane is cut it must reach the factory as soon as possible

and not more than forty-eight hours after cutting. Small railways have been built across the estate using mini-locomotives to bring the cane to the factory.

On arrival the cane is weighed, chopped and crushed. The juice is squeezed out and treated with lime and sulphur, heated and clarified. The clear juice is boiled and the crystals separated from the dark brown molasses. Finally the sugar is dried, graded and put into bags.

The plantation contains a small town. It has its schools, hospitals, canteen, shops and a theatre-cinema. There are homes for the manager and foremen and different kinds of workers. About 9 000 workers are employed on the estate, as well as factory and administrative staff. They are provided with housing and there are thirty-two camps which are dotted over the plantation. On the higher parts where the soil is too thin for growing sugar, eucalyptus trees have been planted to provide firewood and timber for the building of the labourers' houses.

This single plantation produces a large part of Uganda's sugar. The average amount of cane per hectare per crop has increased from 86·5 to 123·5 tonnes (from 35 to 50 tons per acre). This is partly due to the use made of water pumped through 72 km (45 miles) of main pipe from Lake Victoria and 64 km (40 miles) of aluminium feeder piping for the overhead sprinklers.

The climate and soils of the wet plateaus are equally suited to farming by the intensive methods* of cropping of the smallholder, or the large-scale farming of the plantation.

Work to do

1. Make a chart for the year's work in Buganda on a different pattern from the one in this chapter. You can find out how to do a block chart if you look at Figs. 5 and 6 in chapter 2 (pages 8 and 9). Draw your circle chart like this:

   Draw a circle of 5 centimetres radius (10 centimetres diameter).

   Allow 50 millimetres for writing names of months.

   Divide into a smaller and a larger circle (inner for crops, outer for rainfall).

   Rule lines to divide it up into 12 months.

   In the inner circle show details of each crop:
   (a) when it is planted
   (b) the months it is in the ground
   (c) when it is harvested

   Some crops, like coffee, are perennial (producing for several years without replanting; i.e. not annual) so that the picking season only can be shown.

   Measure rainfall along spokes of outer circle. The circles can be drawn larger; this gives more room to show crops.

2. Write about a township or small market that *you* know. Draw a plan to show the position of shops or stalls (see Fig. 50).

   Find out which things sold there today were not sold twenty years ago.

   Why has there been a change?

3. The following rainfall figures (mm) are for Bukoba and Kyerwa (a little further west, but in almost the same latitude) in Tanzania:
   (a) Comment on the differences and try to find out why they exist.
   (b) Draw a cultivation chart of the year's work for one of them if you know the area.

*'Intensive' is used to describe ways of farming that produce many crops from a small area. 'Extensive' is used to describe the farming of a large area. Although yields are good, the land could be made to produce greater areas of different crops.

Bukoba (1 144 m, 3 753 ft above sea-level)

Table 5: Rainfall in mm (inches)

Jan.	Feb.	March	April	May	June	
147	158	249	356	315	86	
(5·8″)	(6·2″)	(9·8″)	(14·0″)	(12·6″)	(3·4″)	
July	August	Sept.	Oct.	Nov.	Dec.	Total
48	86	107	132	161	193	2 052
(1·9″)	(3·4″)	(4·2″)	(5·2″)	(6·5″)	(7·6″)	(80·8″)

Kyerwa (1 402 m, 4 600 ft above sea-level)

61	53	89	150	94	15	
(2·4″)	(2·1″)	(3·5″)	(5·9″)	(3·7″)	(0·6″)	
8	18	81	94	99	79	838
(0·3″)	(0·7″)	(3·2″)	(3·7″)	(3·9″)	(3·1″)	(33·0″)

B. The east coast of Lake Victoria and north-central Uganda (maize—cotton—millet belt)

In some ways the second sub-region is very like the area that we have just described.

The land is still about 1 220 m 4 000 ft) above the level of the sea. It is still plateau with hills rising here and there; many of the same crops can be grown. But everywhere the rain is less reliable and there is always at least one really dry season. In this way it is quite different from the Buganda study.

Because of this difference in climate the banana cannot grow everywhere as it does in the wetter region. It only grows in favoured places. Instead of the banana the basic foods are maize, millets, sweet potatoes and cassava.

The marked dry season makes another difference. When there are no clouds in the sky the sun beats down and the temperatures rise higher than they do in the areas of well-distributed rain. At night, when there is no blanket of cloud, the temperature may fall quickly. Hence temperatures are not as equable as they are in region A. They are less 'equatorial'.

In these areas cotton often replaces coffee as the chief cash crop; surplus maize is also sold.

Two studies from Kenya and one from Uganda illustrate ways of life in this sub-region.

Farming in Nyanza

The first study comes from the lower parts of Nyanza Province, just to the north of Kisumu. The eastern parts of Nyanza are over 1 520 m (5 000 ft) and therefore form part of the Highlands.

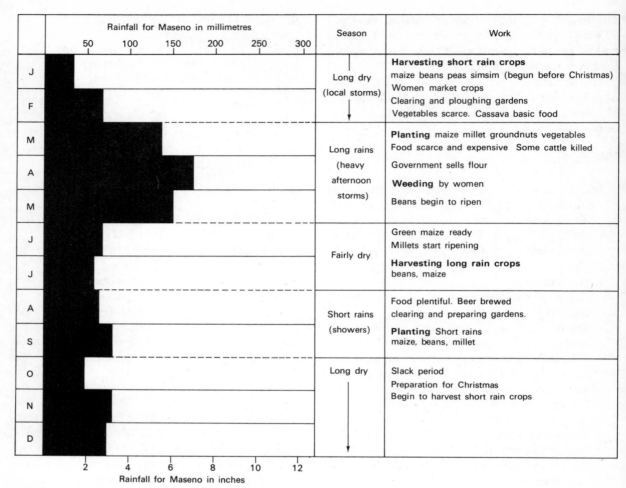

	Rainfall for Maseno in millimetres	Season	Work
J		Long dry (local storms)	**Harvesting short rain crops** maize beans peas simsim (begun before Christmas) Women market crops Clearing and ploughing gardens Vegetables scarce. Cassava basic food
F			
M		Long rains (heavy afternoon storms)	**Planting** maize millet groundnuts vegetables Food scarce and expensive Some cattle killed Government sells flour **Weeding** by women Beans begin to ripen
A			
M			
J		Fairly dry	Green maize ready Millets start ripening **Harvesting long rain crops** beans, maize
J			
A		Short rains (showers)	Food plentiful. Beer brewed clearing and preparing gardens. **Planting** Short rains maize, beans, millet
S			
O		Long dry	Slack period Preparation for Christmas Begin to harvest short rain crops
N			
D			

Fig. 53 Seasonal work in Nyanza

This province carries more than 1·5 million people and is one of the most densely settled parts of East Africa.

It shares the rainfall pattern of the Lake Victoria Basin with two drier seasons and two 'peaks' of rain. Rainfall totals may also be much the same as in the Lake Victoria coastlands further west, but it differs from the southern lake shores where Mwanza has only 890 mm (35 ins) of rain a year. Kisumu, at lake level, in the north-east has 1 200 mm (47 ins) of rain a year. The other special features are that the main dry season is usually more marked and may last for as much as five months: it does not share in the rainfall reliability of the higher lands.

Secondly, away from the lake the relief is more varied. Much of it is 1 520 m (5 000 ft) and even

1 820 m (6 000 ft) with steep-sided hills and valleys. This is much higher than the average 1 220 m (4 000 ft) level of Buganda and the result is lower temperatures. Temperature range is also greater. In both these ways the region loses some of its 'equatorial' character.

Nyanza is one of the most important maize-growing areas of East Africa. Both maize and cotton are produced on small farms. There is such pressure on the land (as many as 400 people to the sq km, 1 000 people to the sq mile in places) that it is important that more food should be grown and stock improved. The diagram on this page shows the relation between farming and climate (Fig. 53).

The Nyanza countryside is full of villages. The holdings are close together between small patches of forest or granite hills. At one time there was

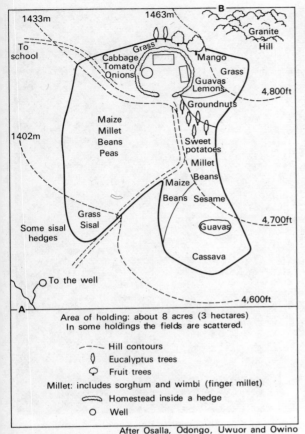

Area of holding: about 8 acres (3 hectares)
In some holdings the fields are scattered.

- - - Hill contours
Eucalyptus trees
Fruit trees
Millet: includes sorghum and wimbi (finger millet)
Homestead inside a hedge
O Well

After Osalla, Odongo, Uwuor and Owino

Fig. 54 A Seme Kowe holding

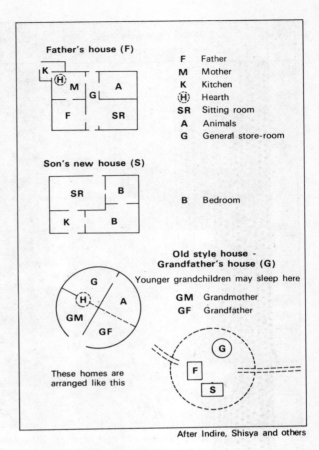

F Father
M Mother
K Kitchen
(H) Hearth
SR Sitting room
A Animals
G General store-room

B Bedroom

**Old style house -
Grandfather's house (G)**
Younger grandchildren may sleep here

GM Grandmother
GF Grandfather

These homes are
arranged like this

After Indire, Shisya and others

Fig. 55 A Maragoli home

plenty of common land. Now most of it is taken up.

Hence changing the crops between different fields has long been a practice. But it is now very difficult to allow the land to 'fallow' or rest, as there is little to spare and it is needed to pasture the animals. Although maize is the chief food, other crops (sweet potatoes, groundnuts and cassava) are always grown in smaller quantities to supplement maize. The cassava especially is useful when food is short.

Both the homestead and the chart of the year's work would be different in other parts of Nyanza. This is because there is such a wide variation of rainfall, soil and tribal custom.

At one time a homestead would always have been surrounded by a strong hedge as a protection against wind and loss of animals. Now this is less common. Round houses are also giving way to rectangular ones. This is shown in Fig. 55.

The future of farming in Nyanza

What the farmer grows depends on his needs in food, on the price he can get for any surplus and on the advice or direction of the government agricultural officers. Nyanza is one of the richest parts of East Africa and the density of population is high. This means that the land must be even better used.

Already a great deal of maize is marketed. One of the features of this area is the great number of small and larger markets where the women especially engage in trade. Other surplus crops may include rice and groundnuts. The chief export crop has in the past been cotton. Some coffee is grown, mainly in South Nyanza.

The great problem is to increase production. To do this it is necessary to maintain soil fertility and to reduce soil erosion. The wise rearing of stock can be a help.

At present farms are scattered in such a way that

79

Meanders on the River Ngaila in West Nyanza. Study the picture and make sure you can see the following: meanders, undercut and slip-off slopes, sand-bars, rapids and a place where the river is about to cut through a narrow neck of land. Make an annotated drawing of the picture to show these physical features. Suggest a reason why the land between the river loops has been cultivated, while most of the other land is used for grazing. In the background are several traditional settlements, enclosed by euphorbia hedges.

drainage of the heavy rain and the use of small mechanical ploughs is difficult. With co-operation the land can be organised in drainage units, heavy rain can be led off, and soil erosion reduced. Gently sloping terraces would allow this; they would also allow machinery to move along the terrace from one holding to another, ploughing the land after annual crops. The fences between these parts of the holdings would need to be movable, but in this way grazing and crop land could be rotated, giving each the benefit of manure.

Work to do

Draw a section from A to B on Fig. 54 to show the position of the homestead and crops in relation to the granite hill (tor), the slope of the hillside and the place from which water is carried.

The Ahero Pilot Scheme, Kenya (Fig. 56)

Water from the higher areas of Nyanza is being used to irrigate the lower areas such as the Kano

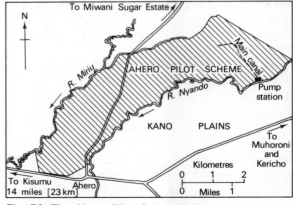

Fig. 56 The Ahero Pilot Scheme, Kenya

80

Plains. The map (Fig. 56) shows the location of this exciting new project. A survey report has estimated that 14 575 hectares (36 000 acres) of the Kano Plains, near Kisumu, could be irrigated. The Ahero Pilot Scheme is an attempt to see how successful large-scale irrigation might be.

The scheme consists of 842 hectares (2 080 acres) of irrigated land. On this 520 tenant farmers are growing rice. Like the Mwea Scheme, described in chapter 12, they have a 1·6 hectare (4 acre) holding each. The organisation, rules and technical control are the same as those at Mwea. One big difference is that since Ahero is lower land (below 1 220 m (4 000 ft)) than Mwea, *two* crops of rice per year should be possible. However, two crops per year may be too difficult, because of the length of growing season of existing rice varieties. The National Irrigation Board which manages the scheme is looking for varieties which need a shorter growing season.

It is still too early to judge the success of the project. However, the first crop yielded two tons of paddy per acre, which is a very encouraging result considering that neither the farmers nor the staff had any previous experience.

Cotton growers of Uganda

Cotton is one of the most important crops in East Africa. It is also one of the chief exports. It is not grown in the wettest parts of the country because too much rain at the time of picking spoils cotton; but Buganda rivals the Eastern Province of Uganda as a producer of cotton.

The people of Teso District in the eastern part of Uganda are smallholders and cotton producers. Like many African peoples they now grow cotton as a cash crop in addition to their food crops. The countryside is gently rolling with granite hills rising suddenly from the plateau. In places the plateau surface itself is granite, of little use as farm land but useful because rainwater collects in hollows, after storms.

Among the Teso, the men and women share the growing of crops. In this area, too, the plough, pulled by oxen, is used to work the land. The Teso are cattle keepers turned cultivators, for they moved into this part of Uganda from Karamoja.

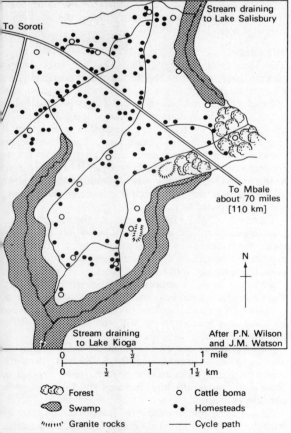

Fig. 57 Kasilang a Teso village

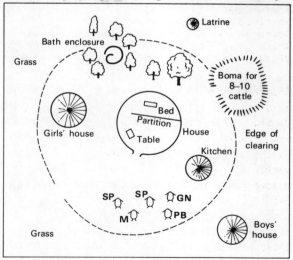

Fig. 58 A Teso homestead

But for the problem of finding drinking water in the three or four dry months, many more people might live in this area. Much of the land bears quite good grass, and cattle, sheep and goats are pastured on this common land. In most places there is enough ground for new plots to be cleared if the present ones become exhausted. The chief problem is to find water during the dry season.

Kasilang is an example of a Teso village (Fig. 57). There is no close grouping of homes, for the people live on their holdings and houses are scattered through the farm land. There are six or more hamlets, each made up from a family group (Fig. 58).

The village occupies the higher ground between swampy valleys, and it forms a natural unit partly because its boundaries are clear. Hence there are two kinds of crop land in the village, the higher parts (called *apokor*) growing cotton, finger millet and vegetables, and the lower ground near the swamp (called *apulon*) where the sandy soils are suited to groundnuts. The lowest land may be used for rice.

The ground is cropped for about three years and then allowed to rest so that the land is used in turn. Different rotations are possible.

Higher land

	Plan 1	Plan 2	Plan 3
Year 1	Cotton	Early cotton	Early cotton
Year 2	Millet, then pulse	Millet, then pulse	Millet, then late cotton
Year 3	Simsim, then cassava	Millet, then sweet potatoes	Millet, then cassava

On the lower ground

	Plan 1	Plan 2
Year 1	Groundnuts or simsim	Groundnuts
Year 2	Millet, then sweet potatoes	Millet, then pulse
Year 3	Cassava	Cotton, then cassava

Work through the year

Table 6: Rainfall figures for Soroti (East Teso) in mm (inches)

Jan.	Feb.	March	April	May	June
18	64	81	183	206	125
(0·7″)	(2·5″)	(3·2″)	(7·2″)	(8·1″)	(4·9″)

July	August	Sept.	Oct.	Nov.	Dec.	Total
117	173	137	112	76	25	1 321
(4·6″)	(6·8″)	(5·4″)	(4·4″)	(3·0″)	(1·0″)	(52·0″)

Detailed study section

The section set in small type is for advanced study. Return to this later if you prefer.

Read the following paragraphs and fill in the information on a seasonal work chart or table like the one for Buganda, page 69.

The driest season comes at the end of November, and in December, January and early February. Teso proper has most rain in April–May but in some places there are two peaks in April–May and August–September. In the dry season cotton is picked and some rice harvested and finger millet and maize are planted; the ground is prepared for more crops. These are planted in the rains of April, May and June. The lowest flooded or swamp land is used for rice and the higher better-drained ground for cotton. This is also the time to earth up the ground for sweet potatoes and to plant cassava.

Cotton is planted from May to September when the heaviest rain falls in the Soroti district, though there is a break in the rains in July.

Through June and July there is a good deal of work to be done weeding cotton, harvesting the millet planted in January; planting beans and sorghum. Cowpeas and sweet potatoes are planted during the second rains.

As each crop is harvested and dried in the sun, it is put into one of the grain stores. These are raised from the ground to protect the crop from pests. There are several millet bins, a rice store, and others for beans or peas, groundnuts and sweet potatoes. Millet is the chief food crop and is pounded into flour.

THE CROPS

The basic food is finger millet (*eleusine*). It is used in making beer and provides the meal for porridge. It is planted in different ways to fit in with the crop that occupies the ground before it. If the crop is cotton, then it can be sown in January before the cotton plant is pulled up for burning. At the end of January or in February it can be sown with the 'grass rains'. These rainstorms sometimes bring as much as 76 mm (3 ins) of rain before the real rainy season begins. Sometimes it can be planted as the cotton is pulled out of the ground. If millet is sown as late as February or March it is usually planted into specially prepared land.

During April and May the rains and the heat give good growing weather, and weeding is a heavy job. At harvest time a flat rock is often used as a drying floor. Other crops are simsim (sesamum), sorghum, groundnuts and cowpeas, the last sown in the second rains.

Cowpeas form an important and varied item of diet. The young leaves can be cooked as a green vegetable; the seeds can be ground to a flour to make porridge; they can be made into a sauce to eat with the *atap* (finger millet porridge).

Sweet potatoes are also sown in the second rains on small patches of ground near the homestead. They too have a great many uses and can be eaten fresh or boiled, or dried and ground into flour. Bananas and fruit trees grow near the compound.

Cassava, the chief famine crop, is more often grown by bachelors, who say that they find it less work than other crops!

otton bolls ready for picking.

eshly picked cotton near Gulu, Uganda, ready to
taken to a co-operative ginnery.

otton

otton, the chief cash crop, is planted any time
tween May and September. The average yield
47–55 kg per hectare (250–300 lb per acre). The
st yields come from planting at the beginning of
ne and as much as 19–28 kg (100–150 lb per
re) *more* cotton is picked from a hectare planted
early June than from a hectare planted in
ugust. The great difficulty is to get the land cleared
d ploughed in time.

Cotton is an annual crop which needs about
ght months in which to grow. The first flowers
grow at the base of the plant and the younger ones
near the top. When it opens the flower is white,
but the second day it turns red and then withers.
Soon after the pod or 'boll' begins to form and
the lower ones may be ripe while there are still
flowers higher up. By November the bolls are a
good size and during the dry weather they turn
brown and hard and split to show the white cotton
lint inside.

As soon as it is showing, the cotton lint is
quickly picked, in case a sudden storm splashes it
with mud. It is put in sacks and taken to the cotton
stores opened by the ginnery companies in the
village and then to the ginnery where the seed is
separated from the lint. Selling cotton helps a man
to pay his tax, to send his children to school and
to buy the extra things that he cannot grow or
make for himself, for example, his bicycle or radio.

Developments in farming

The pressure of work at ploughing time is leading
many Africans to seek new methods. For example
in Acholi and other areas similar in some ways to
Teso many tractors are now at work. Sometimes
they are privately owned, or they are shared under
a co-operative or group-farming scheme.

Tobacco as well as cotton, is sold from this
area, and there has been an increase in tobacco
production. African farmers are building their
own curing barns.

The pattern of work on the land through the
year in Acholi is very similar of that of Teso. The
controlling factor is the rain which comes at
slightly different times and this changes the time
of harvest.

Work to do

1. If you live in Uganda use the set of rainfall
   figures nearest to your home to make a work
   chart for the year and then compare it to one
   in a different district. The instructions for
   drawing a circular cultivation chart are in
   Fig. 77.
2. If you live in a cotton-growing area in another
   country, make a work chart using local
   rainfall figures.
3. Those of you who know the drier parts of
   East Africa where cotton is grown can write
   more fully about growing and selling cotton.

Make a plan of a smallholding that you know yourself; make a table of the work done through the year similar to Fig. 48 on page 69. (Buganda chart).

Table 7: Rainfall for three Uganda weather stations in mm (inches)

	Jan.	Feb.	March	April	May	June
Kitgum	8	25	76	132	175	150
	(0·3″)	(1·0″)	(3·0″)	(5·2″)	(6·9″)	(5·9″)
Masindi	28	55	102	157	150	102
	(1·1″)	(2·2″)	(4·0″)	(6·2″)	(5·9″)	(4·0″)
Mbale	23	51	91	168	168	127
	(0·9″)	(2·0″)	(3·7″)	(6·6″)	(6·7″)	(5·0″)

July	August	Sept.	Oct.	Nov.	Dec.	Total
178	180	140	112	145	36	1 245
(7·0″)	(7·1″)	(5·0″)	(4·4″)	(6·7″)	(1·4″)	(49·0″)
112	137	140	119	117	43	1 270
(4·4″)	(5·4″)	(5·5″)	(5·7″)	(4·6″)	(1·7″)	(50·0″)
117	137	112	81	61	43	1 194
(4·6″)	(5·4″)	(4·4″)	(3·2″)	(2·4″)	(1·7″)	(47·0″)

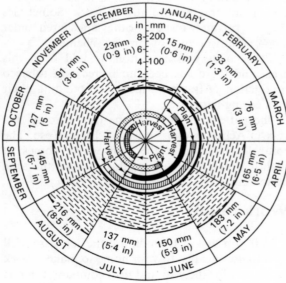

1 mm on paper represents 10 mm of rain

■ Millet
▦ Cow peas
▒ Cotton
▥ Maize
▭ Planting time for each crop
▭ Harvesting time for each

Fig. 59 Cultivation chart for west Teso

The miombo woodland.

C. The miombo woodland of west and south Tanzania

The woodland (see photograph above) is found in two blocks in Tanzania, and covers most of the western and southern parts of the country. At first sight these areas appear to be suited to development because they receive enough rain.

The main check to settlement is the tsetse fly. The result is that these areas include some of the most thinly peopled parts of East Africa. Some parts are almost empty of people.

The following quotation gives a good impression of the miombo country:

'A very large proportion of the country is dotted with miombo (trees) from which people obtain bark for grain bins, and *kemba* or bark rope for building purposes; it is a favourite place for the honey-hunter. A month before the rain sets in, the miombo-covered hills burst all at once into flaming reds, pinks and coppery tinges of all hues as the *Brachystegia* trees flush into young leaf, and within a week all the riot of colour has blended into a forest of the freshest green carpeted with a legion of flowers, scenting the air.

'In full leaf this miombo is delightfully cool and shady and the scanty grass is pleasant to walk through. The trees are 30–40 ft [9–12 m] high and more or less flat-topped. The activity of the honey bees among some of the tree tops is quite phenomenal.

'In the dry season what a change! The whole

...elling a tree in the miombo woodland.

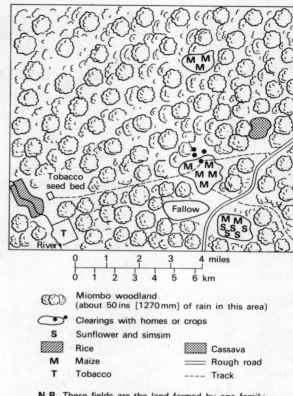

Fig. 60 Cultivation in the miombo woodland

...miombo forest becomes entirely leafless, while ...rass fires burn up all the grass and leaf litter. ...he suns beats down unmercifully and whichever ...ay one turns one sees the same view: the grey ...tems of the miombo trees fading into the shim- ...ering distance. The buzz of insect life has ...isappeared except for the sharp hiss of the tsetse. ...rown dry pods up in the tree tops will split ...uddenly and scatter their seeds, while overhead ...e bark of an eagle catches the attention.' (B. D. ...urtt, 1942.)

Most of the people who live in these areas are ...und in the clearings in the woodland. These ...earings may be on a large scale, as in the case of ...e town of Tabora. In some cases scientific ...earings have been established where the number ...f people, crops and animals is carefully planned ...o as to keep the tsetse fly away. Elsewhere there ...e small clearings made by families. The Songea ...ttlement shows a small family clearing (Fig. 60). ...ee also chapter 2, Fig. 6.) The success of ...bacco growing at Urambo and Tumbi (chapter ..., page 131) shows that the land of the miombo ...odland can produce good crops. The first need ... that experiments should continue in order to ...d out how best to clear and farm the land, and ... try out different crops; the second need is for ...ney to do all this.

Table 8: Rainfall for Songea in mm (inches)

Jan.	Feb.	March	April	May	June
274	231	259	112	15	3
(10·8″)	(9·1″)	(10·2″)	(4·4″)	(0·6″)	(0·1″)

July	August	Sept.	Oct.	Nov.	Dec.	Total
0	3	3	10	48	178	1 130
(0·0″)	(0·1″)	(0·1″)	(0·4″)	(1·9″)	(7·0″)	(44·5″)

85

Chapter 8: The dry plateaus

The dry plateaus differ from those already described in the uncertainty of their rainfall and the low totals received. They have a long and difficult dry season, in some places lasting for six or seven months. This is well shown by the rainfall figures, for example, 529 mm (20·8 ins), from Seke station at 1 215 m (3 985 ft) in Sukumaland, on the railway between Tabora and Mwanza.

Table 9: Rainfall for Seke in mm (inches)

Jan.	Feb.	March	April	May	June
71	76	99	76	43	1
(2·8″)	(3·0″)	(3·9″)	(3·0″)	(1·7″)	(0·06″)

July	August	Sept.	Oct.	Nov.	Dec.	Total
2	2	3	15	48	69	529
(0·07″)	(0·09″)	(0·1″)	(0·6″)	(1·9″)	(2·7″)	(20·82″)

Sukumaland*

The countryside (Fig. 61)

The people of Sukumaland live in a countryside of wide rolling plains broken by hills of granite, often called tors. Such a landscape of *ngulu* is also found in other parts of Africa, in the Sudan and Northern Nigeria. At their foot there are long gentle sandy slopes which flatten out to form part of the great plateau of Africa about 1 220 m (4 000 ft) above sea level. A little below this level are shallow basins of darker *mbuga* soils, where rivers flow during the rains. Here some water can usually be found even during the dry season. There are few trees. They are still found among the round granite rocks of the tors; but in the open country only the baobab trees are left, and small thickets for the supply of fuel. Near the foot of the rocks are signs of older homesteads. The newer homesteads are set further out on the plain in the middle of grazing and cultivated land. They are nearer the

*Freely adapted from *Sukumaland* by D. W. Malcolm, O.U.P. 1953.

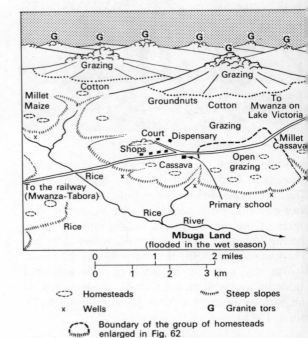

Fig. 61 The landscape of Sukumaland

wells and nearer the road to their neighbours and to school.

The homesteads (Fig. 62)

Each homestead has a euphorbia or thorn hedge. Within the hedge there is room to build homes for the whole family with a separate boma for the cattle and separate grain stores. Beyond this is a little meadow where the calves can graze and where firewood can be stored. Beyond this are the fields for growing crops, separated by their little walls of milkweed, and the fallow or resting land and the grazing land. Several homesteads form a village.

Agriculture

The people of Sukumaland are cultivators who

86

Baobab trees, a familiar sight in areas of East Africa so dry that trees have developed their own method of storing moisture. Notice the bare, stony appearance of the ground, and the bare outcrops of rock on the distant hill.

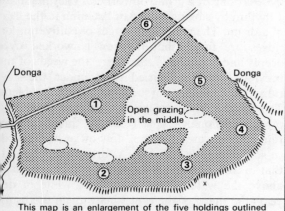

This map is an enlargement of the five holdings outlined in Fig. 61   Each holding has its own farmland and homestead. It also shares the open grazing and the reserve pasture.

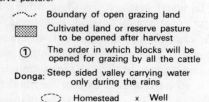

<table>
<tr><td>·····:·</td><td>Boundary of open grazing land</td></tr>
<tr><td>▒▒</td><td>Cultivated land or reserve pasture to be opened after harvest</td></tr>
<tr><td>①</td><td>The order in which blocks will be opened for grazing by all the cattle</td></tr>
<tr><td>Donga:</td><td>Steep sided valley carrying water only during the rains</td></tr>
<tr><td>⌒⌒</td><td>Homestead   x   Well</td></tr>
</table>

Fig. 62 Rotation grazing

...ave learned about stock rearing. They have become skilled cattlemen and keep the animals in good condition even during the dry season. The combination of cattle rearing and cropping is a very good one for Sukumaland conditions. Perhaps the biggest problems are rainfall and water supply.

Only about five months in the year are rainy, and planting and growing has to be fitted into this short season. For the rest of the year there is a constant struggle to keep things going until the next rains. From mid-May through to November the ground dries up under the scorching sun. Strong winds lift the soil and whirl the dust into 'dust devils'; nearly always there are five or six severe dust storms near the end of the dry season. The weather gets hotter and hotter, the air is filled with thunder. Then about the middle of November the rains break. The first warning showers make it possible to hoe the hard ground. The maize, the millet seed, the cotton and later the groundnuts, are planted. The first 'little rains' last only six weeks, for January is a drier month in some places and is very hot. Then in February the heavy rains come. These normally last through March and April and well into May, so that these months form the main growing season. The harvesting begins in late May and June and finishes in July and August. Through June, July, August, September and October the sun beats down from a cloudless sky.

From June to October the main problem of feeding the cattle must be faced. During the rains water is free for all. During the dry season it must be controlled by the headman. Some cattle have to walk as much as 24 km (15 miles) every third day to get water. But despite the problem of feeding and watering animals, the Sukuma find them a very good investment. They give hides, meat, milk, ghee (clarified butter), calves and manure. So the arable land profits too, and crops are better on land that has been walked by cattle or to which manure has been carried. Cattle are so important that if a man inherits some but has no pasture for them he will lend them to someone else until he himself has made a homestead. The important thing is to keep enough animals to crop the grass so that it stays short and sweet, but to avoid overgrazing. Where the Sukumaland grass is short, there are fewer ticks. One great advantage of the traditional co-operation in the village is that as soon as the crops are harvested the *whole* of the land belonging to the village can be thrown open to cattle to graze what is left. To make this more useful the land is often opened for grazing one section at a time (Fig. 62).

Thus the grazing can be controlled; all the land

will get a share of the manure; all land will get a rest; and if the use is timed, the last section of grazing land will last until the onset of the next season's rain. This is called 'rotation grazing'. Without cattle the land could be used for only half the year. This is a practice that would bring great benefit if it could be used in other parts of East Africa where there is a long dry season.

The growing of food and cash crops has to be crowded into a few short months, and rotation of crop land is not usual. Instead several crops are sown together in rows on the same ground (for example sweet potatoes with maize between). The advantage of inter-planting is that beans or groundnuts or any member of the same plant family can restore nitrogen to the ground and help to keep a balance in the soil. According to the nature of the ground cassava, sweet potatoes, maize, millets, sorghums, cowpeas, groundnuts (including Bambara groundnuts), sesame, tobacco, vegetables, cotton and even rice may be grown. Maize growing is on the increase as it may be a cash or a food crop.

Sukumaland does not include the miombo area to the west, or the drier Masailand to the east. But the people of Sukumaland have many things in common with the Nyamwezi of Tabora and the Western Province. The Wasukuma occupy the dry plateau but not the very dry lands where the water supply is not enough for their way of life. This change from dry to very dry is important in East Africa; it marks the change from a more settled agricultural life to a nomadic pastoral life. The dry plateau, with rainfalls of over 635 mm (25 ins), can produce crops; the very dry plateau cannot usually do so without irrigation. The map shows which parts of East Africa are too dry for settled agriculture (see Fig. 36).

Developments in cotton production

Practically all Tanzania's cotton exports, worth about £11·7 million in 1969, come from farms in the Lake region, which has Sukumaland at its centre. In 1950 the cotton crop in this region was only 40 000 bales. In 1963 it was 220 000 bales, so that cotton became the second most valuable export of the country. Since 1963 cotton production has continued to expand, except for temporary setbacks in 1967 and 1968 due to poor weather.

Several factors have been important in this rapid increase of cotton output. Firstly, the price for cotton on the world markets improved. Sukumaland began to grow more cotton. Later, prices fell slightly and so farmers had to grow still more to maintain their income. In this way the total production doubled between 1955 and 1959. Secondly, the Sukuma farmers, being cattlemen, saw cotton production as a way of obtaining cash to buy more cattle. In ten years up to 1962, cattle numbers doubled in the Lake region. A further advantage over other cash crops, such as rice and maize, is that cotton gives a better return for the amount of work needed to produce it.

In central Sukumaland the farmers have developed a special method of cultivation. Ridges 50 cm (20 ins) high and 1·5 m (5 ft) apart are constructed. The hard work involved in building these is done by a group of workers. They maintain a rhythm by singing a song or listening to the beat of a drum. The main advantages of cultivating on ridges are firstly that the soil is worked over deeply and thoroughly. Secondly, the weeds of the previous year are buried deep under the new ridges, and so do not become such a problem. Thirdly, the ridges are not parallel, but cross each other occasionally. One result of this is that in rain-storms water does not flow off at high speed, so soil erosion is reduced. A further advantage is that in wet years the roots of the plants are raised above the water lying in furrows, while in dry years the shape of the ridges helps them to absorb more rainfall. The latest development is *tie-ridging*. This consists of making cross-ridges 2–3 m (6·5–10 ft) apart between the main ridges. In this way a series of small hollows is formed, which holds the rainfall, and also prevents soil erosion.

But preparing the ground and planting is always a race against time. In the dry season much of the ground is so hard that it cannot be hoed until it rains. The two grain crops must be planted first, because life depends on them. The cotton is then planted bit by bit at intervals of two to three weeks. This gives early and late crops. The big disadvantage is of course that late planting gives smaller yields. However, there are two advantages. One is that since the rainfall is unreliable, there is more chance of some crop if planting is spread. Another is that cultivation using hoes is hard work and takes much time. If the cotton planting is done at intervals it makes the work easier to do. A large family means many hoes, but more hands also mean more mouths to be fed and there is a limit to the amount that a family can cultivate. Since about 1964 group farming schemes have been started which use tractors to cultivate. Once the land is ploughed it is divided into plots of 0·8–1·6 hectares (2–4 acres) for each farmer. In these schemes only cotton is grown. The family still has to do all the work of sowing, weeding and harvesting. However, spraying against disease and insects is done for the entire block of 60 to 120 hectares (150 to 300 acres). Tractor-drawn sprayers and even helicopters are used for this work.

Co-operative schemes work well, partly because of the tradition of mutual help in Sukumaland. Many farmers are now members of their local co-operative society and this enables them to get up to half of their requirements on credit.

The Masai

The Masai occupy the wedge of arid country extending from Nairobi into Tanzania, between Mt Kilimanjaro on the east and Lake Manyara and the Rift Valley on the west (Fig. 63).

A traditional Masai settlement (Fig. 64)

Any one family may own 150 cattle and some have as many as 500. As one encampment may contain only one family or up to twelve or fifteen families it is a problem to find and maintain enough pasture for all the animals every year. In addition to cattle there are sheep, goats and donkeys.

The semi-permanent *enkang* or kraal is usually found on the higher slopes. Every *enkang* or kraal is protected by a high thorn barrier of bushes cut from the scrub of the savannah. This guards both the people and their cattle from lions at night. The thin branches that serve as the framework of the home also come from savannah thickets, being woven into a shape that can then be thatched with grass and plastered with clay and dung to water-proof it. The men cut the branches for both thorn fence and for the home, but the hut was usually built by the women (this was true formerly, but now it is more often built by the men). Fig. 64 shows what it is like.

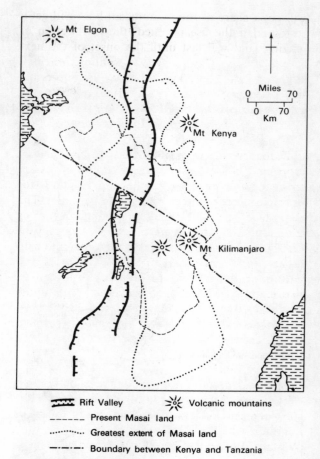

Fig. 63 Masai lands

Legend:
- ~~~~~ Rift Valley
- ☀ Volcanic mountains
- ------ Present Masai land
- ··········· Greatest extent of Masai land
- —·—·— Boundary between Kenya and Tanzania

Each family has its own entrance to the enkang, and as a man usually has more than one wife the first wife places her home to the right of the entrance and the second wife to the left.

The pattern of Masai society

If his father so chooses any young man may become a warrior or *moran* when he is old enough to join an 'age-group'. An age-group extends over several years and therefore includes men of different ages. When another group of youths is ready to take on warriorhood, the existing age-group retires, many of them becoming tribal elders. The age-group serves the whole of the Masai, not just one village, and the brotherhood of the age-group lasts all one's life; a man can always seek shelter of those who were his companions when he later travels over the Masai territory. The young

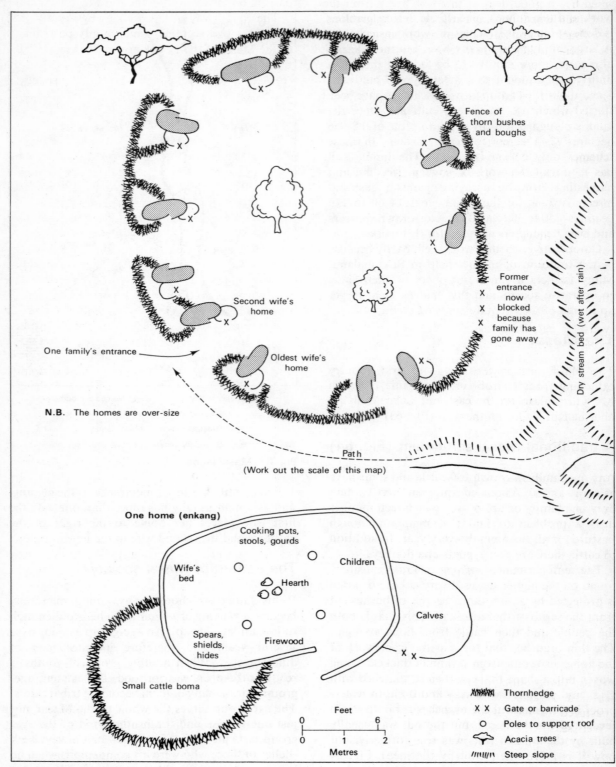

Fence of
thorn bushes
and boughs

Former
entrance
now
blocked
because
family has
gone away

Dry stream bed (wet after rain)

Second wife's
home

One family's entrance

Oldest wife's
home

N.B. The homes are over-size

Path
(Work out the scale of this map)

One home (enkang)

Cooking pots,
stools, gourds

Children

Wife's
bed

Hearth

Calves

Spears,
shields,
hides

Firewood

Small cattle boma

Feet		
0		6
0	1	2
Metres		

Thornhedge

Gate or barricade

Poles to support roof

Acacia trees

Steep slope

Fig. 64 A traditional Masai settlement

men live a good deal of their life away from the main settlement herding cattle on their migrations, and tracking and killing lions and other game that threaten the herds; their temporary settlement is called a *manyatta*.

Masai warriors still use only their spears and short swords to kill lions and leopards; their only protection is the large buffalo-hide shield. All aspects of life – hunting, initiation, marriage – are accompanied by traditional ceremonial and song. When a lion is killed the paws, tail and mane are brought back; to wear a lion-skin cap is a sign of courage.

Most Masai prefer the food provided by their herds, the richest in protein of any in Africa. It would, however, be wrong to suppose that the diet of all Masai regularly includes blood. Milk is perhaps the most important food; it is stored in milk pots made from a single piece of wood, and butter is churned in a gourd. The custom is, however, changing in some areas where all but the warriors eat some maize flour, millet, beans or potatoes and honey, and drink African beer, bought in exchange for meat and hides.

Migrations of the pastoral Masai

The Masai way of life is very well suited to the local conditions, for cultivation is difficult without irrigation in much of their territory. They, more than any other people, have made a success of living in one of the most difficult environments in Africa.

Although they move for part of the year, most Masai families think of one part of the country as their 'home', the place to which they return. The pattern of their settlement is governed by the need to find pasture for their herds and flocks.

Use Fig. 65 to make a calendar of migration in the following way. First, rule a page of your exercise book into three columns. At the top of the first column write 'Month'. At the top of the second column write 'Higher land in north-west: rainfall 1 200 mm (50 ins)'. Head the third column 'Rift valley in south-east: rainfall 500 mm (20 ins)'. Write the months of the year down the first column. Against each month when animals are pastured in the north-west (see Fig. 65) write 'Wet season: pasture on higher land' in the second column. Against each month when animals are pastured in the south-east, write 'Dry season:

pasture on lower land' in the third column.

The Masai way of life is changing rapidly. The preceding two sections, which apply particularly to the Masai of the Narok area in Kenya, describe the situation *as it was in 1955*. The section headed 'Present and future changes' on this page suggests the trend in Masai affairs.

Present and future changes

The Masai have already earned considerable respect as cattle keepers. Mating of cows and of ewes is restricted so that calving and lambing will only occur during the rainy season, for at other times they may die of thirst and lack of grazing. A Masai selects his bulls with great care in order to produce animals specially adapted to hot dry conditions. For example he prefers a humped Zebu cow with a long 'dewlap' under the neck and this is now proved to be of importance in cooling the animal. He also has a large number of bulls to the number of cows, which some people think is needed in tropical countries in order to maintain a high fertility rate. He has some ability to recognise and treat disease, and formerly induced immunity from rinderpest, a serious disease, early in life by infecting cattle with a mild form. The chief problem is one of overstocking, for cattle have a prestige and ceremonial value. While the Masai use their donkeys for load-carrying, and the red-haired, fat-tailed sheep or goats for domestic milk and meat supplies, cattle numbers remain high until reduced by starvation and drought.

During the last fifteen years there have been changes in Masai life, partly as a result of education. Most Masai children now attend primary school. Boys who go to secondary school share less in the traditional life, but they do so during the school holidays, when they also care for cattle.

In some areas modern brick homes are now built, with corrugated iron roofs, pumped water and sometimes dynamo electricity. Though the basic diet still includes milk and meat, other foods are now enjoyed. Many people grow potatoes, beans, maize and millet; and tea, sugar and tinned foods are bought at the store.

In Tanzania the Masailand Development Plan set out to improve the Masai district as a ranching country. The two great problems are water and tsetse fly. A government publication says: 'The

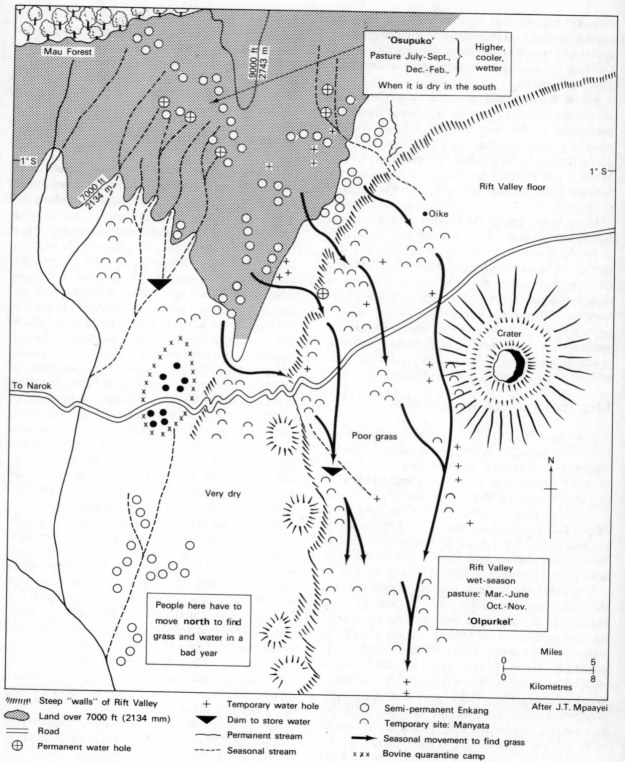

Mau Forest

9000 ft
2743 m

1° S

'Osupuko'
Pasture July-Sept.,
Dec.-Feb.,
When it is dry in the south

Higher,
cooler,
wetter

Rift Valley floor

1° S

● Oike

7000 ft
2134 m

To Narok

Crater

Poor grass

N

Very dry

People here have to
move **north** to find
grass and water in a
bad year

Rift Valley
wet-season
pasture: Mar.-June
Oct.-Nov.

'Olpurkel'

Miles
0   5
0   8
Kilometres

After J.T. Mpaayei

'''''''''	Steep "walls" of Rift Valley	+	Temporary water hole	○	Semi-permanent Enkang
	Land over 7000 ft (2134 mm)	▼	Dam to store water	⌣	Temporary site: Manyata
	Road		Permanent stream	➔	Seasonal movement to find grass
⊕	Permanent water hole	- - -	Seasonal stream	x x x	Bovine quarantine camp

Fig. 65 Former Masai migration and settlement

92

nomadic Masai make the best possible use of limited natural water supplies. At the end of the wet season they disperse cattle to feed on grazing near rain ponds and other temporary watering points. As the dry season advances these dry up and cattle have to be gathered on grazing around permanent watering points. Even these fail in drought, and cattle die.' Hence the Government is developing water schemes and the Masai Council has itself suggested taxation to meet part of the cost.

Despite the changes, cattle are, as always, the centre of Masai life. The Masai people still preserve their traditional tribal life, strong loyalties and self-discipline.

Commercial ranching

From what has been already stated, it is very clear that the Masai have regarded their pastoral activities as a way of life rather than as a source of profit. Now great efforts are being made at Government level to introduce the Masai in Kenya to a commercial ranching economy.

During the disastrous 1960–1961 drought and floods in Kenya the Masai lost half of their cattle.

This, more than anything else, has shown to them the need for reliable water supplies and conservation of grazing. They occupy the southern part of the four-fifths of Kenya which is arid or semi-arid, and which has been largely neglected until recently. It has been said that no one follows a nomadic life out of choice, and that given water and land the Masai will abandon their old seasonal movements. This remains to be seen. Certainly many are already settling down with the help of the Government.

Much effort is now going into the development of the rangelands, as areas suitable for cattle ranching are called. There is also a world shortage of meat, so that a ready market is available for beef.

An important scheme which is typical of the general situation is the Kaputiei Group Ranch Scheme, which plans to develop 283 400 hectares (700 000 acres) of Masailand in the area south-east of Nairobi near Sultan Hamud (Fig. 66). Already more than twenty ranches averaging about 14 170 hectares (35 000 acres) *each* have been marked out. Each ranch will belong to an individual clan of thirty to forty families, and will be big enough to support their combined herd. Out of consideration for the traditional ways of the Masai, the ranches will not be fenced. They will be divided by a

An over-used watering place in Masailand, near Magadi. Cattle are herded to this gorge over a large area, and several herds can be seen in the distance.

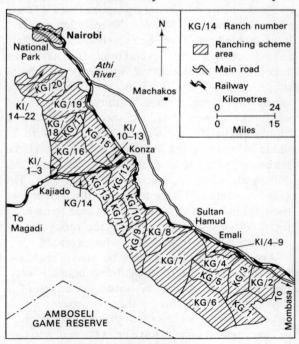

Fig. 66 The Kaputiei Ranching Scheme

93

ploughed ditch, the boundaries keeping as near as possible to the usual grazing areas of one clan. About 20 000 Masai, comprising a fifth of the tribe, already live in this area and should share in the scheme.

The total project, which includes rangelands near the Taita Hills as well as the Masailand area, will take twelve years to complete and will cost £4 million. Most of this money will be used to provide dipping equipment, improved water supplies, technical assistance and disease control, and to purchase pedigree and good local stock. Twenty-five Sahiwal bulls were introduced into the scheme in late 1968 and they are being crossed with the local Masai Zebu to get better grade animals.

One of the most important jobs of the technical staff will be to control stock numbers. Following the 1961 losses some areas were actually understocked, but in future care will have to be taken to prevent overstocking. Eventually 36 000 head of cattle will be available for beef each year from Kaputiei. It is therefore obvious that the Masai, who will own their ranch land for the first time according to both custom and statutory law, will be involved in a very large commercial undertaking.

The first ranch to be set up was at Poka, 112 km (70 miles) south of Nairobi. There thirty families have a herd of 2 000 on nearly 12 145 hectare (30 000 acres) of land. Several difficulties have been encountered, an important one being the choice of ranch managers. Each of the families has a leader, but there cannot be thirty managers. In addition, running a 12 145 hectare ranch is a highly skilled business and an effort has to be made to ensure good leadership. Also, individual herds on Poka are unequal. The richest man has 500 head, while the poorest has only two. The bigger owners will have to reduce the numbers of their animals and allow the poorer men to increase theirs, otherwise some parts of the ranch will be overgrazed while others will be undergrazed.

Another difficulty is that because the Masai have had little tradition of doing manual work, they have had to employ outside contractors to build cattle dips and other relatively simple constructions. This has often proved expensive.

Government officers have been trained, and they are helping the local Masai to understand that a

fairly limited herd of good quality is more valuable than large numbers of undernourished beasts. Without a doubt progress is being made and scheme officials expect ranches to double the beef output of their herds in a very few years.

In addition to developments in stock raising, there are also other developments in agriculture in the Masai area.

The Masai wheat scheme

The Mau Highlands are different from the areas just described because they have a higher and more reliable rainfall. They have for a long time been recognised as one of the most valuable agricultural areas of Kenya, to be compared only with the Kikuyu Highlands and Trans Nzoia. About 405 000 hectares (one million acres) of land is capable of intensive crop and stock development; and because of the variations in altitude, many different crops can be grown. Masai families have traditionally used parts of the Mau Highlands for grazing when lower level pasture is scorched and dry. During the last sixty years, while all other highland areas of Kenya were being developed, traditional Masai rights to their pasture lands were recognised, and so the Mau and the Trans Mara plateau behind it received little outside attention. But just as modern Kenya cannot allow its rangeland pastures to be used haphazardly, so the government has recognised the need to involve the Masai people of this area in land improvement.

After Independence the government decided that the Narok district should support wheat crops, and in 1964 Masai leaders began to consider a scheme for wheat and sheep rotation on the Mau plateau and in other suitable areas. In a pilot project on Purko Sheep Ranch at Mau Narok, a local farmer had been growing wheat since the mid-1950s. Then drought in 1965 caused a shortage of wheat in Kenya, and the Masai were encouraged to allow their land to be cultivated. By 1966 there were over 3 250 hectares (8 000 acres) of wheat in the area. At first all the work was carried out by 'share-croppers', who were entirely responsible for the wheat-growing and harvesting, and who gave the Masai part of the profits in return for permission to use their land. But in other parts of the world this sytem is not favoured, because under it there is always a danger that the share-cropper will misuse the soil and soon exhaust it, since it is not his land and he has no lasting interest in it. Following initial operations in 1967 personnel and funds became available in 1968 which helped the government to take over from the share-croppers. Now a tractor hire service is available which breaks and cultivates the land, sows seed, fertilisers and insecticides and harvests the crop, all on a contract basis.

The yield in some parts has been very high, about 40 bags per hectare (16 per acre), comparing favourably with the best wheat growing areas in the country. The average is about 25 bags per hectare (10 per acre), which is considered good. It is probable that eventually wheat will be grown on only the highest yielding land, and other crops will be planted on remaining areas. One great difficulty which has upset the early stages of the scheme is the state of roads in the area. On some occasions much of the harvest has been lost because the earth roads had become almost impassable due to heavy rains and the weight of the lorries used for moving grain. However, most roads in the area are being given a gravel surface, and the road from Njoro to Mau Narok through Elburgon a tarmac surface.

The main purpose of having such a scheme in Masailand is to use the crop as a means of developing the area, and help the Masai people. Another reason is that Kenya spends up to £200 000 a year to buy wheat and wheat flour from abroad. Wheat plantings at present scattered throughout Upper Masailand give local people the incentive to fence the land and cultivate it.

The success of the scheme is shown by the encouraging response from the Masai. Once a farmer has established himself, he will be encouraged to rear animals, especially sheep. Then the government hire service can move on to other holdings, plant wheat, and again provide money to enable the owner to continue on his own. The final phase should see the withdrawal of the government service, with the Masai able to continue without assistance, growing a wide variety of crops, and enjoying all the benefits of a modern cash economy. But if the high level pastures are fenced and planted, they will no longer be available for the traditional seasonal grazing, shown in Fig. 65.

The Masai ranching studies and the study following show the kind of development that may

be possible in other parts of East Africa.

In all areas the new Masai schools place the emphasis on animal husbandry and improvement of water and grazing in relationship to numbers and this should allow the best use of the land. Some clearing and aerial spraying will reduce the area infested with tsetse fly and make it available for stock. The Masai already ask for inoculation for their beasts, against nagana, black-quarter and other diseases. Where this happens they lose fewer animals by disease; planning must now take place so that they do not continue to lose them by starvation.

It is very important that this dry land should be put to its best use because it covers about a quarter of the territory of East Africa. Successful practice in Masailand may help the pastoralist in every part of Africa to rear his animals with greater profit.

Detailed study section
The section set in small type is for advanced study. Return to this later if you prefer.

THE ANKOLE–MASAKA RANCHING SCHEME, UGANDA

The map (Fig. 67) shows the location of the ranching project in eastern Ankole and north-western Masaka District. It is in a part of Uganda where the rainfall reliability is low, and mean annual rainfall totals are also near to the minimum for safe cultivation. Banana trees

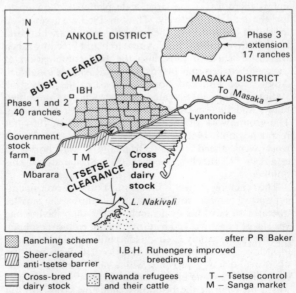

Fig. 67 The Ankole Ranching Scheme

95

do well only in favoured places such as gullies, or at the foot of slopes where water collects and soil has accumulated due to soil creep after burning.

Originally this area of Ankole was part of a pastoral Bahima kingdom. Great herds grazed the rolling hill-bush country, and the landscape was dotted with the Hima kraals which are still seen further west today. At the end of the last century, the area was overtaken by a great outbreak of rinderpest. The virus swept through, often at a rate of 16 km (10 miles) per day leaving as many as 90% of the cattle dead in its wake.

The rinderpest disaster was followed by a series of waves of tsetse fly carrying trypanosomiasis, (see Chap. 4). The type of fly was *glossina morsitans*, one of the savanna species so deadly to cattle. As cattle numbers were lower because of rinderpest, the bush had become thicker and more widespread, and this provided a suitable habitat for the tsetse flies.

The successful reclamation of Ankole was begun in July 1958 and this early phase concentrated on killing off the game animals which acted as a host for the fly. This was followed in 1963 by the spraying of 1 550 sq km (600 sq miles) with insecticide, clearing an area as far south as the Mbarara–Masaka road. This, however, was not a secure barrier for it was persistently crossed by game animals from the south and it was decided that the tsetse-cleared area to the north would have to be protected by a 5–6·5 km (3–4 mile) sheer-cleared zone south of the road. Several giant tractor-crawlers were brought in to clear the bush by dragging between them a length of anchor chain. Then hand labour worked over the whole area of the future ranching scheme. In all about 16 200 hectare (40 000 acres) were cleared to provide the barrier, and a great deal more (1 550 sq km, 600 sq miles) for the ranch itself.

Such widespread clearance would obviously be wasted unless there was some large scale planned follow-up to use the land productively. Thus in 1963 a survey team looked at the area from the point of view of ranching and issued a favourable report. A research and breeding ranch was established to look into the best combination of crossing between four breeds: the local Ankole longhorn. Angus, Red Poll and Boran (Kenya) cattle. A pasture station at Muko investigated the destruction of unwanted plants and the spreading of desirable types of grazing. The groundwork of roads, etc., was started in 1964 but it was not until 1966 when money became available that work went ahead in full. Originally it was hoped to establish 127 ranches but lack of finance reduced this number to 57.

The ranching project is unlike most other Government-supported projects in Uganda, for it allows the smaller operator to have his own ranch, rather than having one very large ranch worked by Government employees. Each unit is approximately 13 sq km (5 sq miles) and rectangular in shape. The occupant, either a local farmer or a co-operative society, is provided with a valley tank to provide clean drinking water and water for the spray or dip. Water was a problem at the beginning, but now dams are full and the supply is reliable. He is also provided with the

Cattle at Aswa Ranch, Uganda, passing through a spray. This will keep the animals free from ticks for a short time.

frame of a house, a fence and the network of ranch roads. He is obliged, under the lease, to enter with a minimum of 200 head, 100 of which must be breeding females. Some people have now as many as 800, the maximum supportable until grazing is further improved and weed and bush growth checked.

Regulations are strict, otherwise one farmer can endanger the entire project. For example, burning is discouraged but had been started by new members who brought with them traditional ideas. It encourages the growth of species of bush which the cattle cannot eat. In particular 'blue citronella' is a weed increased by burning and overgrazing and promises to become a more serious problem as stocking increases. It covers up to 25% of some areas. The lease requires the owner to clear a fire-break around his ranch. He is supposed to spray/dip his animals regularly against ticks and enforce the various management regulations laid down.

The ranch scheme was planned in three parts, all of which are complete. Part I and II involved 40 ranches in Ankole and Part III, 17 in Masaka. A group of ranches has an animal husbandry officer.

To the south of the main road the Government has a project for raising dairy animals for the national herd. Although the ranching scheme does not go in for dairy produce, bulls will be sold to the ranchers. Further south still, Rwandaise refugees and their cattle have been settled as a barrier against tsetse reinfestation from the south.

A market has been built at Sanga on the main road and the markets are advertised in Kampala and Masaka; butchers who attend buy on a weight-quality basis. So far the markets are very well attended for the butchers know the animals are of a high quality, clean of parasite infections, have a high meat/bone ratio and a good flavour. On average, 40% of the beef sales goes to Kampala, 40% to Masaka, and 20% to Mbarara.

Progress: By 1969, all but 3 of the 57 ranches had been occupied and there were about 20 000 head of stock on the ranches. With the controlled grazing some animals are reaching 450 kg (1 000 lbs) liveweight against 360 kg (800 lbs) or so locally. More important, these animals are maturing in 36 months or so against 4–6 years locally, so the turnover is great. The maturing time depends partly on the season that the calf is born in. Tsetse has been

wiped out and ticks are reduced. Seventy-five per cent of all farmers now have a working dip-race. This is a tank full of disinfectant through which the cattle are driven.

The very dry plateaus: the future in irrigation

More than a quarter of East Africa is very dry land. It has so little rain that it is semi-desert. During the short rainy seasons the land is green but for most of the year it is so barren that much of it is called *nyika*–the wilderness. The area is very thinly peopled, mainly by pastoralists including the Karamojong and the Turkana. The marginal areas (sub-desert) can be developed for stock ranching, or as game reserves. But irrigation may in future provide the best chance of development. Irrigation schemes such as the Mobuku in Uganda, or the Galole irrigation scheme in Kenya provide examples.

The Galole irrigation scheme

At Galole, on the river Tana 130 km (80 miles) south of Garissa and almost due east of Nairobi, there is a *pilot* cotton irrigation scheme which

An inselberg in Karamoja 100 m (330 feet) high.

ie village in northern Karamoja. Note the strong, carefully made fence around the houses, and the typical ppearance of the surrounding vegetation in the dry season.

97

may help to determine the agricultural future of a very large area of Kenya's arid lands. Over the period 1963–66 a Food and Agricultural Organisation team conducted a survey of the Tana River Basin. They found that about 101 200 hectares (250 000 acres) are suitable for development under irrigation. However, it was realised that a large amount of further research was needed before a final decision could be made on the development of the Tana. Therefore it was agreed that the existing scheme should be used as an example (or *model*) of the process by which an area can be developed. It was fortunate that this decision was made, for the Galole scheme had been in serious difficulty. Water was pumped from the Tana, and this, added to the remote location of the scheme and its small size, made it uneconomic. Also, considerable trouble was experienced with pests, and the 485 hectares (1 200 acres) became overgrown with weeds. Because of these drawbacks the cotton yield was very disappointing, and the Pokomo plotholders were becoming disheartened.

The in 1966 a determined effort was made by the National Irrigation Board, helped by a Dutch aid team, to make the scheme more successful. It was completely overhauled, with new housing and improved drainage systems installed, and great care given to pest and weed control using pesticides and weedkillers. It has been found that early sowing of the cotton seed and the application of nitrogen fertilisers are very important, and lead to a remarkable increase in yield. The result is that plots are producing an average of 680 kg (1 500 lbs) of cotton per acre per year. This is over five per cent better than it was only a few years ago. Other crops have been introduced successfully, especially groundnuts, kenaf (a plant for fibre, like jute) and sugar-cane, and these, with cotton, are likely to form the basis of any new schemes. Now the 247 plots are supporting about 3 000 people. Their cash income is low compared with some other schemes like the Mwea rice scheme (chapter 12, page 129). But it must be remembered that the people of this area have often had to depend on famine relief, so that an income of about shs. 1 500/– per family a year is an improvement.

The main result of this effort is that the Galole scheme has been improved and developed. Now it is a high quality pilot scheme. It will be valuable as a demonstration of what future farmers can do in the rest of the Tana basin. It will also serve as a training ground for the many staff that will be required. Still more important, it may suggest a way of developing many other arid areas of East Africa.

Work to do

1. Make sure that you know what is meant by: tors, rotation grazing.
2. Draw a section to show the change in relief, soils and land use from the tors to the *mbuga* in Sukumaland.
3. Make a work chart for the year based on the rainfall figures for Seke.
4. Find out what a pilot scheme is and note other examples.

Chapter 9: The highlands of East Africa—the importance of height

The lands that rise above the level of the plateau are very important in the life of Africa. They are regions of heavier and more reliable rain, so that crops do not fail because of drought. Secondly, temperature changes with the height of the land, allowing a variety of crops to be grown. Thirdly, the higher mountain lands often have fertile volcanic soils, so that they bear good crops. It is for these reasons that the mountain lands of Africa carry some of the higher densities of population, while the dry lower plateaus may be thinly settled.

The map (Fig. 36) shows the location of these highland* areas.

1. **In Kenya:** the land bordering the Rift Valley and westwards into Nyanza; the slopes of Mount Kenya and the Aberdare Mountains north of Nairobi. There is a smaller mountain area, the Teita Hills, which forms a green island or oasis in the dry plateau west of Mombasa.

2. **In Tanzania:** the Southern Highlands; small areas near Morogoro and Mpwapwa; Mount Kilimanjaro and Mount Meru and the areas near them; the Usambara and Pare Mountains; the borders of Rwanda and Burundi.

3. **In Uganda:** Kigezi and the Ruwenzori Mountains with their foothills in the west; the slopes of Mount Elgon in the east.

The following studies are chosen to represent the highland areas of East Africa:

1. The Kilimanjaro and Meru area in Tanzania: changing land-use with height.
2. Kigezi, south-west Uganda.
3. Four studies in the Kenya Highlands:
   (*a*) the Kikuyu Uplands.
   (*b*) Settlement schemes in Kenya.
   (*c*) Large and small-scale tea production.

*In this book 'highland' is land over 1 520 m (5 000 ft) above sea-level. In Tanzania land below 1 520 m may have similar characteristics because the area is further from the Equator.

(*d*) Nakuru: the growth of a town.
4. The Southern Highlands of Tanzania.

The Kilimanjaro and Meru area in Tanzania: changing land-use with height

Climate

Wherever mountains rise above the level of the East African Plateau, they receive heavier rainfall. Hence, when they occur in dry areas they form fertile 'oases' where crops can be grown. Such a zone of well-watered land covers the lower slopes of Mount Kilimanjaro in Tanzania. The south-east slopes have most rain, coming in March–May and November–December. The north-west slopes also have two rainy seasons but not at the same time as the south-east. The south-west and north-east are both drier areas.

The rain-bearing winds blow in most strongly from the Indian Ocean in March–April–May,

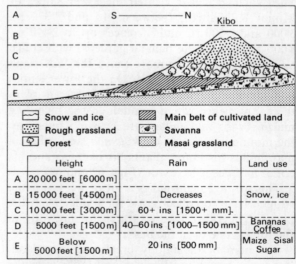

Height		Rain	Land use
A	20 000 feet [6000 m]		Snow, ice
B	15 000 feet [4500 m]	Decreases	Snow, ice
C	10 000 feet [3000 m]	60+ ins [1500+ mm]	
D	5 000 feet [1500 m]	40–60 ins [1000–1500 mm]	Bananas Coffee
E	Below 5 000 feet [1500 m]	20 ins [500 mm]	Maize Sisal Sugar

Fig. 68 Section from north to south through Kilimanjaro to show vegetation zones

mainly to the southern side of the mountain. As the land gets higher, the rainfall increases from 380–510 mm (15–20 ins) in the Masai Steppe (tropical grassland savanna) at the base, to 1 520 mm (60 ins) or more a year in the forest zone halfway up the mountain. At the same time the temperature decreases so that above 3 000 m (10 000 ft) it is too cold for trees and at the summit there are permanent glaciers. Mount Kilimanjaro shows this succession of vegetation zones as clearly as any mountain in East Africa. Mount Kenya also shows it but the vegetation is different.

In the Moshi–Arusha area the rain is not spread over the whole year as in Buganda. It is related to the movements of the monsoon winds. Long before the coming of Europeans the Wachagga brought water by furrows from the melting snows of Kilimanjaro to irrigate bananas and coffee during the dry seasons (July to October and in January and February). As the drier lower slopes have been cultivated, the furrows have been extended until they now spread across the plain for 16 km (10 miles) or more, to the point where there is not enough water to fill them. The furrows are expensive to maintain and some have fallen into disuse. Larger irrigation schemes which are more economic are being developed for the lower, drier plateau areas.

The use of the land

The Wachagga have cleared the lower slopes of Mount Kilimanjaro (between 915 and 1 370 m, 3 000 and 4 500 ft, and in places up to 2 440 m, 8 000 ft) to cultivate banana gardens, with coffee as a cash crop. To be more exact, the Wachagga cultivate two kinds of land. On the lower slopes immediately above the savannah-covered plain there are fields where annual crops, including maize, beans and millet, are grown. Higher up the mountain slopes is the *kihamba* land, where a man builds his home, plants his bananas and his coffee and keeps his cattle (Figs. 68 and 69).

This arrangement makes a lot of work, for the women have to collect grass for fodder from the plains. They also have to search for firewood in the forest zone or in the bush.

The man of the family breaks the new land, builds the house and kitchen, and looks after the cash crops and the water furrows. In the old days

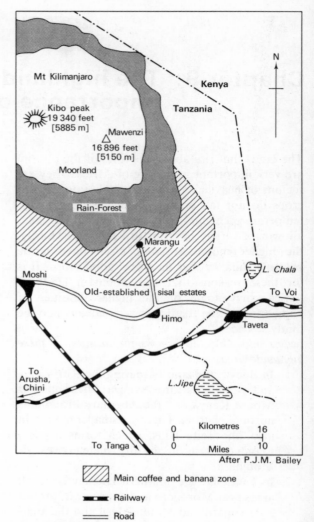

Fig. 69 The Marangu area

when he had more than one wife, every wife owned one kihamba and she had her own house there. A family usually has three or four cattle and about ten goats.

The bananas take three years to establish. They are used as food and in the making of beer. They are also used as fodder. The stems of the banana trees are very succulent and are fed to the cattle; this saves giving the cattle so much water, but means that the banana stems are not available as a mulch for the coffee.

The kihamba land is owned by the family. It may be divided among the sons, or, according to the older law, the larger share is taken by the youngest son. This was the custom because the

100

Coffee berries ripening under bananas on a Wachagga kihamba.

older children were thought to be in a better position to make their own kihamba if the father died.

The result of the customary law of inheritance and the fourfold increase in population has been to break down the old holdings (about 12–16 hectare, 30–40 acres for a family) to an average of 1·6 hectare (4 acres). Some are very much smaller than this. Fig. 70 shows a fairly typical 1·6 hectare holding in Marangu district. Such a kihamba would have about 200 banana trees and 600 to 800 coffee bushes inter-planted, enough to earn about £150 a year.

The traditional Wachagga house shown is round; but the house now built is often a large bungalow, typical of the new homes springing up everywhere, made of cement blocks with a sheet metal roof.

Coffee growing

The grey-brown volcanic soils of Kilimanjaro, like the volcanic soils of Kenya, are well suited to coffee. They are light and moisture-holding, and less acid than most African soils.

Two major types of coffee, Arabica and Robusta, are grown in East Africa, each with different climatic requirements.

Of the two, Arabica is grown on Mount Kilimanjaro because of the height of the cultivated land. Not only does it bring a better price than Robusta, but coffee grown at higher altitudes is less liable to disease.

The climatic needs of Robusta are very different from those of Arabica. It is a large bush whose roots are found mainly near the surface. It there-

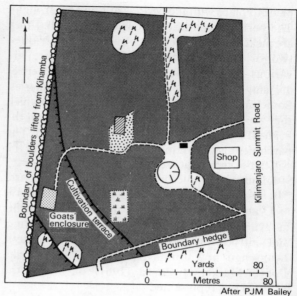

Msonge hut, bed-space for wife, four children; stalls for two cows and two goats

Coffee under bananas

Grass plot

Poultry pen

Onion plot

Sugar-cane clumps

Coffee pulping machine

Fig. 70 A Wachagga kihamba

fore does not like either the dry spell that suits Arabica or soils which dry out easily. In addition to a constant humidity, it prefers higher temperatures, and so flourishes below 1 220 m (4 000 ft). These conditions are best found round the northern and western shores of Lake Victoria.

Whether the type of coffee is Arabica or Robusta, whether it is grown on a plantation or on a small-holding, the bush requires the same kind of attention. The seedlings or cuttings are shaded from the sun in nurseries. When the bushes are twelve months old, they are transplanted into the fields in which they will finally grow. For the best results, they must be carefully pruned. This is, however, less important for Robusta than for Arabica. The weeds must be kept down between the bushes and mulching with banana leaves protects the ground from both the sun and soil erosion.

The time at which the flowers set varies from

101

place to place with the periods of rain and drought. The berries ripen after about eight months; they are picked as they ripen. This may cover a period of two or three months. After picking there are various possible processes. Sometimes the berries are sun-dried before being sold to the hulleries. Sometimes they go directly to the tanks in which they are fermented. Once the pulp is free from the beans it is washed away. The beans are dried. The parchment is then removed in the hulleries and the coffee put into bags (see also chapter 7).

Kilimanjaro coffee reaches a very high standard. The research station for the whole of Tanzania is at Lyamungu. Its nurseries carry out experiments in pruning, mulching, irrigating and manuring, and introduces good varieties to the farmers. Lyamungu now forms part of the Tanganyika Coffee Marketing Board (1961) on which the K.N.C.U. is represented.

Marketing coffee

The Moshi area pioneered co-operative marketing in East Africa. The original well organised African co-operative society was called the Kilimanjaro Native Co-operative Union (K.N.C.U.) and undertook much of the processing and marketing. Processing is now completed at over fifty pulperies at local centres or by the Coffee Curing Company, to which many large farmers belong. The centres remove the parchment skin, cure, polish, grade, pack and sell the crop. Auctioning of coffee goes on in Moshi, the chief centre, and railways take the crop to Mombasa and Tanga.

Formerly the bulk of the farmland and the people were concentrated between 1 220 m (4 000 ft) and 2 150 m (7 000 ft). Now new irrigation technology and industry are helping to settle the lower slopes and plateau. But it is still true that there is a densely settled zone between the lower, drier land and the highest land which is too bleak for cultivation. This pattern is repeated on the slopes of many highland areas in East Africa.

Moshi, 809 m (2 650 ft), above sea level, is a growing town of 27 000 people, and many new buildings. Not only are there new schools, community centres, clinics, hotels, shops; there are considerable developments in industry. The Tanzania Bag Corporation's new factory is supplying 2·8 million bags each year to coffee growers. This is half the total requirement of the country, and the factory will eventually be doubled in size to supply the entire market. Among many other new processing and service industries, a timber workshop in the town is operating in conjunction with a new sawmill at Rongai, West Kilimanjaro.

The future in agriculture and industry

There is no doubt that the Kilimanjaro-Meru area is fortunate. It has good natural conditions and resourceful people.

In addition to the coffee producing *vihamba* on Mount Kilimanjaro and Mount Meru, other land is worked by large private or government companies. Near the base of the mountains larger scale irrigation is opening up land for the cultivation of sugar, cotton and coffee in large company or government estates, or in smallholdings. For example, there is a large and important sugar estate at Arusha Chini, run by the Tanganyika Planting Company, the largest sugar factory in Tanzania. The second largest is the one operated by the Kilombero Sugar Company. The National Agricultural Company Ltd has a vast ranch on the 'saddle' of the land between Mount Meru and Mount Kilimanjaro. It is 32 430 hectares (80 000 acres), and carries at present 8 000 cattle and 7 000 sheep.

Where land is being settled by formerly landless people it is proving equally productive and flexible. In this way, decreases in crop values are being balanced.

Kigezi, south-west Uganda

Kigezi is an excellent example of the fact that higher lands in East Africa carry higher densities of population. Much of the Uganda plateau near Lake Victoria is between 910 and 1 220 m (3 000 and 4 000 ft) above sea level. In Kigezi the height of most land is between 1 520 and 2 750 m (5 000 and 9 000 ft) above sea level. Kigezi occupies just over 2 per cent of the area of Uganda and is one of the smallest districts. Yet it has 7.5 per cent of Uganda's population. The district has many problems arising from the large number of people and the small area of agricultural land available.

Fig. 71 and the photographs show typical valley scenes described in the following passage.

Fig. 71 A valley in Kigezi

This picture of a Kigezi hillside was taken in 1955. The terraces had not been established very long, and are therefore still quite steeply sloping. Lake Bunyoni can be seen in the background.

This picture was taken only a few years ago at roughly the same place. Repeated cultivation has moved soil to the edge of the terraces which have thus become flatter.

The rounded hills form parallel ridges with wide swampy valleys in between. The valley floors are at about 1 830 m (6 000 ft) and the hills rise up about 450 m (1 475 ft) above them. The hill slopes are convex, i.e., they are steep at the bottom but become more gentle towards the tops, which are flat and uniform in height.

Because the land was hilly and so heavily farmed, terracing was introduced and at first enforced by law. The terraces run in horizontal strips, ideally about 15 m (50 ft) wide (though less in the steeper parts), and separated from one another by grassy banks, called *bunds*, often edged with elephant grass. As the soil shifts, it builds up against the stems (which are like thick canes) and the fields become more level. The drop between each field becomes steeper, but soil erosion is reduced because the soil stays on the terrace.

The houses and the roads line the sides of the valleys just above the swamps. But in places where the population density is very high the houses are found in clusters higher up the hillsides. This brings the problem of having to fetch water from far down the hillside since there are few springs on the upper slopes.'

Probably the biggest problem facing the people of Kigezi today arises from the rapidly increasing population: the population has doubled from 1935 to 1961. Although farmed land has been extended, the increasing population has led to less land being available for each person. In the area near Kabale the amount of land drops to less than 0·2 hectares (0·5 acres) per person.

Another farm problem arises from fragmented holdings. On average a farmer in Kigezi has six plots of land. Although some farmers have consolidated farms, others may have as many as thirty pieces of land. To take an example of this: a piece of land may lie as much as 10 km (6 miles) away from the homestead. Traditionally the farm land is split up equally between the sons of a farmer so there is continuing fragmentation. Yet another problem is the decrease in the resting (or fallow) time between crops.

The problem of over-population is being tackled in three ways.
1. Men find work elsewhere (e.g. Kilembe mine) and send money home.
2. There is a government policy of resettling people in northern Kigezi and some voluntary migration.
3. Swamp land is being reclaimed.

The farming activities are related to the two rainy and two dry seasons. The mean temperatures remain fairly steady throughout the year at about 17°C (63°F). The annual range is 3°C (5°F).

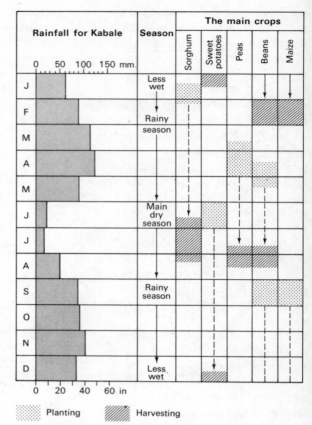

Fig. 72 Crop seasons and rainfall in Kigezi*

*Crop rotation is practised, mainly involving sorghum, beans and maize, since sweet potatoes occupy only a relatively small part of the farm.

Use Fig. 72 and the following paragraphs to work out when each crop is planted and harvested. Which would you regard as the busiest time of the year? What jobs are done in the dry season?

'The sorghum harvest is the highlight of the whole year's activities and after that there is a quieter period. The sorghum begins to ripen to a rusty red in late June and the harvesting continues into August. Sometimes the heads are cut off and the stalks left for the cattle to graze on, a valuable supplementary food during the dry season. Sometimes the stalks are cut and the heads then cut off before the stalks are carried to the compound for use as thatching.

Onbushera (porridge) and *amarwa* (beer) are prepared from the sorghum. After the seeds have been threshed and winnowed apart, they are placed in sacks, with ash from the fire, in the swamp for about twenty-four hours. The ash makes the sorghum turn from red to black. The sack is removed from the water and the grains kept moist within the sack for another three days. As a result of this process the grains sprout. They are laid out to be dried in the sun and lastly they are pounded to remove the small shoot. The grains are now ready to be turned into porridge and beer, the basis of the people's diet. One or two cows, perhaps six goats and some chickens are kept.

In the dry season, in July and August, the papyrus is cut for use as thatching, and making into mats and 'rope'. Houses are planned and built. Wattle and eucalyptus trees provide the wood for building, as well as wood for burning and making into charcoal.'

Cash crops are being introduced into Kigezi: of these four, coffee (mainly Arabica), tea, tobacco and vegetables are gradually gaining some importance. Perhaps the most interesting of these developments is the vegetable growing in reclaimed swamps in the south-east part of Kigezi, as shown in Fig. 71. The Water Resources Department has dug main drainage channels which lower the water table so that the papyrus dies.

A wide variety of different types of vegetables are being grown including cabbages, carrots, lettuces, artichokes, egg plants, leeks and some soft fruits such as strawberries. Tomatoes and onions have been tried but do not do so well. The advantage of vegetable growing is that a farmer can obtain perhaps four or five crops a year from one piece of land, particularly if he grows seedlings first. He can vary the vegetable according to the market prices, and he obtains an income every time he produces a crop, not just once a year, as with coffee. Each farmer belongs to a co-operative of which there are thirteen so far. From it he obtains special seed and advice, and he sells his produce through it. Fifteen years ago many of the vegetables sold in Kampala came by lorry from the Congo. Now eighty per cent of the vegetables come from Kigezi, arriving still very fresh after a six-hour journey by lorry along the tarmac road. In addition, the Kigezi Vegetable Co-operative Union has signed contracts with large organisations such as hospitals, restaurants, schools, hotels and prisons, for bulk supplies in order to obtain a ready sale.

Of course there are many problems. Farmers are having to learn how to grow strange plants. There is a steady demand from the towns and production has to be kept up throughout the year. So vegetables are grown on hillsides during the rains, and in cleared swamps in the drier weather. The next step will be to build a dehydration unit near Kabale to produce dried vegetables for sale even in the distant villages of northern Uganda.

The Kenya Highlands

The Kenya Highlands form the largest area of continuous mountainous country in East Africa. Extending almost from Lake Victoria in the west to Mount Kenya in the east and beyond, the Highlands cover nearly one-fifth of Kenya. Although only a fifth of the area, these mountain lands carry four-fifths of the people; but as we have seen, the density of the population varies greatly from place to place.

Everywhere the land is over 1 500 m (5 000 ft), and much of it is between 2 000 and 2 500 m (7 000 and 8 000 ft) above sea level. The great volcanic mountains Kenya and Elgon rise to 5 200 m (17 000 ft) and 4 300 m (14 000 ft). Because the land is so high it is cooler than most equatorial regions.

The Kenya Highlands, in common with all the areas that rise above the plateau, have heavier and more reliable rainfall totals. The Rift Valley divides them into two main sections. Both of these have double rains but there are slightly different patterns in each.

Not all this area is well watered; parts are only suited to ranching, and the pasture is poor. Rainfall and water supply are the key to development.

The Kikuyu, one of the largest tribal groups (over one million people) live mainly on the middle slopes of Mount Kenya and the Aberdares (4 000 m 13 120 ft). Most of the settled land is between 1 520 and 2 130 m (5 000 and 7 000 ft) above sea level, some even higher. These highland areas are volcanic in origin consisting of lavas poured out during the Rift Valley's development. Mount Kenya was built up around a central vent, so that its shape is roughly conical, while the elongated Aberdare range accumulated as the result of lava-flows from fissure eruptions, that is, from long cracks. The soils developed on these volcanic rocks are for the most part fertile, fine and easy to work, and hold moisture well. It is a land of ridges and valleys, produced through erosion of the lava-flows by the many streams. These have been fed with the melting snows of Mount Kenya and the frequent rainfall.

Reorganisation of agricultural holdings

The Kikuyu live in six districts, Murang'a, Kiambu, Kirinyaga, Nyandarua, Nyeri and Thika. At the beginning of the century their shamba clearings in the forest were only in Murang'a, Kirinyaga and Nyeri. However, as the tribe grew bigger, the Kikuyu bought land by agreement from the Wanderobo, who were hunters rather than farmers. This new district of Kiambu was south of the Chania River towards the Ngong Hills and the present site of Nairobi. It brought an important change into the custom of the tribe. The new land had to be bought, and was therefore owned by those who paid for it; other Kikuyu land was held by the elders and could not be bought or sold. If a man in the south wanted to sell his land his family and clan had first right to buy it before it could be offered to a stranger. Some Kikuyu families became tenants on the new land and farms were soon made, leaving bush for grazing and forest for fuel and timber. The Kikuyu people have lived in these places for several hundreds of years, but for a shorter time in Kiambu.

After Independence much land which had been taken over by European farmers was returned (see the following section on settlement schemes).

The traditional Kikuyu pattern of land-use consisted of dispersed groups of homesteads, with the land held by one family scattered in many separate pieces. This resulted in waste of time and effort in moving from one plot to another to plant, cultivate or harvest, and made improvements (such as terracing to prevent soil erosion) difficult to carry out. However, since the early 1950s much of the land has been surveyed and reorganised so that a family still has the same areas of land but it is in one block. This is known as *consolidation*.

Consolidation was assisted by the creation of 'emergency' villages into which the Kikuyu were gathered during the Independence struggle. Some of the better villages have remained, and have become rural centres, with perhaps a school, a community development centre, a church and a clinic. Many other families have returned to build new homesteads on their own land. The position and size of the new smallholding was agreed between the family, the agricultural officer, the surveyor and the elder (or chief) of the tribe. In this way the best use can be made of both the land and a man's time. Each new holding sits on the side of a hill so that it has some of the level land at the top and some of the valley land as well as the slope (Figs. 73a and 73b).

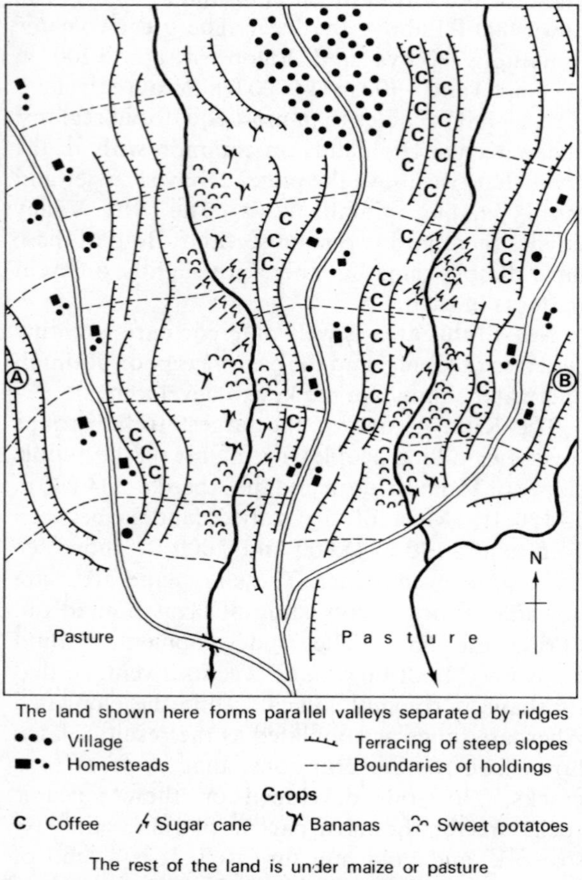
A
B
N
Pasture
P a s t u r e
The land shown here forms parallel valleys separated by ridges
Village
Terracing of steep slopes
Homesteads
Boundaries of holdings
Crops
C Coffee
Sugar cane
Bananas
Sweet potatoes
The rest of the land is under maize or pasture

Fig. 73a Kikuyu resettlement holdings

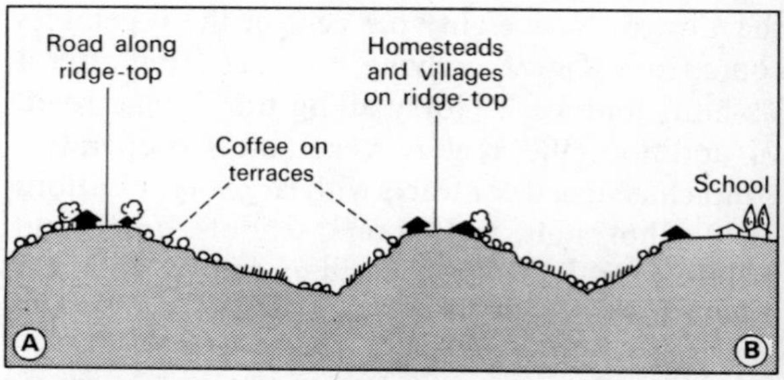
Road along ridge-top
Homesteads and villages on ridge-top
Coffee on terraces
School
A
B

Fig. 73b Section from A to B (see Fig. 73a)

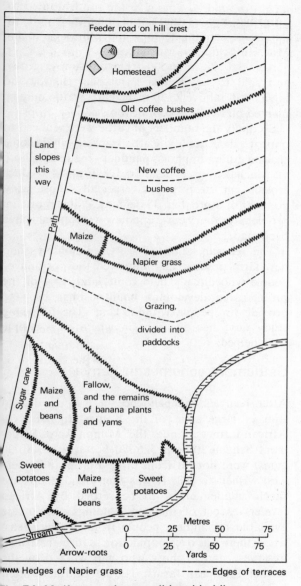

Feeder road on hill crest

Homestead

Old coffee bushes

Land
slopes
this
way

New coffee
bushes

Path

Maize

Napier grass

Grazing,
divided into
paddocks

Sugar cane

Maize
and
beans

Fallow,
and the remains
of banana plants
and yams

Sweet
potatoes

Maize
and
beans

Sweet
potatoes

Stream

Arrow-roots

Metres			
0	25	50	75
0	25	50	75
		Yards	

~~~ Hedges of Napier grass   ----- Edges of terraces

Fig. 74 Mr Kamunyu's consolidated holding near Nyeri

Study Fig. 74. It is a plan of Mr Kamunyu's smallholding (which was consolidated about 1958. It is 2·5 hectares (6 acres), slightly larger than the average. Note that it includes the land right down to a stream. It is essential to have a plentiful supply of water nearby for domestic use, otherwise much time and effort is wasted carrying it from distant wells or streams. It shows how the varying kinds of land on the slope are used to grow different crops. Note in particular how the coffee bushes

have been planted on the well drained terraces of the valley sides.

When it was planned, the new holding was divided into fifteen parts, and the Agricultural Department suggested crops for each. Since then the number of people living on the shamba has fallen from six to three. The eldest three children are either working, or at boarding school. Originally 1·2 hectares (3 acres) were given to subsistence crops. Now, since there are fewer mouths to feed more attention is paid to cash crops. Only 0·4 hectares (1 acre) of maize is grown, and this gives a surplus for sale in addition to the amount eaten at home. The area planned for coffee in 1958 has been doubled. The coffee bushes are carefully looked after, and spraying is done regularly.

There are two good quality cows, a sow and several goats on the shamba. These are the responsibility of Mr Kamunyu's wife. The family is very proud of the cows, for these are still rare in the area. They provide milk for sale, and also for use at home. Profits from the milk go partly to repaying the loan with which the cows were bought. In addition to his income from milk and coffee, Mr Kamunyu rears piglets from time to time. His overall profits for the year are about shs 3 000/–. From this he pays school fees and taxes, and buys goods not produced at home, especially refined sugar, salt, paraffin, cooking fat and tea.

In the future he hopes to plant all the area below the coffee with grass, so that he can have another cow. He feels that cows need little attention compared to crops, and yet are very profitable.

Farming practice

The chief food crops are maize, beans, pulses, sweet potatoes, sugar cane, fruit and vegetables. Nearly everywhere mixed cropping is practised and the varied crops help to restore plant foods to the soil. At first sight a Kikuyu holding appears overcrowded with the different crops, but this has some advantages. Completely covering the ground reduces weeding, saves moisture, and reduces soil erosion. It is also one way of giving a varied and balanced diet from a relatively small farm; it means too that if any one year is a poor year for one crop and it fails, there is a chance that the other crops may survive. In some places consolidation of

Month	Rain	Season	Work on the land	Planting	Harvesting
Jan.	1·5″ [38 mm]	Short dry Season	Preparing land for planting. Uproot maize stalks for cattle		Last of crops planted in short rains (picking coffee)
Feb.	2·5″ [64 mm]				
Mar.	4·9″ [125 mm]	Long rains		Maize and pigeon peas 1. 'Chop and plant' maize with panga 2. Beans a few days later when maize sprouts 3. Sweet potatoes (cuttings) on low land a few days later	
Apr.	8·3″ [211 mm]				
May	6·2″ [158 mm]		Weeding. Earth up sweet potatoes. Maize-peas nearly full grown (ground covered)		
June	1·8″ [46 mm]	Long dry season			Beans
July	0·6″ [15 mm]				Maize and sweet potatoes
Aug.	1·0″ [25 mm]				
Sept.	1·2″ [31 mm]				
Oct.	2·1″ [53 mm]				
Nov.	4·3″ [109 mm]	Short rains			Beans and sweet potatoes
Dec.	3·4″ [86 mm]				

Fig. 75 Work through the year on a Kikuyu holding

holdings has resulted in increased yields of maize, up to three times the former amount.

The table (Fig. 75) shows the relationship between rainfall and the work on the land throughout the year. It is incomplete.

Three developments have improved farming and provided work. The first was the introduction of cash crops. Coffee was recommended on land between 1 585 and 1 830 m (5 200 and 6 000 ft) and seedlings are provided by the Agricultural Department. A beginning was made with a small number of trees. Elsewhere pineapples are an easier crop and they produce money more quickly. Co-operative organisations send their pineapples to the Thika canning factory and others go to the Mua Hills cannery, Machakos.

Above 1 980 m (6 500 ft) pyrethrum is grown and sold to the Kenya Pyrethrum Board, and higher still (above 2 130 m 7 000 ft) wattle may be planted on land too cool or too steep for crops.

Secondly the numbers of cattle were reduced to improve their quality. Cattle tracks easily become erosion gullies but grass paddocks made like those at Machakos (see chapter 12, Fig. 84) reduce erosion on steep slopes, especially those at a gradient of more than 35 degrees. Water is often a problem for dairy cows and new water points have been made.

The reorganisation of scattered holdings and new farm practice has improved the position of people who already held some land. One of the problems in developing countries has been to provide for people without land. The following study describes one way in which such people were helped.

Settlement schemes in Kenya

After Kenya's Independence, it was decided to transfer large areas of the Kenya Highlands to African farmers. Under the 'Million Acres Settlement Scheme', about 526 370 hectares (1 300 000 acres) were bought from those European owners who wished to sell. It was then divided up into much smaller units, to be settled by African farmers. Most of the new holdings were made available to landless people from nearby areas, where there was over-population in former African 'reserves', and to those who had worked on the former European farms. The new farmers often had no experience of agricultural methods, and no capital to develop their land, but were helped to overcome both problems. Now about 30 000 families have received plots on 135 different schemes and are producing a variety of crops and dairy products.

Different types of scheme have been organised because some districts do not provide the same opportunity for producing a living for the people who farm them. Some are 'high density schemes', where the land is very productive, and is worked *intensively,** providing for a greater number of

*See note page 77.

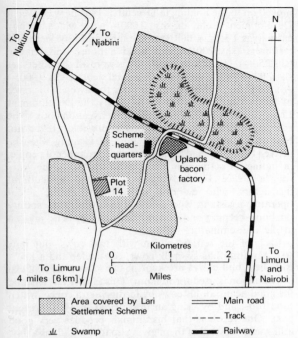

Fig. 76 The position of the Lari settlement scheme

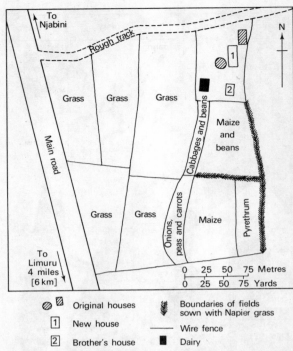

Fig. 77 Plan of Mr Mwaniki's plot at Lari

Mr Mwaniki's holding at Lari. Compare this photograph with the map, Fig. 77. The grazing plots are in the foreground; the maize and vegetables are to the right of the buildings.

people on holdings averaging 4–6 hectare (10–15 acres) each. Other holdings of 8–16 hectare (20–40 acres) form part of 'low density schemes' with fewer people and larger holdings. In addition, co-operative settlement schemes have been developed in those areas where it was economically unwise to divide up the large farms. This was especially the case in cattle ranching areas, such as Machakos district. Elsewhere *extensive* farming had been practised, such as in the Ol Kalou area, where there was large scale wheat and sheep farming. In these areas the land is now owned and farmed co-operatively, and the large holdings remain intact.

Lari settlement scheme (Fig. 76)

A good example of a high density scheme is Lari (Fig. 76), about 40 km (25 miles) north-west of Nairobi, at a height of 2 350 m (7 700 ft) above sea level. It consists of 702 hectares (1 733 acres) divided into 107 farms, all owned by Kikuyu. The farms range in size from 2·7 to 16 hectares (6·7 to 40 acres), the reason being that even within this one scheme some parts are much more productive than others. There is a large swamp in the centre and farmers need a larger acreage of this type of land to make a living compared with those in the better drained parts. It was intended that the main products should be pyrethrum and dairy cattle, those with large plots concentrating on dairying, while those with small plots were more concerned with horticulture. It was hoped that each plot should produce annually a total of shs 2 010/–, made up of shs 800/– for subsistence, shs 810/– for loan repayments and shs 1 400/– for profit.

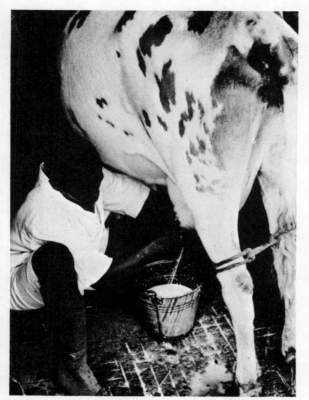

Mr Mwaniki milking one of his pedigree cows.

Mr Mwaniki examining his crop with the Lari Settlement Officer.

Detailed study section

The section set in small type is for advanced study. Return to this later if you prefer.

Fig. 76 shows Plot 14, the holding of Mr. W. Mwaniki on the western side of the area. He has a total of 4 hectare (10 acres), and uses it as shown in the sketch map. When he moved on to the holding in December 1963 he was given a Development Loan of shs. 2 000/- with which to buy cattle (shs 1 550/-), cultivate the land and buy seeds and fertilizers (shs 200/-), and build a house and fencing (shs 250/-). His plot was valued, as were all the others, at shs 7 000/-, so he began with a total debt of shs 9 000/- Although he has been given 30 years to pay back the price of the holding, and 10 years to re-pay the Development Loan, there is a 6½% interest charge per year on both, so he is trying to clear the debt as soon as possible. He did not have much experience of this kind of farming when he arrived but he has had the assistance of a number of people, including the settlement officer (who for two of the years was a Peace Corps volunteer), several agricultural instructors, who de-horn and castrate cattle, a co-operative assistant, who advises the co-operative society on book-keeping and general financial matters, and an artificial inseminator.

Each of the settlers began with two cows, but now Mr. Mwaniki has six milk cows, one heifer and a heifer calf. Few bull calves are kept in the scheme as artificial insemination is used throughout. This farmer has ensured the good health of his cows by feeding extra concentrated foodstuffs, and by using an insecticidal spray to prevent ticks. One result is that his animals produce very good milk yields, several of them giving up to five gallons a day. In addition to marketing milk, the Lari Farmers' Co-operative Society Ltd organises bulk buying of wire for fencing, concentrated cattle food, seeds, fertilisers and insecticides. Some pigs are being reared.

Mr. Mwaniki has built his own dairy, and has put most of his efforts into producing a steady supply of milk. But, as shown in Fig. 77, he grows 1·4 hectare (3·5 acres) of maize and vegetables for the subsistence needs of his family, his mother, wife, three children, and a brother who is attending a nearby secondary school. Other farmers have developed vegetables such as cauliflower, cabbage and lettuce for the Nairobi market. There is an experimental plot on the scheme to find out what other marketable crops can be grown, such as asparagus and artichokes. Some of the best quality horticultural produce is now appearing in the markets of European cities, flown there by jet cargo aircraft (see chapter on relief and communications).

Larger farm units

Large farms, many over 400 hectares (1 000 acres) still exist in the Kenya Highlands. Farming is extensive rather than intensive.

Grains are grown over large areas. Above 2 000 m (6 500 ft) the cooler conditions favour wheat, barley and oats. Below 2 000 m maize is more important (see Fig. 78).

To prevent exhaustion of the soil, a form of rotation is used. Grass (called a ley) is sown on the arable sections and cattle are turned in to graze.

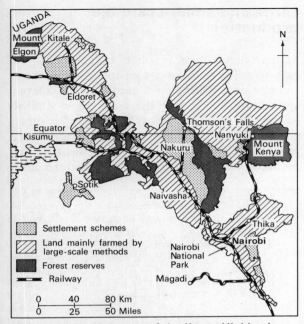

Fig. 78 Land use in part of the Kenya Highlands

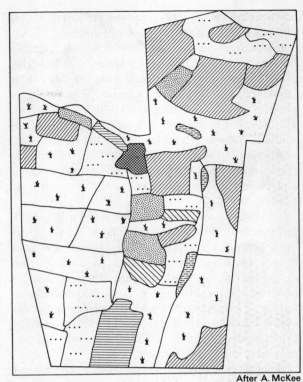

After A. McKee

Key:

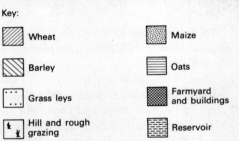

Wheat	Maize
Barley	Oats
Grass leys	Farmyard and buildings
Hill and rough grazing	Reservoir

Fig. 79 Karuna Farm, Moiben

In this way the ground 'rests' and the dung of the cattle restores fertility. Meanwhile the parts of the farm under grass are ploughed for crops. By careful planning the land use can be changed year by year to maintain fertility and improve yields. Fodder crops, millets and sunflowers are also grown. Pyrethrum is important over 2 130 m (7 000 ft).

But large areas are unsuited to arable farming and here ranching is often the chief use of the land. Cattle in Kenya are of very mixed origins. While there are some pure-bred herds of European stock, most are mixed breeds. They are European crossed with Boran (African) or Zebu (originally from Asia) cattle. Many of them are well suited to local conditions.

The drier areas are used for beef cattle and many hectares are needed for each beast. In the poorer areas it may be 4 to 10 hectares (10 to 25 acres) per animal; in the best it is still 2·4 hectares (6 acres) and extra feed must often be given to the cattle during the dry season.

Dairy cows are kept for both milk and butter production. The supply of skim milk has encouraged pig rearing. Bacon pigs are very useful and profitable animals on the farm. They use up surplus milk and need only simple housing.

Karuna farm (Fig. 79)

This case study shows that much capital and agricultural knowledge is required to run a large farm. Many such farms are today owned by a group of Kenyans who employ a manager. Others are bought and divided up into smaller farms by the joint owners.

This is a fairly typical large farm. The map (Fig. 79) shows its layout. It is 32 km (20 miles) north of Eldoret, on the Uasin Gishu Plateau and covers 1 392 hectares (3 480 acres). It is a 'mixed' farm: over 440 hectares (1 100 acres) are cultivated, and 400 hectares (1 000 acres) are natural grazing, including grass leys. Of the remainder, about

111

560 hectares (1 400 acres) are over 2 273 m (7 578 ft) and are suitable only for poor hill grazing.

Conditions on the farm are especially suitable for the growing of wheat. About 400 hectares (1 000 acres) are sown each year in May and harvested in October–November. The yield is about 1 480 kg per hectare (1 320 lbs per acre). The wheat is entirely a cash crop. That is, it is all sold and none is grown for use on the farm.

About 28 hectares (70 acres) of maize are produced as food for the eighty-five farm workers and their families, who live on the farm in four groups.

The other main activity of Karuna Farm is milk and beef production. The farm is self-sufficient in foodstuffs for the animals. Four hundred tonnes of silage are produced each year from maize leaves and stalks. Grain straw is used as bedding or mixed with molasses and used as fodder. Twenty-two hectares (55 acres) of barley, and 4 hectares (10 acres) of oats are grown for cattle fodder. Surpluses go to the Kenya Farmers Association Mills at Eldoret.

A seven year rotation is practised. Four years of cropping is followed by three years temporary grass. This 'rest' period enables the soil to recover its fertility. To prevent soil erosion, the land has been shaped into broad terraces which are ploughed along the contour.

There are over 650 cattle on the farm. Two hundred and fifty of these are steers, which are reared for four and a half years and then sold to the Kenya Meat Commission. About 220 are cows, half of which are producing milk at any one time. Much of the milk is sold to a creamery in Eldoret. The rest is 'separated' into cream and skim milk. The cream goes to the dairy to make butter, while the skim milk is fed to pigs.

The farm has a contract with Uplands Bacon Factory to supply 300 pigs each year. The pigs are reared for six to seven months, mostly fed on skim milk.

Over £9 000 worth of machinery is owned by Karuna Farm. This includes seven tractors, four combine-harvesters, mowers, a terracer/grader and much other equipment, including an oxy-acetylene welding plant for carrying out repairs.

Fig. 79 is less helpful than many in this book. What extra details would help you to make more use of the information in it?

Large and small-scale tea production

Modern agriculture is often organised as an industry. The following case-study shows how complex an organisation is needed to run a large agricultural estate. Like the sugar estate studied on page 75, the tea estates at Kericho and in other parts of East Africa are truly large scale enterprises. However, the latest development in tea production shows that small farmers can also

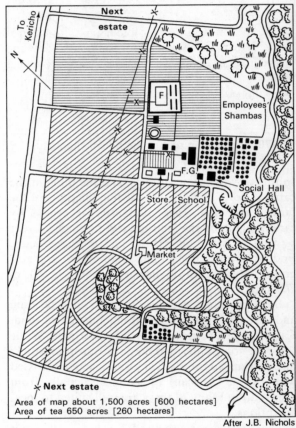

Area of map about 1,500 acres [600 hectares]
Area of tea 650 acres [260 hectares]

After J.B. Nichols

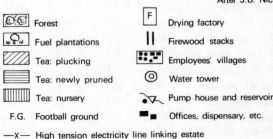

Forest	F	Drying factory
Fuel plantations	II	Firewood stacks
Tea: plucking		Employees' villages
Tea: newly pruned		Water tower
Tea: nursery		Pump house and reservoir
F.G. Football ground		Offices, dispensary, etc.

—X— High tension electricity line linking estate to hydro-electric station

Fig. 80 A Kericho tea estate

grow tea, with the help of a co-operative society.

Kericho tea estate (Fig. 80)

Perhaps the most difficult thing about starting a plantation is the great expense before any money can be earned. Nearly all plantations are a few years old before they produce a crop. During this time the land is cleared, the plants are grown and then planted out; constant weeding and care are necessary.

Tea likes a well-drained acid soil. It does not like stagnant water at its roots, so many tea plantations are found on hillsides. On older plantations trees were grown at intervals to shade the tea and prevent water loss. Now tea is not shaded, because it has been found that the trees themselves use up more water than they save.

In East Africa these conditions are best found in the highlands. The most important area for large-scale tea production is in Kenya at Kericho. Kericho district lies at about 1 980 m (6 500 ft) above the sea and within a degree of the Equator. Hence the climate is equable and the heavy, well-distributed rainfall averages 1 956 mm (72 ins) a year. Plucking can be carried on all through the year. Despite these advantages there is one serious disadvantage in this environment: the Kericho area is liable to severe hail storms.

As in the case of sugar or sisal estates it is important to grow enough raw material to keep the processing plant busy. An economic unit includes from 400 to 480 hectares (1 000 to 1 200 acres) serving one drying factory. The estate itself is larger still to include labour camps, fuel woods, forest and so on. It might be run as one estate or divided into two 200 or 240 hectare (500 or 600 acre) units each with a manager, an assistant manager, ten to fifteen supervisors, and clerks, drivers, etc., 200 to 300 pickers and fifty to eighty more general labourers. A well-run estate allows about one labourer to every 0·8 hectares (2 acres) of mature tea.

A typical Kericho estate draws its labour from several places: 150 might be Kisii men from South Nyanza, 100 Luo from South and Central Nyanza, and about 50 Kipsigis. There would also be wives from the same tribes, who are employed on a temporary basis.

The workers are usually housed in well-built

Tea pluckers remove two leaves and a bud from each stem. Notice the stick which the man on the left is using to keep his plucking at a constant height. He is throwing a handful of leaves into the basket on his back. The tea bushes are often very wet, so both men are wearing waterproof overalls. What are the buildings in the background?

stone houses with at least two rooms. Permanent senior staff have three- or four-roomed homes with electric light.

Such a community has its social hall, canteen, a school for the children, a football ground, dispensary and a shop. After a year's continuous work a man is entitled to two weeks' leave with pay and a free travel pass to his home.

Detailed study section
The section set in small type is for advanced study. Return to this later if you prefer.

HOW TEA IS GROWN
Clearing forest land for tea is difficult and expensive. The trees are cleared by heavy tractors. The trunks and branches are cut up and the wood is used for fuel in the tea factories. All the old tree roots must be taken out because they soon become infected. Couch grass chokes the young tea shrubs unless it is completely killed or removed. Then the ground must be terraced and limed.

Meanwhile leaf-cuttings from selected tea bushes are planted in the 'nursery' where they stay for one year until they have rooted and grown to 23–31 cm (9 to 12 ins) in

An aerial view of a tea estate near Kericho. The tea bushes in the foreground have grown to form an almost continuous 'plucking table'. On this estate shade trees were planted: this is unusual today because it has been found that trees take up more moisture themselves than they conserve. In the middle of the photograph is the factory, and to the left are some of the workers' houses.

height. The plants are grown in polythene bags which are removed when the young plants are planted in the field.

When the young plants are ready pits 36 cm (14 ins) deep are dug in readiness for the young plants. They are then planted out on the contour in rows about five feet apart and three feet between the plants. On flatter land a different pattern may be used.

The bushes bear a good crop about two and a half years later. During this time the important thing is to train it into a good 'plucking table'. If the bush is well pruned it grows many short branches. These are topped off at 38 to 46 cm (15 to 18 ins) above the ground so that the fresh young shoots growing from the branches form a thick mass of tender green at about 61 cm (2 ft) from the ground. Thus plucking is much easier than from an uneven bush of greater height. Another aim of pruning is to make all the bushes join together. This protects the soil and helps to prevent weed growth. Chemicals are used to kill weeds which grow between the tea bushes.

It is a great temptation to gather a heavy crop as soon as the fifth year is reached, but later yields may be damaged if this is done; the best results come from gradually increased plucking. Groups of pluckers move along the rows between the bushes, swiftly throwing the leaf in their baskets. They work for seven to eight hours each day.

When the tea has reached a mature state, plucking can be carried on at intervals right through the year. The interval depends on the weather, the age of the bush and on the plucking policy; the interval varies between one and two weeks. The estate aims at plucking two leaves and a bud only from the plucking table and quality

Tea being withered inside the factory.

depends on this. It is only when a mature bush is ready for a major pruning that plucking really stops.

After every four years in production the bush is pruned right down to a new level; a good time of the year for doing this is in April or a little later. After pruning, yields once again increase.

A 200 hectare (500 acres) estate produces over two million pounds of green leaf every year, and this means that every hectare (2·5 acres) of mature tea produces over 454 kg (1 000 lbs) of dried tea each year, and often as much as 680 kg (1 500 lbs). Fertilizers are used every year to increase the quantity of leaf produced.

PROCESSING TEA

Lorry roads intersect the estate so that the plucked leaf may quickly be brought to the factory in specially made lorries or trailers. Any delay or damage spoils the leaf. It is weighed and then passed straight up to the top floors of the factory, called the withering lofts. It takes twenty-four hours to carry green tea down floor by floor through all the stages to dried or 'made' tea, as it is called.

There are five main processes. First the leaf is spread to dry in withering troughs which are 15 m (50 ft) long, 1·5 m (5 ft) wide and 0·3 m (1 ft) deep. Drying out the

Leaves of a tea plant damaged by hailstones.

Protecting the tea crop by 'seeding' hail clouds. An aeroplane flies under the cumulonimbus clouds, back and forth for several minutes. A bracket fitted to each wing carries eight flares: these burn and give off sub-microscopic particles of silver iodide which are taken up into the clouds by the natural updraughts (see page 5). The silver iodide crystals cause the water drops to fall as rain rather than as hail. Unfortunately, the method cannot always be a success. In March 1969 hailstones up to 4·4 cm (1·75 inches) in diameter fell in the Nandi Hills area. They caused damage to tea estimated at £70 000, despite the efforts of two aircraft, which could not get through the clouds. At least 113 400 kg (250 000 lbs) of tea were destroyed.

moisture causes the leaf to lose weight, so it must be carefully controlled by cool or warm air currents.

Then the withered leaf is passed to machines that crush it enough to free the juices, for these are necessary for the third stage, fermenting. Fermentation, or souring, takes three or four hours according to the size of leaf particles.

Fourthly it goes to the drier which finally dries it and it is then left for the last cooling stage. The next day it can be graded and packed into large chests for export.

Such an estate calls for great skill in organization. There must be enough fuel for the boiler houses, engineering shops for repair work, a water supply, and often a special hydro-electric power plant. All this is in addition to the employment of the right number of pluckers and other workers, the provision of houses and the other needs of the labour force.

This helps to explain why, in the past, production of tea and of other plantation crops has been in the hands of a small number of very large companies. A Government-controlled scheme now enables an increasing number of African small-holders to plant tea. The green leaf produced by these small farmers is processed in central factories and the made tea from these factories is of the highest quality.

Hail in the Kericho area

At low temperatures raindrops freeze to form ice-drops called *hail*.

Kericho is reported to be the only place in the world where hail falls at all seasons, and hail is so common that Kericho district is said to be *hail-prone*. Hail does more damage than any other single factor, and about one million kg (2 200 000 lbs) of tea are damaged each year in the Kericho and Nandi areas. Strong winds whip the hailstones into the tea bushes. It is this that causes damage rather than the size of individual hailstones.

Modern technology is being used to reduce hail damage. A *hail suppression scheme* has been started at Kericho.

The kind of radar screen which observes aircraft is being used to watch clouds. The unit has been set up on a high ridge so that cloud movements within a 240 km (150 miles) radius can be spotted on the radar screen. A round-the-clock watch is kept on the towering cumulo-nimbus clouds which form almost daily over the forests of the Mau plateau and carry the hailstones which can do so much damage to the tea. When hail clouds threaten the tea areas, aircraft are sent up.

Tea from smallholdings

In the last six years the growing of tea on small-holdings has become very important. The cost of producing tea on smallholdings compares very favourably with that of tea grown on estates. On a tea estate over half of the cost of production is for labour. On a smallholding the farmer and his family cultivate and pick the crop, so labour costs are low, and the overall profit is high. A great advantage over other smallholder crops such as coffee is that the tea grows more or less continuously throughout the year. It therefore provides a steady cash income, unlike seasonal crops which can only be harvested once or twice a year.

Tea growing is being encouraged in all three East African countries. In 1968 Kenya had 18 000 hectares (45 000 acres) of estate tea, and 10 800 hectares (27 000 acres) of smallholder tea. By 1973 Kenya hopes that there will be a total of 24 800 hectare (62 000 acres). Thirty new factories will be needed to process this tea. Their distribution is an indication of the main areas of expansion. Fifteen will be west of the Rift Valley, that is, six in the Kisii area, five in the Kericho district, two in Nandi and two in Kakamega.

In Uganda tea production is increasing yearly

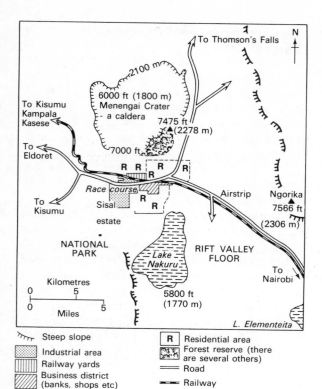

Fig. 81 Nakuru

Key:
- ꭣꭣꭣ Steep slope
- Industrial area
- Railway yards
- Business district (banks, shops etc)
- R Residential area
- Forest reserve (there are several others)
- ══ Road
- ▬▬ Railway

in estates and small farms. Most of the new tea is in Toro and Bunyoro in west Uganda. There, large areas which are sparsely populated receive the high rainfall totals necessary for tea. Most of the smaller farmers are 'outgrowers' for tea estates. This means that they send their tea to an estate factory to be processed. This is similar to the sugar scheme in the Kilombero valley described in chapter 12. By 1972 there will be about 18 000 hectares (45 000 acres) of tea in Uganda.

For many years tea has been grown in the Southern Highlands of Tanzania. In recent years small-holder production has been increasing in importance, both there and in Tanga Region. There is a good example of a small-holder tea scheme on the western slopes of the Usambara Mountains. Twelve hundred small farmers have each planted a small area of tea on their land. But the total is 400 hectares (1 000 acres) of tea. This is the first phase of a much larger development project. The aim is to encourage each farmer to plant 0·4 hectares (1 acre) with tea, and then possibly to increase this as he gains experience. Each family should be able to look after 0·8 hectares

(2 acres) of tea in addition to food crops. One condition for a farmer joining the scheme is that he must be a member of a co-operative society such as the Usambara Co-operative Union, through which he gets his plants and fertilisers. As in Uganda, the small-holder tea is sold to commercial factories. However, the Tanzania Tea Authority is building a factory at Mponde mainly for the small-holders.

Coffee production has been restricted by agreement with other countries (see chapter 10). Sisal is less profitable. Those East African farmers who live in areas suited to tea growing have now the possibility of producing this valuable cash crop.

Nakuru: the growth of a town (Population 47 800 in 1969) (Fig. 81)

Towns are growing up all over East Africa. Crossroads with one or two shops are becoming hamlets; others are growing into townships with filling stations, bars, a post office and many shops and other buildings. The Swahili word for 'shop' is *duka*, and these new townships are often called *duka towns*. Some, in especially good situations like Tabora, Mwanza, Kisumu, Moshi and so on, are becoming really urban settlements. Nakuru, larger than most, shows how towns develop (Fig. 81).

Nakuru (1 830 m, 6 000 ft above sea-level) is situated on the railway line from Mombasa where one branch continues to Uganda and the other to Kisumu. Menengai, an extinct volcano, lies to the

Table 10: Temperatures in °C (°F) and rainfall in mm (inches) for Nakuru

	Jan.	Feb.	March	April	May	June
Temperature 0°C	18·5	19·5	19·5	19	18·75	18
	(65°F)	(67°F)	(67°F)	(66°F)	(65·5°F)	(64°F)
Rainfall in mm	18	38	66	127	114	84
	(0·7″)	(1·5″)	(2·6″)	(5·0″)	(4·5″)	(3·3″)

	July	August	Sept.	Oct.	Nov.	Dec.
Temperature 0°C	17·5	17·5	17·5	18	18	18
	(63°F)	(63°F)	(63°F)	(64°F)	(64°F)	(64°F)
Rainfall in mm	112	104	69	56	38	31
	(4·4″)	(4·1″)	(2·7″)	(2·2″)	(2·5″)	(1·2″)

north, blocking the Rift Valley, and Lake Nakuru to the south. Its moderate temperatures make it an ideal place in which to live.

Its position, giving easy contact with different areas, has made Nakuru a good choice for an administrative centre and it is the headquarters for Rift Valley Province. This is partly the reason for the many organisations gathered there. These include the main banks of East Africa, the offices of the Kenya Farmers Association, and others. There are schools and educational institutions; the Egerton Agricultural College is only 11 km (7 miles) away at Njoro and Nakuru is such an important farming centre that it has sometimes been called the agricultural capital of Kenya.

Its position on the railway and as a sales centre has helped to stimulate industry, especially that related to agriculture, for example, the Rift Valley Cigarette Company. More industries are likely to develop, for Nakuru is the obvious place where farmers from the surrounding district can get their tractors serviced and obtain spare parts for all kinds of machinery. So big firms like Massey-Harris and others have depots and workshops there.

Such a centre is always a place where people go to shop. There are hotels where people coming from a distance can stay, and bars, clubs and sports fields for leisure time.

This pattern of growth of a town is in some ways a sample of what may happen over much of East Africa. Any small place that is conveniently situated for transport develops shops, garages and repair shops, buys and sells produce from the neighbourhood, has a Post Office and perhaps a bank, and one or two places in which to eat or stay. Sometimes it is the headquarters of the administration; often it is a good place for a school. Small industries grow up.

The places best suited to serve the needs of the district grow more quickly; some have special advantages, like being on the railway or near power or mineral sites. The items found in the town or village reflect the nature of the countryside and tell us some of the things going on there; they also tell us how the town *serves* and helps the people who live nearby. Such a town is sometimes called a *service centre*.

A study of the city of Nairobi is included in Part Three, page 159.

The Southern Highlands of Tanzania

The Southern Highlands of Tanzania form the second largest block of highland country within East Africa (excluding Rwanda and Burundi). In some ways they resemble the other highland areas. They have for the most part a high rainfall. They are cool on account of their altitude and are, in consequence, healthy. Certain favoured parts have a very high density of population.

There are, however, considerable differences between these highlands and those further north. Because they are 10 degrees south, they tend to be slightly cooler than the highlands on or near the Equator. In addition most of the area has one long wet season and one long dry season like the rest of southern Tanzania.

Like the mountains further north they are associated with the Rift Valley system. Here, too, there has been a considerable amount of volcanic activity. The area covered by volcanic rocks is, however, much smaller than in Kenya or northern Tanzania.

But it is *inaccessibility* that above everything marks the Southern Highlands off from the other main highland areas. Mbeya, the central town is 640 km (400 miles) from the nearest railway. Development has been very much slowed down for this reason. The most densely peopled part, the Rungwe district to the north of Lake Nyasa, is more closely linked with Zambia than with Tanzania. The Nyakyusa tend to go to the Copperbelt of Zambia when they go elsewhere to find work.

The Southern Highlands are very much divided up. Each part tends to be different from its neighbour. To the south the Umatengo block is separated from the remainder by the Ruhuhu trough. Umatengo is very isolated and well known for its system of pit cultivation. The area is self-sufficient in food crops and some coffee is grown for export. The Livingstone Mountains are high, wet, cold and largely uninhabited. The Njombe district is also high and cold. The main occupations are the rearing of animals and the growing of wattle. The Iringa plateau is little developed except for the Mufindi tea estates found on the wetter eastern edge. The Mbozi plateau to the west of the Rift Valley grows good quality coffee but in very small quantities; the Ufipa plateau is even more isolated and is one of the most remote parts of Tanzania (see Fig. 36).

Most of the people of the Southern Highlands are concentrated in the country between the northern end of Lake Nyasa and Mbeya. Parts of this area are as productive as any in East Africa. This is due to two things: a high rainfall and a rich soil. In addition the people, the Safwa and the Nyakyusa, are hard-working. There is an enormous variety of geographical conditions and products in a very short distance.

Lake Nyasa is one of the lowest of the Rift Valley lakes (457 m, 1 500 ft). On the eastern side the Livingstone Mountains fall steeply to the lake. Only towards the south is there a small plain in the neighbourhood of Mbamba Bay. Some cassava and groundnuts are grown.

To the north of the lake there is an alluvial plain within the Rift Valley. The low altitude, high temperature and rainfall (2 950 mm, 116 ins) and alluvial soil make the country good for rice growing. A population density of over 100 people per sq km (250 per sq mile) is reached in this region. In addition to rice cultivation a large number of bananas are grown. Cattle are also important. Maize and groundnuts form part of the local diet (Fig. 59).

The rice-growing region ends at about 900 m (3 000 ft). Between 900 m (3 000 ft) and 1 850 m (6 000 ft) the main occupation is the growing of coffee and bananas. This, like the Chagga country and Buganda, is a wealthy area and mainly peopled by Africans. The soils are volcanic in origin and often very fertile, although sometimes thin. The rainfall is between 1 900 and 2 550 mm (75 and 100 ins). The coffee and banana shambas are found among a mixture of grassland, forest and bush on which cattle are pastured. There are several tea plantations in this district. Tukuyu is the main town.

Still higher up the countryside changes once again. Above about 2 950 m (6 000 ft) the Poroto Mountains are closely cultivated by the Safwa. Because of the steep slopes contour cultivation has been introduced (see chapter 2). Because of the height the crops are mainly those of temperate latitudes; maize, important lower down, gives way to wheat and barley. Peas, beans and European potatoes are important. Once again one sees how climate and crops change at different altitudes.

Mbeya lies in a saddle between the Poroto Mountains and the Chunya escarpment. The town itself is at an altitude of about 1 700 m (5 600 ft). In the saddle coffee is the money-earning crop.

The future

Most people realise that the future of this area is related to transport. It is clear that the building of the railway from Dar es Salaam to northern Zambia, and the improvement of the road link (see chapter 5) will completely change the situation in the Southern Highlands.

Two areas in particular are suitable for irrigation: the Buhoro Flats, between the Southern Highlands and the central plateau of Tanzania, and the Kilombero Valley to the south-east of the Iringa Highlands.

Work to do

1. Draw a map of East Africa either from an atlas and show and name all the Highland areas.
2. Study the three plantation crops: sugar cane, tea, sisal. Divide your page into four columns and write the name of a crop at the top of the last three. Then write down the important facts about their production, thinking of such items as: relief, soils, rainfall, temperature, clearing the land, labour supply, processing, transport and marketing. Write these headings in the first column.
3. There are many town studies in this book. Each may be analysed in an orderly way under the headings: site, situation, function.
4. Use the photographs on page 103 to list other changes that have taken place in Kigezi in the interval of fifteen years.

Part three: The resources of East Africa

Chapter 10: Some East African changes

If this book were to have a sub-title, then a very suitable one would be 'The changing face of East Africa'. In recent times these countries have been in a state of continuous change. This is especially true of the last ten years. The rate of change has been accelerating so rapidly that it is difficult in a book of this kind to give a truly up-to-date picture. However, an attempt has been made to focus attention on the main directions in which change is taking place: changes in town life, agriculture, industry, transport, in business organisation and political and trade links. The emphasis is on the development of both natural and social resources, or, in other words, of the lands and peoples of East Africa.

Someone who had not seen East Africa for twenty years would be impressed by the changes in rural and town landscapes, in development projects, by the new responsibilities of the governments and by the way ordinary people are sharing in development. One of the most striking changes is in the character of towns. In the last twenty years they have 'exploded' both in the number of people living in them, in the new houses and multistorey buildings, and in the growth of new towns. Everywhere new building is going on, with new or improved transport links.

An important change has been the movement of people to towns. Many people feel that there are more opportunities to be had in the towns than in the countryside. In some places, for example, the movement to towns is causing difficult problems in planning for the future. Unemployment, overcrowding, and shortage of housing are serious problems. In all three countries the real population of towns is disguised by the fact that many of the

One of the recently built hotels in Nairobi, made necessary by the great growth of the tourist industry.

town jobs are filled by people who 'commute' daily to work from some distance outside the town. This is especially true of Nairobi and Kampala. Very large rural population densities are maintained nearby because many people earn a living in the city. Although Tanzania has one of the smallest urban populations in the world, its major towns have also been growing quickly.

However, the proportion of people who are wage-earners has remained small, and will probably increase only slowly. Throughout East Africa the vast majority of workers are self-employed small-scale farmers. A hundred years ago most of the farm products were for domestic use. Families and villages were largely self-supporting and were engaged in subsistence agriculture. Of course, some products were sold in markets (or exchanged) but on a small scale, and few village people earned much money. Even today when people produce cash crops they do not receive regular wages for their work, but only at certain times of the year at harvests, or from sales in local markets. It is important that standards of living and earning in the countryside should be safe-guarded and improved. For, if money is earned by country people, they can afford to pay for extras, both goods and services, such as electricity or education. This gives work to still more people.

In the earlier stages of development of the three countries, the main aim was to produce as much of the 'primary products' as possible. These were products such as coffee, cotton, sisal and tea, mainly destined for export to the developed countries of the west. They were primary products in that little factory processing was required to prepare them for use and export. So at first little attempt was made to broaden the range of export goods beyond the traditional ones. However, it is now realised that it is dangerous to rely on only one or two cash crops: a much more stable economic position is created by diversifying or broadening the range of products. An example will illustrate this principle.

For many years sisal was Tanzania's most valuable export. The development of artificial fibres elsewhere led to a steady decrease in the value of sisal. In 1962 one tonne of sisal fibre earned £100 sterling; in 1967 it only earned about £65 sterling. Tanzania suffered greatly from the loss of income from sisal (see chapter 6, page 59).

A similar position has arisen in relation to Kenyan pyrethrum. Synthetic insecticides, which are often by-products of petroleum, have challenged the importance of pyrethrin, the extract from pyrethrum flowers. Its economic value on the world market has therefore dropped. However, insects develop immunity to certain insecticides, and some synthetics have proved harmful to people. So pyrethrum may come back into favour.

A further major problem is that for a number of years there has been overproduction on a world scale of some of the primary products. The most notable example is coffee, and this has led to the fixing of 'quotas', or limits on the amount that a country may export. The quota system has not yet been introduced for tea exports, but it is a possibility. Overproduction results in falling prices which harm all producers; and this has been the pattern for most of the important East African exports. This presents a serious problem. So once again it is wise to have a wide range of products and exports. Increasing the variety to some extent ensures against falling prices for any one product or group of products. It also guards against the type of situation which Tanzania had to face when sisal lost its importance because of competition.

Another way to meet competition is to develop the home market, and to process and manufacture as much as possible, and this challenge is being met with enthusiasm and some success. But to develop new products and markets requires know-how, skill and money.

Aid and development

In the years since Independence, a number of countries have been providing aid of various kinds to Kenya, Tanzania and Uganda. Sometimes the aid is in the form of 'capital' or money, given freely or loaned for a specific project, though 'interest' sometimes has to be paid for the use of the money. Most of the new schemes described in the second part of this book have been assisted by interested countries. Two of the agencies involved are the United Nations Development Programme (U.N.D.P.) and the United States Agency for International Development (U.S.A.I.D.). Two of the other interested countries are U.S.S.R. and China. Aid programmes also provide skilled people for technical help in agriculture, water supply, engineering, health and education projects. Such people are not only involved in actual development work, but also help to train East Africans to do the work and take over the responsibility. As an alternative, some countries offer scholarships for Africans to study special subjects overseas.

Although considerable aid has come from 'western' countries including the United Kingdom, East African countries have extended their links to include U.S.S.R. and China. The countries appear to be keeping a balance between 'east' and 'west' and between aid and 'dependence'. For example China is providing an interest-free loan towards the building of the Tan-Zam railway. Both new and old links are sometimes commercial, sometimes political.

Political factors have sometimes been important in bringing about changes. Reference will be made later to the effect which the trade boycott on South Africa has had on some East African exports. We have also seen how new possibilities have opened up through Zambia's orientation towards Tanzania. Within the borders of East Africa, new governmental laws have been made in an attempt to increase the rate of development. Probably the most significant move has been the establishment of what are called *parastatal* organisations.

Parastatals are companies or corporations which, although run on commercial lines, are wholly government owned, or nearly so. They have therefore two main duties: the first is to be profitable, the second, to promote the wise development of the country and its resources. As we shall see these two objectives sometimes clash. Parastatal projects have been organised in East Africa to deal with practically every sector of the economy, and they are chosen because of the long term effect they will have on the overall development of each country.

The Uganda Development Corporation Ltd is a good example of a parastatal organisation. Begun in 1952, it has extended the field of its interest to a point where it now has subsidiary companies in agriculture, food and beverage production, mining and mining exploration, industry, hotels and tourism, banking, finance and commerce. It is involved in fifty-three separate companies. In each it is committed to making a profit if possible, and also to developing its

resources wisely so that there is the maximum benefit to the country as a whole. In Tanzania, separate power, industrial, milling and food processing, sisal, agricultural, tourist, distributive, building and construction, petroleum prospecting, transport, banking, rural credit, insurance, and housing finance organisations have been established.

The objectives of being profitable, in order to have money to invest, and of wise, long-term development for the benefit of the people, sometimes make decisions difficult. For example, which is it better to do: to site a new factory some distance away from the main centres of established industry, which reduces profitability (increased transport costs, etc.), or to site it where it benefits the local community, in terms of employment, wages, and the improvement of communications, water and power supplies?

Parastatals are also important as an example of co-operation between the three countries. The main areas in which they operate across international boundaries are in transport and communication. East African Posts and Telecommunications, East African Railways Corporation, and East African Airways Corporation are some of the main parastatals operating in all three countries.

Some of the changes briefly described here are studied more fully in following chapters.

Work to do

Many institutions and agencies are described by initials and other abbreviations (e.g. E.A.R.H., Tazama). Collect examples from this book and from your own country.

Chapter 11 : The resource base

A country's *resource base* consists of the resources or possessions on which development can be based. This includes much of the natural wealth, such as land, the soils, the climate and its suitability for growing crops, whether the rainfall is adequate, or whether there are water resources in rivers or snows for providing irrigation. It includes the natural vegetation such as forests, and also the mineral wealth of a country. It covers power resources which may be coal or oil, but can be water-power sites where electrical power can be developed.

Location is also a resource. A country (or a town) can be in a good accessible position or not, and this can be an aid to development or a hindrance. For a country wishing to export, a coastline is a resource. But some coasts have good natural harbours which are an advantage, while others have no suitable harbours for large ships.

But none of these things is of much use without people, and it can be argued that people, especially resourceful people, are a country's most important possession.

In this chapter we shall first consider, in outline, the ways in which the land is used whether for forestry, pastoralism or cultivation, secondly, the prospect for mineral development and lastly, people as a resource. All of these will be discussed more fully in later chapters.

The use of the land

Forestry

East Africa both exports and imports timber products. It has been realised that high quality wood is used at home where cheaper wood would do as well. Therefore people are being encouraged to use lesser known inexpensive woods and to export the valuable species such as mvule, mahogany and podo. The forestry departments of the three countries are moving towards a position where they will be able to supply all domestic soft wood needs. The most important single timber product exported is wattle bark. Juice extracted from the bark is used in the tanning of leather. In 1968 the value of wattle bark and extract exported from Kenya was £1 238 000, making it the ninth most important export.

The pastoral areas

Animals are kept throughout East Africa, except in areas infested with tsetse fly. Some areas are better suited to the keeping of animals than others. The coastal area, with its high temperature and humidity, suits the brown tick, an insect which brings East Coast fever. This discourages animal keeping. Cattle are most important to the people of the driest areas of East Africa where cultivation can only be practised with difficulty. The mainly pastoral areas are therefore found in a belt from Karamoja in Uganda, through most of northern Kenya, round the Highlands and into the heart of Tanzania.

A specially designed tractor lifting heavy tree trunks in a Kenya forest.

In East Africa, the word pasture can mean a number of different things. At one end of the scale are the pastures of the highlands, in some cases rich, productive and scientifically managed, with herds of cattle as good as any in the world. At the other end is the short, dry, poor grass of the Nyika, of which many hectares are necessary to keep even one beast. Until recently, the standard of animal rearing has been low. Now this pattern is changing rapidly, as the studies of the Ankole ranching scheme (page 95), the Masai scheme (page 93) and the dairy farm in Bunyoro (page 74) have shown.

In East Africa there are three kinds of cattle keeper: the nomadic pastoralist, the cultivator-pastoralist and the rancher.

The nomadic pastoralist

Certain of the peoples of East Africa have always depended mainly on cattle keeping. Among these are the Masai and Turkana, Suk, Samburu, Boran and Somali of Kenya. The Hima and Karamojong are cattle keepers in Uganda. Among these tribes cattle are still a symbol of wealth. Thus it is the numbers that count, even if the animals are small and wretched. Now that such diseases as rinderpest are being successfully controlled, the numbers of cattle are increasing. This has brought about overstocking and soil erosion. The result is that, as in many parts of Africa, there is a real danger of pasture land turning into desert.

The cultivator-pastoralist

Many peoples who either grow some food or depend mainly on cultivation also keep cattle. The animals serve various purposes. They may be used as an indication of wealth and for bride price. They are also used for meat and milk, depending on the customs of the tribe. In these areas a considerable slaughtering and meat-selling industry has developed. In Tanzania, important stock routes have developed for taking the cattle to market. These lead from the cattle-rearing areas, such as Sukumaland, Gogoland, Singida and Kondoa, to the consuming areas, such as Bukoba, Nairobi and Korogwe. From the producing areas in Uganda, mainly Lango, Teso, Karamoja and Ankole, the cattle are brought to Jinja and Kampala.

The rancher

Until recently, large scale cattle rearing was confined mainly to the Kenya Highlands. There the type of activity carried on depends very largely on the amount of rainfall available. Dairy farming is most popular in the cooler and wetter parts of the Kenya Highlands and milk, butter and cheese are all produced and sold throughout Kenya. A subsidiary activity, the rearing of pigs, has also become important. The Uplands Bacon Factory near Limuru now supplies most of the needs of East Africa for bacon, ham and lard.

The drier areas are better suited to beef rearing and the keeping of sheep. In all three countries co-operative and private ranches are changing large areas of little used land into cattle country.

The Kongwa cattle ranch

In Tanzania, following the collapse of the ground-nut scheme (chapter 12, page 128), a vast ranch was established at Kongwa in 1951. The experience of recent years has been that the region can produce high quality beef cattle, gaining good prices in Dar es Salaam markets. Today the ranch has around 11 000 cattle on 40 500 hectares (100 000 acres), of which fifteen per cent to twenty per cent is still uncleared bush.

Every year about 3 000 calves are born between January and April, at a time when grass is most plentiful. This is achieved by allowing the bulls to serve the cows over a three month period only. The bulls used are Boran, that is, a Zebu (humped) type from northern Kenya which has been selected and improved over many years. The calves are separated from their mothers (weaned) after seven to nine months. The castrated male stock, the steers, are then reared until they are about four years old when they reach about 450 kg (1 000 lbs) weight. They are then killed and dressed in a slaughter-house on the ranch, and the meat chilled in a refrigeration room before going to Dar es Salaam.

In Tanzania, the National Agricultural Company Ltd, a subsidiary of the National Agriculture and Food Corporation, is responsible for the management of eight vast ranches. These total 340 000 hectares (842 000 acres) and carry around 70 000 head of cattle. Another 101 200 hectares (250 000 acres) are being acquired for five new ranches.

The progress made in using the pastoral resources

of the Kongwa area of Tanzania is typical of vast tracts of country throughout East Africa. Today the expansion of beef production is one of the most exciting developments taking place. Uganda's second five year plan (1966–1971) stated that livestock production was the most important part of the programme for widening the range of agricultural produce. There is a need to supply more and better quality meat and milk for domestic consumption, and there are also valuable markets abroad. In addition, as the standard of living and income of East Africans rises, and as the population increases, demand will grow.

The least useful part of East Africa is found in the north and east of Kenya. Here the pastoral areas gradually become poorer and poorer until they turn into desert. In some years, parts of the desert are used as pasture. But huge areas are necessary and the peoples have to move around to the places where grass is growing.

Cultivated land

Fig. 82 is the same diagram as the one used in the first edition of this book. It has not been possible to find new percentages. This shows how difficult it is to find and *match* for three countries, satisfactory, up-to-date statistics. Such statistics depend on surveys, land censuses and collection of data, an expensive and time-consuming business. If, also, three countries go about this *independently* the land-use counts for different kinds of land may not match. You will see that they do not in the 1955 diagram.

Nevertheless Fig. 82 is a very useful 'visual aid' for comparing the way the land is used in the three countries. We also use it to make the point that in any future survey (in which a computer and air or satellite photography may well be used) a plan should be agreed between the governments which really does produce figures which can be usefully compared. Such *accurate* assessment of resources is the basis of future planning. Can you get information from your Government?

Find out more about R.A.M., (Resource Allocation Methodology) a form of computer mapping.

The most striking feature of the diagram (Fig. 82) is the very small proportion of the area under cultivation, about 4 per cent (compare France thirty-one per cent and Denmark sixty-nine per cent). Many of the reasons for this have been considered in Part one. They include inadequate rainfall, the effect of the tsetse fly and poor communications. The questions of water supply must also be considered. Many parts of East Africa have sufficient rain for the growing of crops but water

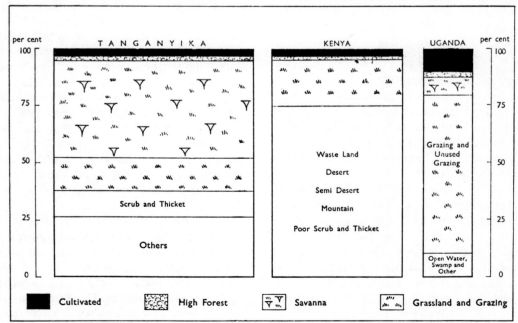

Fig. 82 East Africa: main land use (1955)

124

for drinking and other purposes must be found during the dry season. Development of these areas depends greatly on the sinking of boreholes and the making of small dams. Large sections of the dry central areas of Tanzania are being opened up in this way.

In the last fifteen years the area of cultivated land has been increased in many parts of East Africa. Among the methods of increasing the area of productive land is irrigation. In Tanzania, irrigated agriculture has been practised for a long time in the Arusha and Kilimanjaro districts, but recently several new schemes have begun. The largest project is at Mbarali, on the Usangu plains which are a part of the Great Ruaha basin. Experimental crops are being grown there to see if this whole area can be similarly used. In addition to the Ruaha, the main rivers which offer possibilities are the Rufiji, the Kilombero, and the Pangani. The Pangani is already supplying power and water for irrigation.

However, careful surveys already carried out have shown that vast capital investment would be required. For example, it will be possible to develop 610 000 hectares (1 507 400 acres) of irrigated land in the Rufiji valley, but the estimated cost for this in addition to providing a hydro-electric power scheme, would be shs 2 800 million (about $100 million). It is unlikely that much of this area can be irrigated for some time. Nevertheless, the resources are available, and in the long term much of this land will probably be brought under irrigated cultivation.

In Kenya, where the need is greatest, the possibilities are fewer. The highly successful Mwea-Tebere rice scheme, north-east of Nairobi, and the newly developed Kano plains scheme near Kisumu indicate that even small rivers can produce enough water to irrigate large areas. Also, the small scheme on the Tana at Galole has for some time been regarded as a pilot project to find suitable crops for the eventual cultivation of up to 101 225 hectares (250 000 acres) in the area.

Uganda's needs are not so urgent. Already small schemes are operating such as the one based on the Mobuku River. The Nile and the Semliki have great potential, if needed in the future.

As a whole, East Africa is not short of cultivable land, although there are some areas where there are so many people that more food is needed.

The Kikuyu areas south of Mount Kenya, Kigezi in Uganda and the Rungwe district in Tanzania are areas with a high density of population so that some form of emigration is necessary. In general, Kenya has less good land unused than the other two countries. Tanzania has plenty of land though this is still little used because of tsetse flies. Uganda for her size has more unused fertile land than either of the other two countries.

The future

Improved land use is the key to the future in East Africa. As it has not the power and raw materials for the development of large-scale industry, prosperity is more likely to come through improvements in agriculture and village life. In order to find out the best way to use the cultivated, pasture and forest lands, it will be necessary to continue the research work done by the government departments of agriculture and by other bodies such as exist at the universities and the East African Agriculture and Forestry Research Organisation. Already education is playing its part in teaching the younger generations that a scientific approach to the use of the land is important. It is important that young people should discover that work on the land can be both profitable and satisfying, for this is how most East Africans can easily be employed for a long time to come.

Chapter 12 describes some of the problems of development.

Minerals

It has already been pointed out that the land is one of East Africa's most important resources. Unlike some other areas such as Zaire and the Rand (South Africa), it has not as yet proved rich in mineral resources. Although the Basement rocks are similar throughout Africa, the East African part has been covered to great depths in many areas by volcanic rocks. However, some valuable mineral deposits have been uncovered, and it is possible that further exploration will lead to the discovery of more.

Later, in the chapter on development in industry, the main mineral workings will be described. In passing, it should be noted that a single mineral discovery can be very important to a developing

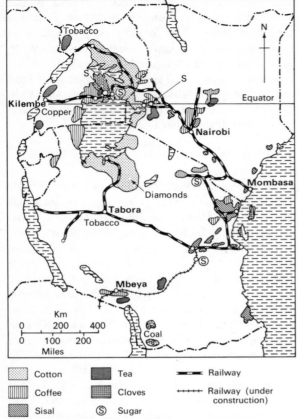

Fig. 83 The main producing areas of crops and minerals

Map legend:
- Cotton
- Coffee
- Sisal
- Tea
- Cloves
- Ⓢ Sugar
- ▬▬▬ Railway
- ┼┼┼┼ Railway (under construction)

Map labels: Tobacco, S, S, Equator, Kilembe, Copper, Nairobi, Diamonds, Mombasa, Tabora, Tobacco, Ⓢ, Ⓢ, Mbeya, Coal

Scale: Km 0 200 400 / Miles 0 100 200

country. For example, diamonds from Mwadui are Tanzania's fourth largest export. In Uganda, Kilembe copper is about twelve per cent of all exports, and the third most valuable.

The people

In any country the people are an important resource. People can only play a full part in the development of their country if they are healthy and energetic, and properly trained. Since much effort is going into the agricultural sector of the economy, this is where most government assistance, advice and training has been available. Many traditional crop practices are valuable and so village elders have been able to give help in teaching the young generation. In addition, new methods and crops have been introduced. It is here that agricultural extension workers are most useful. One important feature of farming in Tanzania has

been the recent use of the ox-plough. This is much more easily and cheaply introduced than the tractor plough. Oxen and men are being trained to plough in a much more effective way than is possible with a hoe.

East Africans have from early times developed along community lines. The extended family system ensured that there was a basis for co-operation in work. From this traditional foundation have come the modern co-operative activities which are flourishing throughout East Africa. In Uganda the group farms, in Kenya the co-operative societies and in Tanzania the ujamaa villages all show that the people recognise the value of helping each other.

In the cities and towns young people have shown themselves to be adaptable to new demands. The proportion of people living in urban areas has increased rapidly, and is continuing to increase. Fifty years ago very few East Africans lived in towns. In 1962 only 8·6 per cent of Kenya's population lived in towns. By 2000 it is expected that thirty per cent will be urban dwellers. These figures are a measure of the ability of people to adapt to a different way of life, and in many cases to a new job as well.

Change sometimes brings problems: but forward-looking people think about problems and possible solutions. Their ideas often give a boost to development: ideas move mountains. People are indeed a country's greatest resource.

Work to do

1. *For your own country* try to find out percentages for the areas in different types of land use. Compare the present position with that in Fig. 82.
2. Find out approximate percentages for *your own region*. How does it compare with the national situation?

126

Chapter 12: Changes in agriculture

We have already said that a hundred years ago farm families earned little money because they produced crops and other goods mainly for home use. It is absolutely essential that small farms earn as much as they possibly can to provide a higher standard of living for people who live in rural areas, as well as to benefit those living in towns. It is also important if the nation is to expand its trade. There are many examples in Part two of the ways in which farm land has been 'improved'. Refer back to the section on Kigezi (page 102) and the Kenya Highlands (page 105). The two plans which follow show how different a farm looks after it has been replanned (Fig. 84).

Work to do

1. Use the information in Fig. 85 to draw a section

(similar to Fig. 49 or Fig. 68) to show the crops grown at different heights. Columns 3 and 4 can be put together to give:

(a) Plateau
(b) Lower mountain slopes
(c) Higher mountain slopes.

Large scale projects are often better known because they are reported in the press. However, even if large projects are important, they are of little use if between them there are stretches of arid and unproductive countryside, with poor villages and hungry families. The real benefit to the people themselves, and to the country, lies in the remarkable changes that have taken place, especially during the last ten years, in thousands of small farms all over East Africa. While this is true, there is also a place for large scale, major

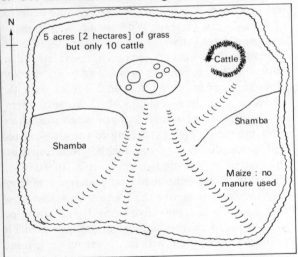
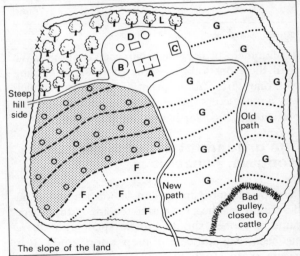

Size: about 11 acres [4·5 hectares]

Thornhedge of cattle boma
Huts and grain stores
Erosion gullies
Old sisal hedges
o Banana pits

.... Young sisal banking up paddocks
--- Edge of bench-terraces growing coffee
F Famine crops – cassava or sweet potatoes
G Sown grass paddocks and vegetable plots
C Covered cattle shed

A Main house
B Spare hut
D Stores
L Pit latrine
Fruit trees

Fig. 84 The left-hand diagram shows a Wakamba smallholding; the right-hand diagram shows the same smallholding reorganised

Altitude	Below 4000 ft [1200 m] (plateau)	4000–5000 ft [1200–1525 m]	5000–5500 ft [1525–1675 m]	5500–6000 ft [1675–1830 m]
Rain (2 rainy seasons)	15–25 inches [380–630 mm] Very uncertain Lower hence hotter, so a greater loss by evaporation	25–30 inches [630–760 mm]	30–35 inches [760–900 mm]	35 inches [380–630 mm] or more Higher, cooler, so less lost by evaporation
Crops	Maize is grown but a poor crop because rainfall is too low. Beans Millet Sorghum Pigeon peas Little possibility of cash cropping (No coffee)	Maize Beans Millet Fruits (cash) Vegetables (irrigation) Castor oil Grams (Some pineapples over 4500 ft) [1370 m] (cash)	2 crops of maize Sorghum Wheat (cash) Beans Grams Bananas **Horticulture** (cash) Tomatoes Cabbage Cauliflower Strawberries Peaches Citrus fruits Mangoes Onions European potatoes Pineapples and coffee are new development. Tobacco	Maize grown, but takes up the ground too long Wheat (cash) Beans **Horticulture** (cash) Tomatoes Cabbage Plums Apples Coffee up to 5800 ft [1768 m] (cash) Wattle (cash)

Fig. 85 Crop levels near Machakos

development projects in a balanced economy. We shall therefore look at some of these, beginning with one started about twenty-five years ago which was *not* a success. So much was learned from this project that it is worth studying it in detail.

The groundnut experiment at Kongwa, Tanzania

Perhaps the most important lesson learned from the failure of the groundnut scheme is that large sums of money should not be spent until there has been long and careful preparatory study. It is necessary to study the soils, rainfall and water resources, the labour supply, markets, communications and many other things. This in itself is expensive and takes time, and people wonder if it is really necessary. Let us see.

The area discussed lies to the north of the Central Line railway in Tanzania, between Mpwapwa and Dodoma. It is occupied by the Wagogo, most of whom live at the foot of the hills (where the rain is a little heavier) and water can usually be found in the dongas (valleys) and gravels.

The study that follows shows how difficult it is to make a success of agriculture on the margins of the dry and very dry zones.

The United Kingdom was very short of vegetable oil after the Second World War. In 1947 it was decided that oil seeds might be grown on a large scale in Tanzania.

When some of the Wagogo fields near Mpwapwa were squared off and the yield counted it seemed that they were producing 180–360 kg of groundnuts per hectare (1 000–2 000 lb per acre). Twenty check counts were taken in different places. All were good. At first it was planned to start clearing in some of the other parts of Tanzania, but only Kongwa was near to the main railway line across Tanzania and the port of Dar es Salaam where the heavy tractors and bulldozers could be unloaded. There were no reliable rainfall figures for Kongwa but the vegetation was good and soil tests were taken – unfortunately in the wet season, for the soil feels very different in the dry season.

Water was a difficulty from the start. Boring was expensive because of the hard granite bedrock of the African plateau. When water was found it was sometimes salty.

Homes for workers were the next problem. Wood and grass thatch were scarce, so the red clays and sands were made into bricks with the addition of a little cement. Alas, the soils themselves were to set almost as hard when they dried after the rains. This hardening of the tropical red soils made ploughing very difficult, and lifting roots in the dry season almost impossible. In addition the gritty soils contained small sharp grains of quartz which wore out the root-cutting blades, so that some lasted only five hours! The soils too were so hard that at harvest it was not possible to lift the whole plant with its nuts from the ground as the harvesters can do in the U.S.A. A large part of the crop broke off and stayed in the ground. Indeed, it was found that the land could not be cleared or planted, nor the crop lifted, in the dry season. European farmers found that they, like the Wagogo, could work the land for only half the year.

In the past some writers have said that the problem of developing Africa was that it was hard to make good workers out of 'Africans who had been quite happy for centuries to tend their shambas during the wet season and do nothing all the rest of the year round'. It is worth quoting Alan Wood in *The Groundnut Affair*, who said, 'Now the sun and the soil of Africa were imposing just the same timetable on the latest invaders. Much of the work could *only* be done during half of the year.' So the expensive machinery would have to stand idle during the remaining months.

Troubles did not stop there. Clearing the bush had to be done in the rains so that the trees and roots would come out in one piece; that meant waiting a year for the next rainy season for planting. In the dry season tremendous winds blew dust storms through the area. The engines on the Central Line ran out of water; then when the rains came railway embankments and roads were washed away. Some of the workshops were on *mbuga* land and were flooded after heavy rain. This same mbuga land, said to be useless for groundnuts, proved to be some of the best land in the end.

If the planners could have read correctly, from the Wasukuma and the Wagogo, the meaning of African customs of land use, they might have been warned of some of the difficulties. However, the lesson was learned that this area is really better suited to cattle rearing than cultivation, and much progress has been made since then along these lines (see chapter 11, Kongwa ranching).

We shall now look at four agricultural development schemes that seem to be working well:

1. The Mwea irrigation settlement scheme, Kenya.
2. Tobacco growing in central Tanzania.
3. Sugar growing in the Kilombero valley.
4. Cooperation through ujamaa villages.

These schemes show how land can be developed by providing irrigation water, how land in the miombo woodland is being used for tobacco growing and the possible future use of the land if it can be freed from tsetse flies. Then a study of the Kilombero Sugar Company's development in Tanzania shows how far-reaching agricultural change can be: it creates towns, develops industries, demands good transport and provides a variety of jobs where few existed before. Lastly, the importance of co-operative organisation is explained

through a study of ujamaa villages. Throughout Africa these are examples of ways in which village people share responsibility and work together to complete tasks that are too large for one individual. The K.N.C.U. (chapter 9) is an example of co-operation for commercial purposes, and the Wasukuma and many other groups show how this can be done on a small scale. The new ujamaa villages in Tanzania may be powerful means of promoting co-operation and change.

Mwea irrigation settlement scheme (Fig. 86)

The Mwea irrigation settlement scheme covers an area of 8 800 hectares (22 000 acres), about 96 km (60 miles) north-east of Nairobi, near the foothills of Mount Kenya, at 1 160 m (3 800 ft) above sea level. Water for irrigation is drawn from the Thiba and Nyamindi, two rivers which rise on the slopes of Mount Kenya. The map (Fig. 86) shows the areas of rice growing.

The soils are of two main types, 'black cotton' clays on which all the rice is grown and freely draining clay loam which is more suitable for other cash and food crops.

The rainfall of the area is very unreliable. It has varied from 635 to 1 270 mm (25 to 50 ins) during the past eight years. The 'rains' come in April–May and October–November. Only one crop can be grown per year, during the short

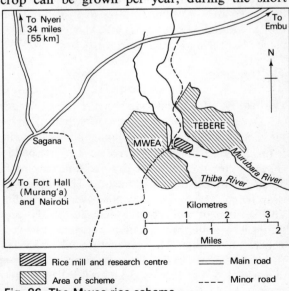

Fig. 86 The Mwea rice scheme

129

April rains. It has been found that the weather is too cool during the long rains for rice to grow successfully.

The scheme was started during the emergency of the 1950s when the colonial government was seeking projects on which to employ detainees. The main part of the scheme began in 1954. By mid-1967 1 734 families had been settled on a total of 3 088 hectares (7 719 acres) of black cotton soil. It had been levelled into 0·4 hectare (1 acre) units for rice cultivation, and had been provided with complete irrigation water distribution systems. The settlement was divided into three blocks, Tebera, Mwea and Thiba, the first two being of about 3 000 hectares (7 500 acres) each and Thiba 2 800 hectares (7 000 acres). Within this total, the 3 088 hectares (7 719 acres) of irrigated paddy-land were divided up into 1·6 hectare (4 acre) holdings. Each farmer had four 0·4 hectare (1 acre) fields, each surrounded by a small bank of earth, called a *bund*, to keep the water from draining away. Altogether a livelihood was provided for about 8 000 people coming from other parts of Central Province. No tests of agricultural ability were applied to prospective settlers, and in fact none of the tenants had had any previous experience of rice cultivation. Anyone without land could apply to join the scheme.

Each tenant has on his holding a permanent nursery of 0·04 hectares (0·17 acres). This nursery is cultivated by hand and is carefully maintained. Seedlings are transplanted after five weeks, when they are about 15 cm (6 ins) tall. Harvesting takes place about five months later.

Cultivation

The paddy fields are flooded to a depth of 10 cm (4 ins), and a fleet of twenty tractors then ploughs the entire acreage. Each tenant plants, weeds, reaps and threshes his own crop. When the paddy is nearly ripe the fields are drained and reaping is done by hand using small sickles. Threshing and winnowing is carried out by hand over a tarpaulin. The settlement collects the bagged paddy and brings it into the three collecting centres at Mwea, Tebera and Thiba. There it is weighed and dried either in the sun or in a diesel-driven drier. It is then cleaned, put into 72·5 kg (160 lb) bags, and stored. Yields are quite high, averaging about

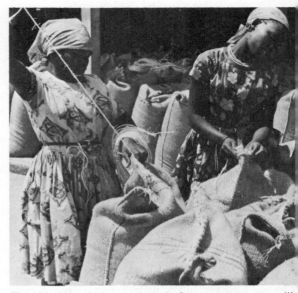

The dried rice is bagged ready for transport to a mill.

75 bags per hectare (30 bags per acre). One individual holding has yielded over 145 bags per hectare (58 bags per acre), which may be a world record.

In the early years, the rice had to be taken to other centres, especially Mombasa, for more processing. Then in 1969 a new rice mill was opened at Mwea. It was paid for largely by the farmers themselves.

The settlement provides very full services to the tenants, including the mechanical cultivation of the holdings, drying of the crop, and the provision of fertilisers, bags, seed and insecticides.

At present, with the assistance of the West German government, a further 1 200 hectares (3 000 acres) are being brought under irrigated paddy to accomodate 2 597 more families. It has been estimated that the whole scheme will then produce an annual crop worth nearly £K 500 000 from 4 421 hectares (11 052 acres).

Mwea's sound economic position is due to two major factors: the shape of the Mwea Plains, where over 4 000 hectares (10 000 acres) of rice land can be irrigated from the run of the Thiba River, eliminating the need for expensive storage facilities; and the results of several years of sound management, whereby the tenants have come to accept the high standard of discipline required for the success of an irrigation scheme. As a result the scheme has gained a high reputation abroad,

Leaf managers inspecting growing tobacco, near Tumbi, Tanzania.

Inside his curing barn, a tobacco farmer is keeping a careful watch on his leaf during the important flue curing process.

both as an efficient producer of rice, and as an effective system of land use. Perhaps most important of all, it has provided a livelihood for several thousand people who formerly had no farms.

Tobacco growing in central Tanzania

In the Urambo area several schemes are developing which concentrate on the production of flue-cured tobacco. They are especially important because the area lies within the miombo woodland, much of which is infested with tsetse flies (see chapter 4).

Tobacco is made from the leaves of the tobacco plant. It is obtained by withering or 'curing' the leaves in a certain way. The best tobacco is made by flue curing in a special barn. This is a complicated process, and needs skilled farmers. In the schemes at Urambo, Lupa-Tingatinga, Kiwera,

A progressive farmer is constructing a new and larger tobacco handling shed and flue curing barn. Notice the old style curing barn built of local materials in the background.

Tobacco farmers with their produce at leaf buying centre at Kitui, Kenya.

Inside the cigarette-making department of a tobacco factory in Dar es Salaam.

Mpanda and Tumbi small-holders have been taught the required techniques, and many are now master growers.

Rent is charged for each farm, and the scheme provides one supervisor for every twenty-five settlers. The supervisor calls two or three times a week. Each new settler is given a loan of shs 1 300/- to start him off. He needs this to buy fertiliser, insecticides and fungicides and to pay for four months of seasonal labour and transport of firewood to dry the tobacco. Then money previously loaned is deducted when he sells the tobacco. Each settler has 8–16 hectares (20–40 acres). Only 1·6 hectares (4 acres) of this are for tobacco. Some of the remaining land is used to grow food crops. Usually he grows enough to supply about three-quarters of his family's needs. Most farmers till their fields with hoes, though a considerable number have bought tractors with their tobacco profits. Each settler is responsible for his own planting, harvesting, curing and storage. He also packs and sells his tobacco individually, so that he gets paid for exactly the quality that he produces.

The yield from 1·6 hectares (4 acres) of tobacco per year is enough to provide each farmer with a very good income. This is between five and ten times what he would earn without the tobacco.

Farmers who are successful on these small farms then have a chance to run one of the larger farms. These are 60–80 hectares (150–200 acres) and on them a settler can grow up to 8 hectares (20 acres) of tobacco.

Urambo and Tumbi are in the miombo woodland. The plan for using the land outlined by the scheme organisers was a four year rotation of one year of tobacco followed by three years of fallow to give the best yields. However, in practice, the farmers find that clearing the grass fallow is such hard work, that they grow another crop of tobacco immediately after the first one. In this way they halve the work involved in clearing fallow. Then after the second tobacco crop many plant maize to take advantage of the fertilisers still in the ground. But the soils which are suited to tobacco growing are not so good for food crops. Therefore most of the food crops are grown separately from the tobacco.

The rotation that has therefore developed is different for tobacco and food crops. A single food crop is grown on one piece of ground for up to five years. By that time the growth of weeds has increased so much that the patch has to be left fallow up to five years. But five years fallow after food crops, or three years after tobacco, is not long enough for the bush to establish itself again. So it becomes a crop-*grass* rotation not a crop-*bush* rotation, and the bush gradually disappears. This may affect fertility.

Unfortunately the grass cannot be grazed at present because of the tsetse fly. If the tsetse flies could be cleared out this might be a very useful form of development. But a careful watch must be kept to see that soil fertility is maintained.

Sugar growing in the Kilombero Valley (Fig. 87)

It has been recognised for some years that the Kilombero valley could be an important agricultural area. However, the Kilombero River floods each year between December and May, covering a zone over 6 km (4 miles) wide. If this flooding were to be controlled, a very large area of fertile land would be made available for irrigated agriculture. Traditionally the people have subsisted on rice, with some maize and beans, and fish from the river and the lakes which remain at the end of the flood season.

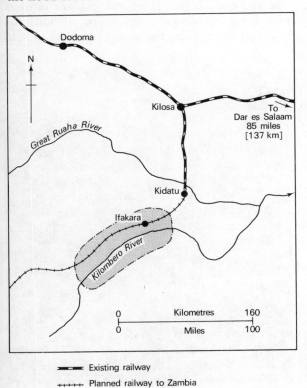

Fig. 87 Kilombero Valley, Tanzania

The first main commercial scheme so far developed in the area is the production of sugar by the Kilombero Sugar Company, a parastatal body (see chapter 10). A well-regulated estate has been made out of 2 800 hectares (7 000 acres) of bush, with communications by road, rail and air and the construction of a modern sugar factory, offices, laboratories and workshops. Although the company's estate is close to the Great Ruaha River, it is actually within the valley of the Msolwa, a tributary of the Kilombero. Water is pumped from the Great Ruaha to supply the overhead field sprinklers. The output of sugarcane has expanded from about 122 000 tonnes to 322 000 tonnes in six years. In particular, the proportion produced by outgrowers has increased greatly.

An important development is the policy of using smaller farmers (or *outgrowers*) to produce about twenty-five per cent of the factory's cane, on about 1 200 hectares (3 000 acres) of land.

Kilombero is not the best or easiest place to cultivate and process sugar cane. The original choice of the site was not determined by economic considerations alone. Broader national interests were taken into account, particularly the need to open up a remote and unprosperous area whose people had otherwise little hope of improved living conditions. Thus the estate company has to face situations not entirely of its own making. One of the main problems is a disease called 'yellow wilt', which struck Kilombero several years ago and has seriously hindered cane production. The disease prevents cane from reaching full maturity so that yields per hectare have been lower than normal. Another major concern is to improve factory efficiency and increase productivity. Research is going on to find the best

Sugar cane being irrigated at Kilombero.

133

kind of cane for this area, and many trial plots have been established. Improvements are also being brought about by training workers and a gradual process of mechanisation. There is still a considerable number of expatriate staff, but this is decreasing steadily as more and more trained Tanzanians become available.

There are three settlement schemes about 19 km (12 miles) south of the main sugar estate, four farmers' associations and six small estates. K.S.C. helps the outgrowers in many ways, by supplying suitable cane varieties for planting, advising on cultivation techniques, assisting in road maintenance. In addition it gives them direct encouragement to meet delivery schedules, which is vital to this kind of scheme.

Tanzania consumes about 76 000 tonnes of sugar per year, and this figure is rising rapidly. Until 1962 demand was met from some local estates and by importation from abroad. Now Kilombero produces about 30 000 tonnes of refined sugar annually and was one of the first producers of good quality refined sugar in East Africa. This allows local manufacturers of food and soft drinks to use Tanzanian sugar for canning and food-stuffs, and results in a considerable saving of foreign exchange. K.S.C. also helps the country's economic growth by employing several thousand workers and by paying taxes resulting from its profits.

Before 1962, job opportunities were very few in the Kilombero valley area. Now, the company directly employs 3 500 workers and thousands more are involved in the outgrowers' scheme, while others earn a living by providing goods and services in the area. At the beginning there was no town, but now a community of 10 000 people exists. Houses, a community hall, a hospital, shops, a church, a mosque, schools and playing fields have been established, giving the new town at Kidatu a settled atmosphere.

Early in the company's history it was able to move its refined sugar out of the region along a new, specially built railway line from Kidatu to Mikumi. In the near future it will have railway links from the south, for the line to Zambia will pass along the Kilombero Valley, extending from Kidatu to Ifakara, Makumbako and on to the border (see map of railways, page 38). This is likely to open the area to a whole variety of new projects.

These will bring to it an importance in the country's economy that was only a dream a short time ago.

Co-operation through ujamaa villages

'Tanzania is a nation of peasant farmers whose ultimate objective must be to become a nation of co-operative farmers . . .' So states a Tanzanian Presidential circular.

The 1969/1974 Five-Year Plan for Tanzania suggests that the hidden wealth of the country lies in its under-used land. Development is to be sought by co-operative activity.

When governments make decisions and direct development there is sometimes a danger that responsibility will be taken away from ordinary people. Yet the traditional extended family system lays emphasis on very valuable qualities: co-operation, mutual respect and the responsibility of each individual within the group. The Tanzanian government is attempting to find a balance between too much freedom and too much direction. The emphasis is placed on the peasant farmers who form the majority of the population: the government provides the means for them to help

Tanzanian neighbours working together to clear a shamba.

themselves in developing the community and the land.

The economic advantages of large-scale farming and the availability of technical advice come easier to those who live in large groups than to those who live on scattered farms. Also, vital social facilities, such as water supplies, medicine and education, can be more economically provided to large units than to small.

Bringing scattered people together to plan and work co-operatively means a basic change in social and family organisation, and in the rural economy. One of the most important objectives of *ujamaa* is to modernise agriculture. This will include a consideration of which crops are most suitable, and most productive, and the introduction of modern farming techniques.

Planning of ujamaa villages includes the selection of leaders and of village sites, research on crop cultivation, and the provision of essential services. Agricultural officers and their teams are busy introducing techniques which will increase production. The surpluses of foodstuffs produced can easily be absorbed by the town markets.

Mseta Ujamaa village (Fig. 88)

One such village is Mseta ujaama village, which was declared the best ujamaa village of 1969. It won a government prize of shs 16 000/– and used

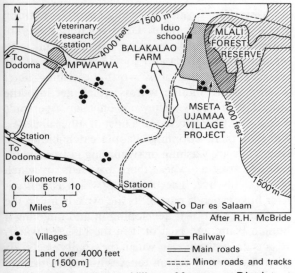

Fig. 88 Mseta Ujamaa Village, Mpwapwa District, Tanzania

The villager in overall charge of the shamba examines the newly planted pineapple crop at Mseta ujamaa village. The Agricultural Officer accompanies him.

this money to buy new agricultural implements.

It lies 24 km (15 miles) east of the township of Mpwapwa, very near Kongwa where the ranching described on page 123 is located. It is in a relatively fertile area of about 600 hectares (1 480 acres) covering hill slopes and plains. Although rainfall totals vary, water is available from springs and streams in the area. In several respects the pattern of climate and cultivation in this area resembles that in Sukumaland (see page 86) and Kongwa.

The population has reached a total of 262 people in fifty-eight family groups. Of the total of 600 hectares (1 500 acres) appriximately 52 hectares (130 acres) are under ujamaa, or co-operative farming, and 18–20 hectares (40–50 acres) are farmed by individuals. The rest has not yet been brought under cultivation.

Each man in the village does some work on the communal shamba: he has a work card on which he is given credit for work done and profits are divided accordingly. Some cash is put aside for re-investment and the improvement of social services. Agricultural officers and extension workers have set up demonstration plots. The officers have planted new strains and shown the advantages of disease control and the use of fertilisers and the ox-plough. At such a plot at Matomondo Mbiri, rice is doing well with the use of fertilisers.

135

Land has been set aside for an orchard. Citrus fruit has already been planted. Two hectares (5 acres) of pineapples (15 000 plants), which are new to the area, have also been planted. The first fruits have now been harvested. They will supply Mpwapwa and the surplus will go to the canning factories of Dar es Salaam via the Central Line which passes within 20 km (12·4 miles). It is hoped to increase production in the next few years.

This could be good cattle country but East Coast fever carried by the cattle tick is a serious problem. There is a plan to build a cattle dip and keep a few dairy cattle and goats. They will graze on the hill slopes. The veterinary research station at Mpwapwa will be able to give advice. Oxen are being trained for ploughing and any farmer can obtain a trained ox merely by handing in one of his own untrained oxen.

Services are important to the development of such a village. Plans to build water furrows to irrigate a 4 hectare (10 acre) vegetable garden by the Water Development and Irrigation Division are at an advanced stage. Villagers themselves are occupied in building earth roads. A small co-operative shop financed from profits already made has been in operation since December 1969. There is a dispensary. Housing is improving as new houses are built according to a standard plan. Each has, or will have, its own garden with a citrus tree. In this way Tanzania is promoting an improved standard of living in the countryside.

We began this chapter with a warning about hasty planning. We finish it with some more warnings on the hazards that a tropical country faces from 'enemies' of a different kind, when trying to improve its agricultural production.

Some hindrances to development

We have already seen that good farming can reduce soil erosion and loss of soil fertility. Thus it can increase the yield of crops both for food at home and for sale abroad. But we now know that it is not enough just to produce *more* food; it must be the right kind of food.

Nutrition

Although it feels more comfortable to have a full stomach, this alone does not give energy and stamina. For full health a man requires a wide variety of different proteins, carbohydrates, vitamins and minerals. Many African diets are lacking in one or other of these, and are often very starchy. *Kwashiorkor*, a disease which comes from lack of protein, not only reduces people's energy, it can cause permanent damage to the liver and other body organs, so that the victim becomes an invalid. It not only makes it difficult for people to work well, it makes them more liable to catch other diseases. Instead of resisting diseases, they become 'disease prone'.

You may wonder whether this is really important and matters to you, but someone writing about the situation thirty years ago showed how serious it was then. It was pointed out that protein shortage in the diet 'kills one child out of every ten born, and can physically and mentally maim the other nine'. Also, protein shortage and intestinal worms can make people more liable to other diseases. It has been common to find a person infected (at the same time) with syphilis, malaria, hookworm, bilharzia and roundworm yet not complaining of unusual ill-health, because what he had to put up with all the time had become so 'normal'.

Thus it is absolutely crucial that everyone understands something about nutrition, for body building foods help people to resist disease.

The invisible enemies

Kwashiorkor is an 'invisible enemy' resulting from undernourishment. Unfortunately there are many other invisible enemies, one of which is so widespread in Africa and some other parts of the tropical world that it is worth describing here. *Bilharzias* are minute worms which get into the stomachs of people. They not only sap a person's energy but they may cause a host of other illnesses, some of them crippling. People catch bilharzias when they are washing or swimming in fresh water lakes or streams, where there are reeds on which water snails live. The bilharzia (which is really a liver fluke) spends part of its life cycle living in the host snail, part of it developing in and infecting a human being and part of it in the infected water. It gets into the water when the snail 'ejects' or when an infected person relieves himself. Once the bilharzia have bored through the skin they get into the blood stream and reach the liver and other organs where they suck blood. They cause dysentery and diarrhoea, headaches and stomach pain as the *first* symptoms. The later ones are still worse.

Illness is always tragic for people but this one is especially bad because people in the African countryside are so dependent on lakes, rivers and streams for all their water needs. Most diseases are kept in check by medical science but bilharzia is spreading to new areas where irrigation ditches are providing new breeding places for the host snail. So new developments may produce new hazards.

There are also a number of *virus* diseases which attack plants, animals and people.

The tragedy is, that tropical areas with their high temperatures are especially liable to diseases which some temperate or cooler climates avoid. Malaria is one of these, so is sleeping sickness and other fevers. The tropical world often gets the tropical *and* the temperate diseases.

Some visible enemies

Even when a country manages to produce good crop yields, they sometimes do not reach the people. The food is consumed by an army of locusts, small birds, rodents (rats, mice, etc.), grubs, bugs, and other insects which eat or damage the crop. These are the predators, the animals and insects that prey on our crops and spoil them.

Perhaps best known is the locust . . . 'hundreds of millions, hopping, marching endlessly, they can at this stage ("hoppers") destroy the pastures of a village in a week. When they become adult, and fly, they can strip a lush field of its crops in a few minutes . . . they plaster the ground with their bright yellow bodies in a round of mating and egg-laying. Within the next month bands emerging from this and similar large egg-fields will emerge as new swarms.' Fortunately the Food and Agricultural Organisation and neighbouring countries unite to fight this deadly enemy.

Sometimes as much as half of the yield of a grain harvest in Kenya has been eaten by flocks of small birds which settle on the field just before it is to be harvested.

All of the hazards mentioned here hinder a country's development. They not only bring misery to people, they reduce the scale of commercial development and the money that can be earned.

Work to do

1. Study the types of land use near your home. Try to explain why the crops grown, or the animals reared, are those best suited to the place in which they are found. What attempts are being made to improve farming?
2. Look in your own area for a holding which shows good farm practice. Use Fig. 84 as a guide and list the improved features.

137

Chapter 13 : Trade and trade links

Chapter 12 described some of the changes taking place in East African agriculture, and some of the related problems of development. One of the greatest changes has been from production for use at home, to production for export. Products must be sold overseas if a country is to earn foreign exchange. 'Foreign exchange' is foreign money needed to pay for goods from other countries. To obtain it, home products must be sold overseas. The difference between what is *earned* from exports, and what has to be paid for imports, is called the *balance of payments* or *the balance of trade*. All countries, like people, want to have a favourable trade balance, with more earned than is paid out!

Before we go on to study the modern developments in industry and towns we shall therefore look at East Africa's trading situation. But first we must distinguish between *production figures* and *export figures*.

Export figures, whether given in cash (£, $, etc.) or in weight (tonnes), record the totals sent to other countries. There is a very much higher total of goods *produced*. Some of these goods are used at home and never enter into world trade figures. It is very difficult to say just what this larger production figure is for many commodities, as no one knows, for example, just how much maize is produced, and some of it is 'exported' unofficially across international boundaries. We only know the figure for *official* exports, and have to make a rough estimate of the very much higher production figure.

Some products almost never enter into East African export figures, for example, bananas. Yet the production of bananas in, say, Uganda, is very important indeed, and is a source of wealth and 'income'. So when export and import figures are studied it is very important to know exactly what is meant if *production* figures are quoted, and how these differ from *export* figures.

Exports

In the nineteenth century very few exports came out of East Africa, with the exception of slaves, ivory and cloves. Trading was largely in the hands of Arabs, who often went far inland in their search for slaves and ivory and set up caravan routes into the interior. The most important of these ran from Bagamoyo via Tabora to Ujiji and from Kilwa to Lake Nyasa. Some coconuts, mangrove poles, gum, copal varnish, rubber and sesamum

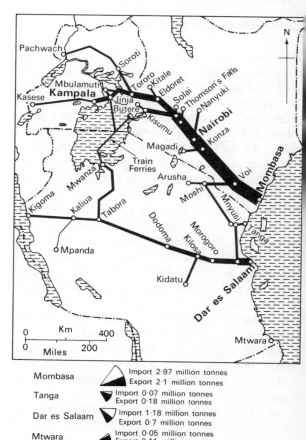

	Import	Export
Mombasa	2·97 million tonnes	2·1 million tonnes
Tanga	0·07 million tonnes	0·18 million tonnes
Dar es Salaam	1·18 million tonnes	0·7 million tonnes
Mtwara	0·05 million tonnes	0·11 million tonnes

Fig. 89 Density of traffic on East African railways

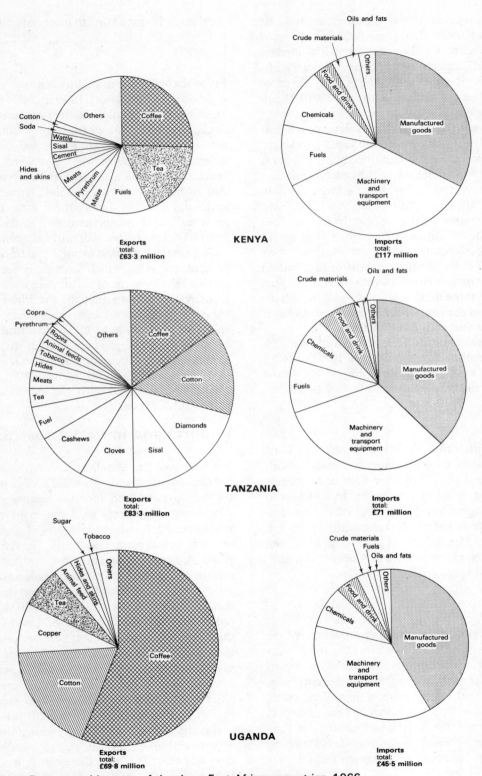

KENYA

Exports
total:
£63·3 million

Imports
total:
£117 million

TANZANIA

Exports
total:
£83·3 million

Imports
total:
£71 million

UGANDA

Exports
total:
£69·8 million

Imports
total:
£45·5 million

Fig. 90a, b, c Exports and imports of the three East African countries, 1966

were also exported but in small quantities. By modern standards this trade was on a small scale. Considerable risks were run: tribal warfare made travel difficult and porters to carry the goods made it expensive. The easiest form of traffic was therefore slaves, who could walk themselves to the coast.

Before much trade could develop, peace was necessary. Once peace was established good road and rail communications had to be built. The great distances from the interior to the coast meant that the goods exported had to have a large value in relation to their weight. The areas that have developed a considerable export have therefore combined the advantages of a climate that would produce either cotton, coffee, sisal, tea cloves or copra (all of them giving an export of high value) with cheap communications with the coast. This has meant that the main areas of development have either been on the coast, near to the main railways, or round the shores of Lake Victoria.

In all three countries agricultural and livestock products account for more than two-thirds of total foreign exchange earnings. Fig. 90 shows the proportions of the main exports from East Africa.

Kenya

In spite of increased variety of crops, the most valuable exports are still coffee, tea, maize, meat, pyrethrum and sisal. Together these form nearly sixty per cent of exports by value. In addition to the major agricultural exports, others of importance include hides and skins, wattle, soda ash and cement. Mineral oil is imported and then exported as refined petroleum products to Uganda, Tanzania and other African countries.

Tanzania

The diagram (Fig. 90) shows the proportions of the main exports. Until 1965 sisal was the most valuable export, but world prices have fallen to such an extent that it is now the third most important crop, after cotton and coffee. Like Kenya, Tanzania's petroleum refinery products now add an important part to the export figures. The importance of Tanzania's new relationship with Zambia has already been stressed in terms of communications and trade routes.

Diamonds are the fourth most important export

Uganda

From the early years of this century, cotton wa Uganda's leading export. In 1956 coffee became th most valuable export and has remained so eve since, except for 1961 when cotton was again temp orarily more important. Prices for cotton hav fallen to two-thirds of what they were only a fev years ago. Cotton also requires much hard work and is therefore not so popular. However, it is successful crop in areas where little else woul grow well, such as northern and eastern Uganda For this reason cotton will probably continue to b an important Ugandan export. The third most im portant crop is tea, which has rapidly been develop ed to take advantage of favourable world prices. I is interesting to note that the third and fifth mos valuable cash crops, sugar and tobacco, do no enter overseas trade at all. Kenya and Tanzani are also trying to produce enough of both thes commodities for their own needs, so it is probabl that Uganda will have to consume all it grows.

Copper is the third most valuable export, so te is the fourth export overall.

Imports and import-substitution

We have seen that the three East African countrie are dependent on agriculture for a large proportio of their exports and income. Similarly they ar dependent on imports as a source of supply fo most manufactured goods. Many of these import could be manufactured at home. The developmen plans for East African industries are therefore con centrating on this *import substitution*, as it is called At present a high proportion of imports are con sumer goods, for example foods and drinks, textiles radios and bicycles. The aim of East African in dustry must be to manufacture these goods at home thus saving valuable foreign exchange. Foreign exchange can then be used to buy expensive an essential 'capital' goods, like heavy and complicate machinery, and the raw materials for manufactur ing, such as metals and chemicals. It is hoped tha eventually the only consumer goods imported wil be very elaborate ones such as television sets and motor-cycles. Eventually these may be assembled i East Africa.

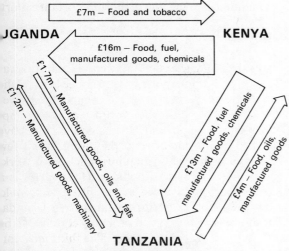

Fig. 91 Trade within East Africa, 1966

Trade within East Africa (Fig. 91)

A very important part of East African trade is carried on between the three countries. The diagram summarises the value of this trade.

The actual range of goods traded is very wide, and it is difficult to describe without going into great detail. This information can be found in the Statistical Abstracts of the three countries, published annually. These should be obtained to keep up to date. However, the most obvious point is that Kenya is the largest supplier, over half of its total being in the form of manufactured goods. The rest is made up of food, drink and petroleum products. Tanzania's contribution to internal trade is very small. The present situation contrasts very strongly with that of fifteen years ago. At that time a much larger proportion of internal trade was in food, drinks and tobacco. Since then each country has been diversifying its own production so that now there is much less need for each to import foods, drinks or tobacco from one of the others.

The East African Community

In 1967 a treaty establishing the East African Community came into operation. Its main effect as far as trade is concerned is to try to establish a common market. Within this, trade is 'free' in the sense that no customs tariffs are charged on the import of goods from a partner state. However, at present there is such inequality in the flow of trade that 'transfer taxes' have been imposed on some goods. It is hoped that the effect of these taxes will be to even up the flow of exports and imports from and to each country. Eventually these taxes should disappear, allowing complete freedom of movement.

The three partner states have also signed an Association Agreement with the European Economic Community (the E.E.C.). This provides complete duty-free entry to the E.E.C. for East African products, with the exception of coffee, cloves and canned pineapples. In return, the East African states have reduced import taxes on some products from E.E.C. countries. The benefits of such an agreement may be enormous in the future. East African goods will be imported by some of the most densely peopled countries of Western Europe. Since no tariffs are charged, produce entering the E.E.C. will have a big advantage over goods from non-member states.

The *turnover*, that is the trade of goods and services, is very important because it provides a country with capital, and people with wages or income. It causes far-reaching changes: new industries, new towns, the modernisation of ports and the improvement of transport. It feeds money back into rural areas as well as towns. It helps to improve everyone's standard of living. The next chapter describes some of these changes.

Trade links

Since early times foreign lands have traded along the East African coast. Chapter 6 tells some of the story of the Arabs, and their movements between East Africa and Arabia. With the establishment of colonial rule much later, Britain became the main trading partner of Kenya, Tanganyika and Uganda. This pattern has lasted until the present day, but we have already seen that valuable new links with the E.E.C. have been forged. Now the E.E.C. countries together form the second largest customer for Kenyan and Tanzanian goods after the United Kingdom. Uganda's most valuable customer is the U.S.A. since the bulk of its coffee crop goes there. The U.K. is second and the E.E.C. countries are third. The E.E.C. is also the second most important supplier, for imports from there are only a little less valuable than those from the U.K.

Substantial exports and imports also pass between many other countries. Although not very impressive at present, links with these countries will doubtless grow stronger. A potentially important partner is Japan. However, it is likely that the most rapid growth will be in trade with other African countries, especially those which share boundaries with the East African countries. Rwanda, Burundi and the eastern parts of Zaire already look eastwards for their supplies. Political upheaval has disrupted Zambia's trade routes, but has encouraged Tanzania to strengthen her southern links. In northern Kenya the construction of a road link to Somalia has begun. Uganda, too, may benefit from trade with her northern neighbour as and when political circumstances permit.

Political considerations are often important in the development of trade. Soda from Magadi in Kenya can no longer be sold to South Africa, but other outlets have been found. Zambia has found a new direction for her trade. The closing of the Suez Canal has resulted in more ships calling at East African ports for supplies. New political agreements may result in trade agreements as well. Thus, Tanzania is looking towards China as an important trading partner in the years to come.

Work to do

1. Study the most important export crop in your area. How is it cultivated? How does the cultivation fit in with the wet and dry seasons? What processes does it undergo to make it ready for market? How is it sent to market? To which countries does it go overseas?
2. Use Fig. 90, page 139 to check the most important exports of East Africa. Use Fig. 83, page 126 to check their distribution. Which of the exports do you expect to become more important? Why is Kilembe copper not marked?
3. Compare exports with imports (Figs. 90a, b, c). Write short notes explaining the strong and the weak points of the trade position of each of the three countries.

Chapter 14 : The development of towns and industries

We have seen that East African exports are at present mainly of agricultural goods; and the imports are almost entirely of manufactured goods and petroleum (Fig. 90). Industrial development in East Africa has still a very long way to go. Examples of heavy industry are few. Only a small proportion of the people employed in each country are in light industry (Kenya 6 per cent, Uganda 4 per cent and Tanzania 3 per cent). Only in a very few cases are the needs of the countries satisfied.

If we consider how and why industries develop we find that six things are important:—

the demand or *market* for goods;
power supplies;
the supply of *raw materials*;
workers, called the *labour* supply;
capital, that is, money for development;
management and 'know-how'.

These factors help to explain the way in which East African industry has developed in the past and the likely direction of future expansion.

The existing industries fall into four main classes:
1. Those processing raw materials.

Raw material	Product	Places
Tobacco	Cigarettes	Dar es Salaam, Jinja, Nakuru, Nairobi
Limestone	Cement	Tororo, Mombasa, Athi River near Nairobi
Leather	Footwear	Nairobi
Cotton	Cloth	Jinja, Mwanza, Dar es Salaam
Wool	Blankets	Nakuru
Sugar cane	Various	Madhvani (near Jinja), Lugazi and Arusha, Chini (south of Moshi), Chemilil, Muhoroni
Oils { cotton seed and coconut }	Soap Margarine	Kampala, Jinja, Dar es Salaam, Mombasa, Nairobi
Rice Wheat { milling } Maize	Flour	widespread
	Soft and other drinks	widespread
Pineapples	Canned	Thika

2. Service industries.

Light engineering–locomotive, motor-car, cycle, repairs.
Industries subsidiary to transport, e.g. tyre re-treading, cycle tyres.
Those supplying domestic needs: paint, asbestos sheets for roofs, beds, kitchenware, canvas and rubber shoes.

3. The making of containers to hold the local manufactured products or imported goods.

Raw materials	Product	Places
Imported metal	Metal cans	Dar es Salaam (meat) Kenya (fruits, meat) Mombasa (oil drums)
Magadi soda	Glass bottles	Mombasa
Fibres	Paper bags Fibre bags	Mombasa, Thika Kenya Uganda

4. Construction.

Timber and woodworking. Making of bricks, cement blocks, etc.

The following factors help to explain the way in which East African industry has developed and the likely direction of future expansion.

The demand or market for goods

Goods when produced must be sold if the manufacturer is to gain any benefit from his work. There must therefore be someone to buy. Within East Africa there are 31 million people. This is a small population by comparison with those of the bigger industrial countries of the world. If goods are to be sold in large quantities they must be wanted by a large proportion of the people, as for example are cigarettes and cotton cloth. Another important factor is the amount of money that the people have to spend. Rich people can buy more than poor. In East Africa the majority of the people cannot afford to buy many manufactured goods. A smaller population which is not wealthy does not give a large market for manufactures. This is one of the main reasons why East Africa has not developed much industry as yet. If the population grows and its wealth increases, then industry may become more profitable.

Power

Most industries require some sort of power to turn their machinery. Normally the chief sources of power are coal, oil and hydro-electricity. For the first two East Africa is not well placed. As far as is known, there is no oil, although exploration is going on at the moment. Coal does exist but, as has been pointed out in the previous chapter, its mining is as yet undeveloped and it will be difficult to exploit on account of its distance from the railway. Even if it were developed, the quantity and quality of the coal would not compare favourably with that of the leading industrial countries, such as the U.S.A., West Germany and Great Britain. Nevertheless in the Songea–Njombe area some development is possible.

For hydro-electric power the position is very different. Africa as a continent has a huge reserve of unused hydro-electric power. East Africa is well off in this respect. A study of the main hydro-electric power plant now working, at the Owen Falls dam, will give an idea of the conditions which favour this form of project.

This dam was constructed during the years 1949–54. It was long ago recognised as one of the best power sites in the world. Lake Victoria gives a large and constant flow of water to the River Nile. The large volume makes for plenty of force behind the water to turn the turbines. The constant supply means that the machinery can operate all the time, whether the season is wet or dry. It also means that a very high dam is not necessary. Some power sites

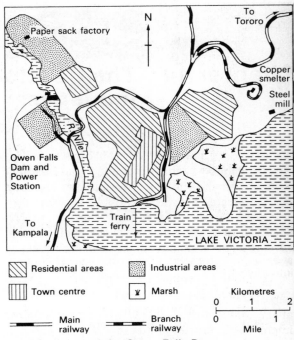

Fig. 92 Jinja and the Owen Falls Dam

Legend:
- Residential areas
- Town centre
- Main railway
- Industrial areas
- Marsh
- Branch railway
- Kilometres 0 1 2
- Mile 0 1

require a big dam in order to store water for dry periods. The site of the Owen Falls is very well suited to dam building. The river flows in a relatively narrow channel between high banks. A long dam is not therefore necessary (the length is only 900 m, 985 yards). The rock on which the dam is built is very hard and makes a firm foundation. The presence of a natural drop in the water, now made larger by the dam, helps to turn the turbines. The dam is situated near to the more densely populated parts of Uganda, so that when the power is produced much can be sold locally. It is taken to Kampala and Masaka in the west, and to Tororo and Mbale and on to Kenya in the east.

At the moment the dam can produce more electricity than Uganda can use but the demand is growing rapidly. Soon more power will be needed, and arrangements are being made to construct another power station lower down the Nile.

As a result of the power Jinja has developed into one of the first industrial towns of East Africa. The trial areas which contain important manufacturing plants. Two large textile mills, both using only locally produced cotton, together employ over 4 500 workers. The factories in the central area

Owen Falls Dam. The electricity station is out of the picture, to the right, on the far bank of the river.

144

Feeding ginned cotton on to the carding machine at a Jinja cotton factory. The next stage is spinning into threads.

make a wide variety of products, ranging from hoes at the tool factory, to matches. Two of the most interesting industries in the town are the steel mill and the copper smelter, which are unique in East Africa. The steel works use large quantities of hydro-electric power to rework scrap metal into ingots. These ingots form the basis of new products such as girders for buildings and steel tubes for metal furniture and bicycles. Nearby is the copper smelter, the largest single consumer of electricity in Uganda. The copper concentrate is mixed with a limestone flux and put into a furnace, while air is blown in to oxidise impurities. The metal is concentrated to almost pure copper (about ninety-nine per cent) and the impurities combine with the flux to form a slag. The copper is then drawn off and moulded into transportable shapes before being railed to Mombasa for export.

To the north of the town a further industrial area is developing. In addition to the textile mill already mentioned, there is a paper sack factory using imported pulp to make bags for the sugar, fertiliser and cement industries. Later the factory plans to use local wood pulp and bagasse (sugar canes from which the sugar has been squeezed) to make the sacks.

Many of the factories in and around Jinja are part-owned by the giant Madhvani group of companies. Their siting at Jinja is to a large extent the result of the availability of water, electric power, communications and labour supply. However, the location of the vast Madhvani sugar estates only 8 km (5 miles) away at Kakira has had an important influence on the establishment of many of the industries at Jinja.

The development of electrical power in East Africa

Owen Falls is the ideal power site. Very few other

Molten steel being poured from the giant furnace at Jinja.

A sub-station of the Halle hydro-electric scheme near Tanga.

parts of East Africa offer the same possibilities. Much of Tanzania has a long dry season (see map, page 7). This means that although there are big rivers their flow varies very much between the wet and the dry seasons. Therefore larger dams have to be built to store water and this is expensive. However, work has begun on developing the hydro-elctric potential of the Great Ruaha river.

Most of Kenya suffers from a lack of rain and permanent rivers. The most promising sources are the rivers flowing from the Kenya Highlands, especially the Tana, and a series of stations is being constructed. At present Kenya is importing electricity from Uganda, but it is possible that this situation may be reversed by 1974. Similarly, the most important hydro-electric scheme in Tanzania, on the Pangani river, depends on water coming from Mount Kilimanjaro.

In summary, it can be said that there is a considerable future for hydro-electric development. In general it is improbable that industry will be held up for lack of electric power.

Raw materials

Normally an industry can operate more cheaply if

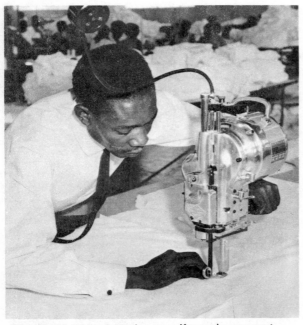

This highly skilled worker at a Kampala garment factory is cutting a pattern through many layers of cloth at one time.

it can get its raw materials nearby. This is particularly true when a bulky raw material loses much weight during processing. This is illustrated by the present nature of manufacturing in East Africa. The cigarette, cement, footwear, cotton and woollen textile, soap, margarine and milling industries all depend on locally produced raw materials.

The extent to which home industries can capture the local market depends to a large extent on whether they can produce the quality as well as the quantity of the overseas product. There is no doubt that many of the home products do match the quality of imported goods. Luckily there is unlikely to be a lack of raw materials such as cotton, sisal, vegetable oil, hides and skins. Therefore once the local demand is satisfied, sales in other parts of East Africa or abroad depend on being able to produce goods of a high quality. Fortunately, there are many indications that large foreign markets do exist, in central Africa, north-east Africa and the Middle East, so that the future for industries based on these raw materials seems bright.

The prospect is less good for heavier industries such as iron and steel and metal manufactures of all sorts. The Jinja works produce only a relatively small amount of steel from scrap metal, and this is used mainly in the construction industry and for bicycles and hoes. It would need a very much larger market than the three East African countries can offer at present to justify a really large iron and steel works, producing steel for bridges, cars, locomotives and ships. The refining of copper on its own has not led to very great industrial growth.

It is still reasonable to hope that mineral oil could be discovered in the sedimentary basins of Kenya and Tanzania, close to the Indian Ocean. Already more than £12 million has been invested in exploration in these areas. This is a measure of the hopes of the oil companies that petroleum will eventually be found. If mineral oil is found the industrial, and indeed, the economic position of the countries could be greatly changed. A large range of chemicals, or 'petro-chemicals' as they are called, can be made. These include such things as medicines, plastics, paints and artificial rubber. However, until oil is found, no great development either of heavy or chemical industry is to be expected.

Frozen fish fillets from Lake Katwe, Uganda, being packed for shipment to other parts of East Africa.

Labour

One factor which may slow industrial development is the lack of skilled labour. Every country in the world which has tried to change a village farmer into an industrial worker has had difficulty with this. People who are accustomed to life in the country, dealing with animals and crops, do not find it easy to settle down to the regular hard work of a factory. They do not understand easily the need to be accurate and precise in what they are doing. If they leave the factory after a short time to return home, the time spent in training has largely been wasted. All these things help to make untrained labour expensive, even if it is poorly paid.

However, many of the young people now working in factories have grown up in towns. Through attending school they have become used to working to a fixed timetable. Also, many are far better acquainted with scientific and mechanical ideas than their parents could be. There are opportunities for learning in small workshops and for full and part-time technical training. In the universities, polytechnics and technical schools skilled and capable people are able to learn the latest techniques of factory production.

Capital and management

To start an industry it is necessary to have the money to put up a factory, buy raw materials and pay the workers. Until recently the majority of Africans have not had enough money for this, or sufficient experience in the running of a factory, and these have had to come from outside. Much foreign money is still required to develop new

Trainee station masters learning how to operate a new railway control system.

The Kenya Polytechnic, Nairobi, where students from all over the country come to study engineering and other practical skills.

manufacturing industries. However, many East African nationals now hold important management jobs. They have either taken courses in Business Studies, or worked their way up from positions as workers on the factory floor.

Development based on minerals

There are several examples in East Africa of the way in which the discovery of an important mineral deposit leads to change. One such example is copper ore from Kilembe, Uganda; another, diamonds at Mwadui in Tanzania. These are by far the two most valuable minerals mined in East Africa.

In each case the mineral has to be mined or quarried, involving heavy machinery, power, a labour force and transport; it has to be processed or refined, sometimes at the site, sometimes after shifting it to a better centre; it has to be moved to market, sometimes exported.

The studies that follow describe the processes of mining, and show the kinds of development that have resulted from working the mineral deposit.

The Kilembe Copper Mines, Uganda (Fig. 93)

The map (Fig. 93) shows the position of Kilembe

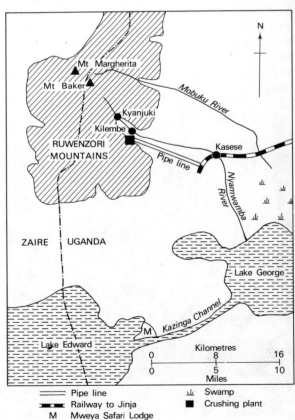

Fig. 93 The location of Kilembe Mines, Uganda

148

The new mining town of Kilembe. Notice how the buildings are confined to the flat valley floor. The shrunken remains of the river which carved this valley can be seen on the far side of the houses. The many large boulders along its bed make it show up in this picture as a light surface.

in the steep sided valley cut by the Nyamwamba river into the eastern side of the Ruwenzori. The river exposes deposits of copper ore within the Basement Complex, which has been uplifted in this area by the block faulting described in chapter five. The geology of the area is very complicated, with many folds, faults and igneous dykes, but the mining company has developed several clever techniques for extracting the ore with the greatest possible efficiency. There are three separate mines, all on one side of the Nyamwamba valley, and at heights ranging between 1 160 and 2 000 m (3 800 and 7 000 ft) above sea level. Workers are trans-

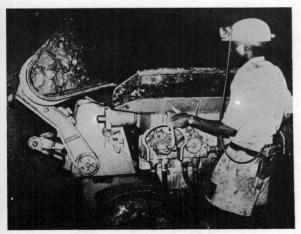

A miner at Kilembe operating a mechanical shovel, which is loading ore on to a conveyor belt. The pack attached to his belt carries a battery which supplies power to the lamp on his helment.

ported up the mountainside on a chair-lift which carries 500 people per hour and covers the distance from Kilembe to Bukangama, one of the mines, in about twenty minutes.

The ore layers vary in thickness between a few centimetres and 30 m (100 ft). They are reached by means of horizontal tunnels, or 'adits', driven into the hillside. Underground there are two separate operations, development and mining. *Development* consists of driving tunnels into the rock so that men and equipment can get in, and ore be brought out. *Mining* breaks up the ore by drilling and blasting. It is removed by small railway trucks. The ore is taken to the concentration plant where it is crushed and reduced in size by grinders. The copper mineral is then separated from the waste products by rotation in water; indeed water is needed at every stage of mining and processing. The concentrate left at the bottom of the water tanks is about twenty-five per cent pure copper, and it is pumped in suspension down an 11 km (7 mile) pipeline to the railway terminus at Kasese, 430 m (1 400 ft) below. There it is filtered and dried to reduce its weight, before being loaded into 36 tonne capacity railway wagons for the journey to the copper smelter at Jinja, 420 km (260 miles) away. By these methods approximately one million tonnes of ore containing about 1·9 per cent copper are mined at Kilembe each year. From this ore 15 587 tonnes of pure copper were extracted at Jinja in 1968.

At present all the copper is bought by a Japanese company, though this contract will expire in 1973. The present known ore reserves will ensure production at least till 1978, but as exploration continues it is likely that new seams will be found to enable the mining operations to continue.

Around the mine and crushing plant quite a large town has grown up. Over 5 000 workers are employed. If each has on average two dependents living with him this would give a figure for the population of about 16 000, making Kilembe the third largest Ugandan town. Kilembe is wholly a mining town, with the entire working population employed at the mine, or in services to the miners. About sixty per cent of the workers are Bakiga from Kigezi and most of the rest come from the neighbouring Toro area. The town's food supply comes from the Bakonjo tribe who live in the area, and supplies of matoke bananas are brought from

An aerial view of Mwadui diamond mine. The camera was pointing approximately south-east: keep this in mind when comparing the photograph with Fig. 96. In the left foreground is the main dump for tailings (sorted gravel). In the centre is the main gravel processing plant. Beyond it is the power house and a small industrial estate. Using the map try to identify other places.

the plains north of Kasese. A dairy cooperative in Fort Portal supplies milk.

In recent years the value of copper exports has varied between eight and twelve per cent of Uganda's total exports, and copper is usually the third most valuable export after coffee and cotton. This shows how important a single enterprise can be in the economy of a country.

The Williamson Diamond Mine, Mwadui (Fig. 95)

The Mwadui mine provides an excellent example of the benefits resulting from the working of a diamond deposit.

The annual income from diamonds in Tanzania is about £6·5 million. They are therefore Tanzania's fourth largest export by value, making up eight per cent of the total. From these figures it will be seen

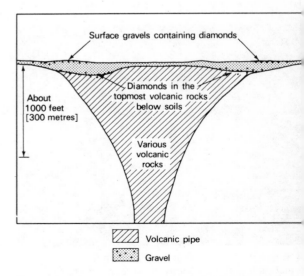

Fig. 94 A simple cross-section through Mwadui diamond deposit

This excavator at Mwadui weighs 300 tonnes, and can lift over 8 tonnes of diamond-bearing gravel in each load.

that the importance of this one industry to the national economy is very great. In addition, the description of Mwadui's activities will show how they contribute to the economic development of the surrounding area.

Since it was discovered in 1940, 2 tonnes of diamonds have been obtained from Mwadui. To obtain this, a total of 40 *million* tonnes of rock has been mined, giving a figure for the average proportion of weight of diamonds to waste material of 1:30 million. This clearly requires the mining, treatment (or processing) and waste disposal of enormous tonnages of ore, and helps to explain why Mwadui has grown into a town with a population of about 7 500.

The diamonds were formed in an intrusion of lava, which solidified to form a plug or pipe, as it is called (Fig. 94). Erosion of the plug has led to a scattering of diamonds and their concentration above and around the pipe. The pipe itself has the largest surface area, 146 hectares (362 acres), of any working pipe so far found in the world. Diamonds are also scattered over a large area round the plug itself.

Detailed study section

The section set in small type is for advanced study. Return to this later if you prefer.

Excavation has so far been limited to two areas within the pipe. The mining is really quarrying at the surface, unlike Kilembe, where the mining is carried on underground. The deepest working at present is only 40 m (130 ft) below the original ground level. Three enormous 200 tonne excavators are used. These have heavy buckets which can scrape up the rock without requiring drilling or blasting beforehand. Heavy diesel trucks which carry 35 tonnes transport the ore to a central crushing station where everything is reduced to a size of less than 10 cm (4 ins). It then goes to the treatment plant on a conveyor belt that is 3 000 m (3 300 yds) long. The main treatment works is one of the most modern and up-to-date plants in the world. It operates twenty-four hours a day on six days of the week, with maintenance being carried out on the seventh. Efficiency is very high, and continuous checks are made, resulting in over ninety-eight percent of the diamonds in the ore being separated out.

Diamonds are dense, hard and they repel water. These three properties are made use of in their extraction. First the ore is passed through separators, where the diamonds and some other heavy minerals sink to the bottom while the remaining ninety-eight percent of the material floats off as waste. The second stage involves the crushing of the two percent heavy minerals with steel balls which reduce the soft materials to pulp, leaving the hard minerals intact. Then the coarse matter is passed over grease-covered belts, to which the diamonds stick. The finer material is dried and then the waste is removed electrically, leaving the smallest

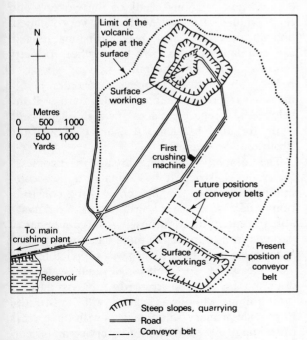

Fig. 95 The diamond workings, Mwadui

151

diamonds behind. Each day 10 million kg (22 million lbs) of material is worked, yet ,after these processes only about 14 kg (30 lbs) of material needs to be handsorted. Finally 450 gm (1 lb) of uncut diamonds is recovered from the day's 'search'. Almost all mining involves moving an immense amount of earth to gain a relatively small product. This is one reason why development often depends on advanced technology.

The quality and size of the diamonds vary a great deal, and these are the two main factors which determine their value. Gem stones, that is, diamonds that can be used for jewellery because of their shape, size, colour and purity make up about fifty percent of production. The remainder have uses in industry, where their usefulness depends on their hardness. Drilling bits for sinking oil wells, and other cutting machinery are often tipped with diamonds to give an efficient cutting edge.

The engineering department, which employs about a third of the total work force in Mwadui, carries out manufacturing, maintenance and civil engineering construction. It generates very large quantities of electric power, and supplies about 454 million litres (100 million galls) of water a

month, as well as being responsible for sewage disposal, refrigeration, public transport, aircraft maintenance, radio and telephone communications and the maintenance of buildings and roads. Its workshop facilities include a foundry and boiler shop, blacksmith shop, workshop for maintaining the heavy earthmoving equipment, and other works.

A very wide range of professional and technical skills are needed at Mwadui, and several departments on the mine run training courses for their staff. In addition, over fifty workers are abroad gaining training and experience. As a result of a training programme the large majority of the workers are Tanzanians and by the end of 1968 only five per cent of all employees were expatriates.

The development of Mwadui and its region

Mwadui is in the countryside 27 km (17 miles) from Shinyanga and 142 km (89 miles) from Mwanza (Fig. 96). Many people are attracted to living in towns, so the standards of living and services have to be high to attract and keep professional and skilled employees, and also suitable trainees. Partly because of this, the town of Mwadui has been developed in such a way as to provide for the social, cultural and religious needs of the workers and their families. Because Mwadui is very isolated, and since careful security needs to be maintained, the company has its own post office, primary schools, a sizeable hospital, various shops, a bakery, an abattoir, a brewery, a dairy and a market garden. Recreation facilities are well developed, and separate places of worship have been built for the Moslem, Roman Catholic and Protestant communities.

The company also helps greatly the people of Shinyanga District. It has donated a new community centre, lent equipment for the construction of dams and cleared bush to make land available for agricultural purposes. A large number of patients from outside the mine have been treated at the mine hospital. Finance was supplied to provide electricity for Shinyanga, and water for domestic use is piped from Mwadui. An agricultural training school was begun in 1967 in Mwadui to provide primary school leavers with three years of training to prepare them for service in agricultural settlements elsewhere. Financial support has

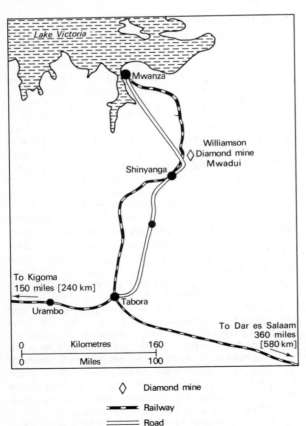

Fig. 96 The position of Mwadui

also been given to the Shinyanga Commercial Institute, from which trained secretarial staff is obtained, and to rural development.

Thus the working of diamonds at this one place in Tanzania provides exports which can earn foreign exchange. More than that, it has spread its benefits over a wide region, providing amenities and encouraging improved standards of living and education.

Although a wide variety of minerals has been found in East Africa, they are not present in large quantities. None of the three countries can rely on minerals for more than a small fraction of the total economy. The relative poverty of mineral resources has resulted in an emphasis being placed on agricultural development, rather than on industry. The following sections summarise the future outlook for mineral production in the three countries.

Other minerals

Kenya

Soda ash from Lake Magadi is still the most important mineral export. This large deposit has been worked since 1919. It results from the evaporation of the water in the lake due to the dry conditions in that part of the Rift Valley. The lake contains the largest natural deposit of soda in the world. It is being renewed by waters from deep underground, so there is little danger of the supply running out. The soda ash is refined to produce sodium carbonate. This is used mainly for glass- and paper-making. The biggest importer of soda from Magadi used to be South Africa. The trade embargo placed on that country resulted in the loss of this important customer. However, new export markets have been built up, so that the amount of soda ash exported is expanding again. Of Kenya's salt, ninety per cent is produced at Magadi. Together these two items make up nearly three-quarters of Kenya's total mineral production. Gold is the next most important of the minerals, though its extraction is scattered and is on a small scale.

Looking to the future, a deposit of lead and zinc at Ribe near Mombasa will probably be exploited. It is in a very favourable position, for it can be exported through the port only 24 km (15 miles) away. Also on the coast, at Mrima Hill, there are possibilities for the extraction of niobium, a rare metal used for making special steel alloys which can withstand high temperatures.

Tanzania

There is very little significant mineral export other than diamonds. The production of gold, for many years Tanzania's second most valuable mineral export, has almost ceased. Cement is the most important mineral produced for home consumption. The Wazo Hill factory north of Dar es Salaam supplies eighty per cent of the country's requirements.

The possibility of oil and coal exploitation in the future cannot be dismissed. Oil exploration is continuing. In the south there may be up to 256 million tonnes of coal, and also a large iron deposit. Unfortunately, the coal is not of a kind that makes good coke, but it is probable that improved communications in the area and new processing methods will encourage extraction.

Uganda

In addition to copper, the exploitation of several other minerals is important. One of them provides cement and fertilisers, essential for farming. In general, deposits of limestone are not widespread in East Africa but large reserves (27 million tonnes) of limestone exist in the ancient volcanic plugs of south-east Uganda, in the Sukulu and Tororo Hills. Notice that this is a similar natural source to that of the diamonds in the volcanic pipe at Mwadui. There is about the same amount at Hima near Kasese, and there are possibly similar deposits in other parts of East Africa. At Tororo, about 130 000 tonnes of cement are produced annually from quarried limestone, while a second cement works is planned for Kasese. The Sukulu rocks also contain quantities of phosphates (202 million tonnes), and there is a growing production of superphosphates to meet fertiliser needs throughout East Africa.

There are important by-products from the smelting of copper. For example, pyrites, which are sulphides, will be processed at Jinja in the future. At present they are being dumped near the smelter, but a new plant will be built soon to extract sulphuric acid from them. Another important product from this process will be cobalt, of which there is an estimated £14 million worth already in the pyrites dump.

Also in eastern Uganda there are 30 million tonnes of magnetite iron reserves, while in Kigezi there is haematite iron ore. Iron smelting therefore

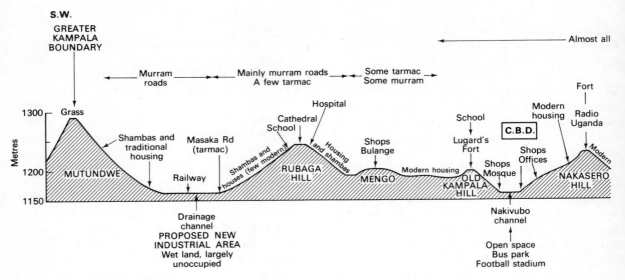

C.B.D. – Central Business District
Bulange – Previously Buganda Lukiko (Parliament) Building
(Now occupied by Ministry of Defence)

Fig. 97 Section through Greater Kampala

appears to be a possibility for the distant future.

Quantities of tungsten, tin, bismuth, beryl, tantalite, columbite, lithium and gold are produced on a small scale.

How established towns develop industries: the need for planning

Introduction

Two examples have been chosen – Kampala and Nairobi. It is, of course, possible to analyse other towns already studied in a similar way.

Kampala (Population 332 000 in 1969) (Fig. 98)

Greater Kampala is the largest town in Uganda. It is sited on a number of well drained, flat topped ridges or hills separated by originally marshy valleys. It includes Mengo which was the capital of the kingdom of Buganda. Each Kabaka used to build his residence on a new hill. These capitals were usually within the fertile lakeshore region where most Baganda live. Eventually, when missionaries came, Kampala became the permanent centre. They built their headquarters near to the Kabaka's palace. Local chiefs had been required to keep a road from their headquarters to the

capital of Buganda in good condition. Hence the Kampala area had an early start as a route focus. The present good system of radiating roads has followed from this.

For a quarter of a century, until 1957, Kampala was the inland terminus of the railway from Mombasa. The railway's extension to Kasese strengthened Kampala's central position. Also, trade across Lake Victoria was encouraged by the construction of a branch railway line to Kampala's outport at Port Bell (though this has now been closed owing to flooding of the port's facilities). Kampala was the natural focus of a relatively prosperous region and as a good route centre it became the market town for the fertile surrounding area and eventually served much of south and west Uganda. The large cluster gradually developed into a business centre. With the growth of population, it became worthwhile starting industries, especially those which provided goods and services for the use of the people. On Independence, the movement of Uganda's government from Entebbe to Kampala gave a further stimulus to its growth and importance.

Analysis of land-use in Kampala

Fig. 97 is an example of one useful way of studying an area. It shows how the use to which the land in a city is put relates to its slope and position.

Study the diagram (Fig. 97).

154

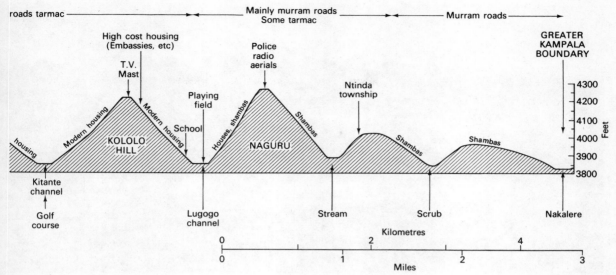

roads tarmac ——————————→ |←— Mainly murram roads ————→|←——— Murram roads ———→
Some tarmac

After C. J. Skinner

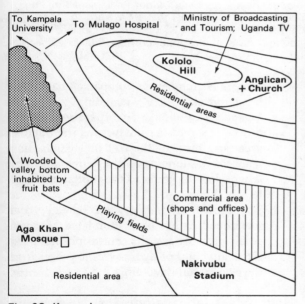

Fig. 98 Kampala

(a) List the uses of (i) the drained valley-floors;
                      (ii) the hill slopes;
                      (iii) the hill tops.
(b) Why have these differences occurred?
(c) Which parts (i, ii, or iii) do you think were developed first?
(d) (i) How close to the central business district (that is, the town centre) is the nearest shamba cultivation?

(ii) What advantages and what disadvantages does this have for the city's growth?

The chief factor responsible for the siting of industry was the railway. This required a low gradient and therefore was built along the gently-sloping valley-bottoms. Fortunately few people lived in this swampy land so homes did not have to be moved. Space was also available for industrial buildings.

The functions of Kampala follow from its central position, its status as the capital, and its size.

155

Downtown Kampala, showing the main area of government, diplomatic and cultural buildings: *1* Kampala International Hotel *2* East African Community Regional Headquarters *3* Kampala Club *4* Parliament Buildings and government offices *5* Residential blocks *6* Kampala Sports Club *7* National Theatre *8* Radio Uganda *9* Jinja Road *10* Embassy House *11* Gomba Motors Building *13* Udyam House *13* Baumann House *14* Kampala Road *15* Shops, offices and cinema *16* City council—new offices under construction *17* Public library *18* Government offices—Treasury *19* Railway station.

1. As the capital and administrative centre, Kampala has the main offices of the various Ministries, in addition to Parliament itself. Also, foreign diplomats from many countries live there, staffing Embassies and Consulates.
2. It is an educational, cultural and religious centre. The expanding university, technical and commercial colleges and schools attract both students and staff from throughout Uganda and abroad. The National Theatre, museum, libraries, mosques, temples and churches provide a focus for the cultural and religious life of the country.
3. Kampala has established itself as the centre of the tourist industry in Uganda. Fine modern hotels, and rapid transport to game parks along good roads, make it a convenient place from which to begin a safari. The international airport at Entebbe is soon to be extended to accommodate 'Jumbo Jets', and these will bring many more tourists through the capital. Even though it is 33 km (21 miles) away from the capital, Entebbe is only a short distance in terms of the time taken.
4. It is beginning to rival Nairobi as a business centre. A number of companies have their headquarters there, including the giant Uganda Development Corporation. In addition, it serves the prosperous surrounding area, and most of the rest of Uganda, as a market and shopping centre. People who have *any* reason for going to the capital are likely to buy things also.
5. The growth of industry has already been mentioned. It has been stimulated by Kampala's growing size, its central position, and the availability of hydro-electric power from the nearby station at Jinja.

New industrial development

Kampala provides a typical example of the way in which industry is now developing in East Africa.

In the past, industry usually had to prepare its own site, bringing in power lines, laying water mains and constructing roads. Now the locations for industrial development are carefully chosen, and the site itself is carefully planned as a trading estate. This is an industrial site already fitted with essential services. Sections of various sizes are offered to industrialists to rent, already complete with roads, sewerage, drainage and power. This

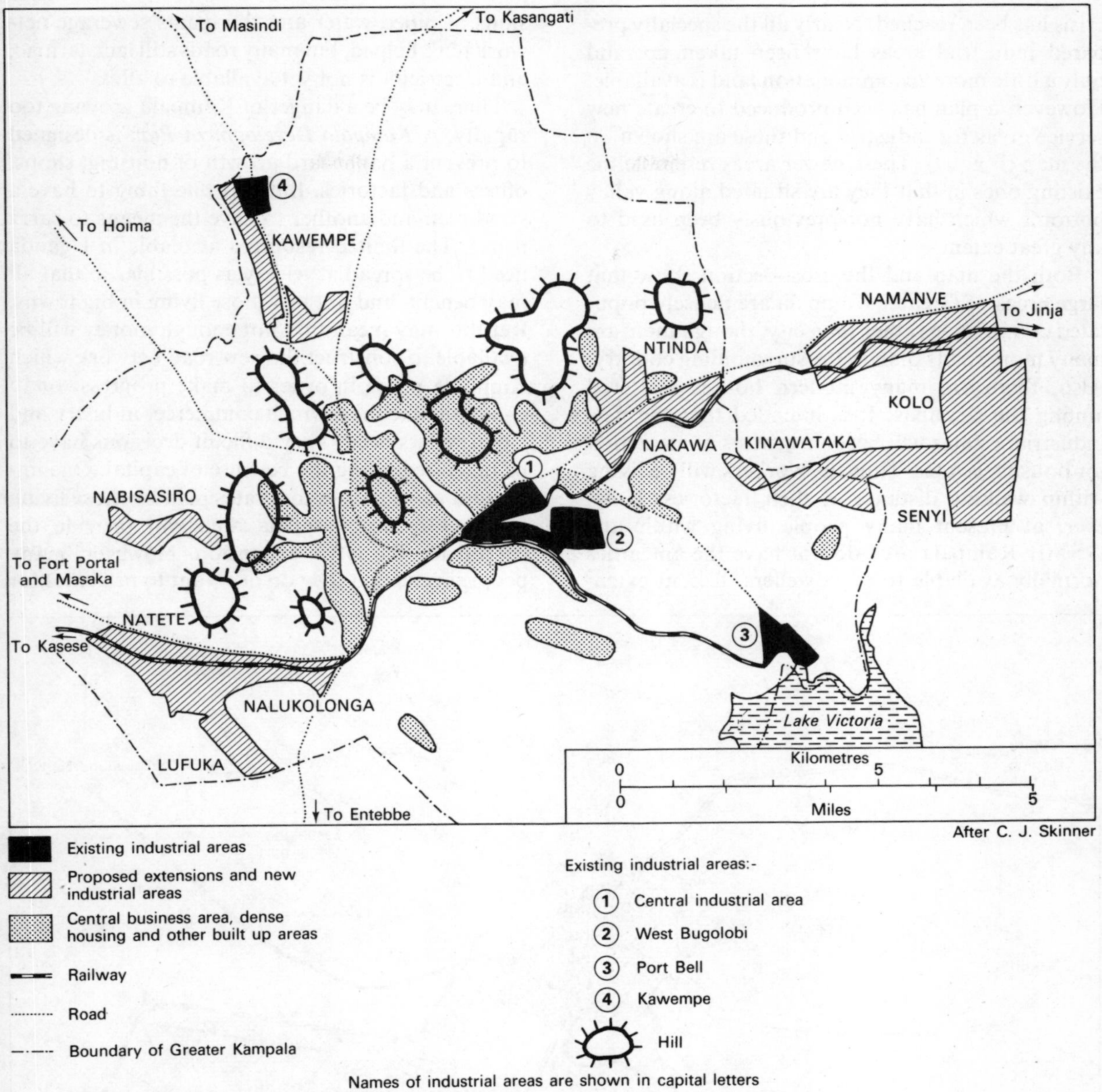
To Masindi
To Kasangati
To Hoima
KAWEMPE
NAMANVE
To Jinja
NTINDA
KOLO
NAKAWA
KINAWATAKA
NABISASIRO
SENYI
To Fort Portal and Masaka
NATETE
To Kasese
NALUKOLONGA
Lake Victoria
LUFUKA
To Entebbe
Kilometres
0
5
0
Miles
5
After C. J. Skinner
Existing industrial areas
Proposed extensions and new industrial areas
Central business area, dense housing and other built up areas
Railway
Road
Boundary of Greater Kampala
Existing industrial areas:-
1 Central industrial area
2 West Bugolobi
3 Port Bell
4 Kawempe
Hill
Names of industrial areas are shown in capital letters

Fig. 99 The industrial and built-up areas of Greater Kampala

development has attracted into Kampala small and medium sized companies, employing up to 350 workers, engaged in what is normally called 'light industry'. In particular, the range of goods reflects the rising living standards of the people in and around the city. Products vary widely but they belong to five main groups, (1) building and construction materials; (2) clothing, footwear and blankets; (3) processed foodstuffs; (4) furniture and household goods; (5) engineering, consisting of vehicle body building, vehicle repair, and welding.

Industry and population are growing at such a rate that the boundary of Kampala has been extended to include an area now known as Greater Kampala (see map Fig. 99). In the 1969 census this area was found to have a population of 332 000, so that it is a very important urban area. Now a crisis has been reached. Nearly all the specially prepared industrial areas have been taken up, and only a little more accommodation land is available. However, a plan has been produced to create new service areas for industry, and these are shown on the map (Fig. 99). These newer areas resemble the existing ones in that they are situated along valley bottoms which have not previously been used to any great extent.

Both the map and the cross-section show that large areas of Greater Kampala are densely populated countryside rather than city, though there are many more roads than in the surrounding country. Also, there are many modern houses scattered among the shambas. It is intended that the new industrial estates will become centres of attraction for housing estates. Thus the workers will be living within walking distance of their factories. However, at present many people living within the Greater Kampala area do not have the amenities normally available to city dwellers. Recent extensions of piped water and the mains sewerage network have helped, but many roads still lack tarmac, and electricity is not yet available to all.

There may be a danger of Kampala growing too rapidly. A *Kampala Development Plan* is designed to prevent a haphazard growth of housing, shops, offices and factories. But it is one thing to have a good plan and another to have the means to carry it out. The limited resources available in Uganda need to be spread as widely as possible, so that all may benefit, and not just those living in big towns. But this may mean that not enough money will be available to construct the new road network which Kampala needs in order to make progress; or to create the facilities which commerce, industry and city dwellers need. Very difficult decisions have to be taken regarding the best use of capital. One important possibility is that rates paid by those living in the Greater Kampala area will provide the capital for the city's expansion. However, many people argue that they do not want to pay rates for

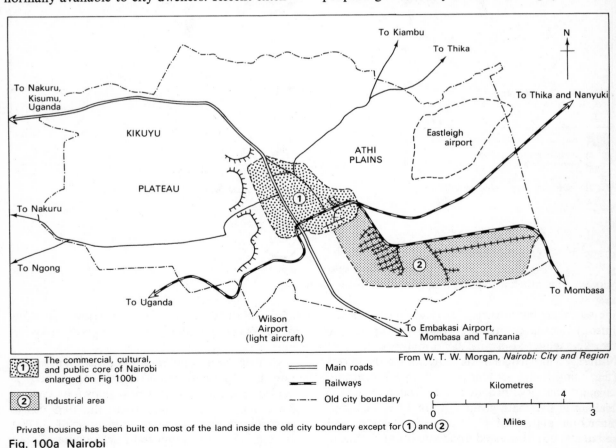

From W. T. W. Morgan, *Nairobi: City and Region*

1. The commercial, cultural, and public core of Nairobi enlarged on Fig 100b

2. Industrial area

Main roads

Railways

Old city boundary

Kilometres

Miles

Private housing has been built on most of the land inside the old city boundary except for ① and ②

Fig. 100a Nairobi

158

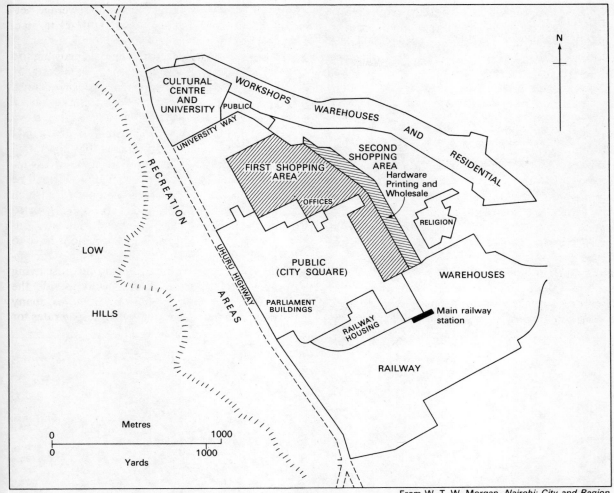

From W. T. W. Morgan, *Nairobi: City and Region*

Fig. 100b The main functions of central Nairobi

such things as light, sewerage and water until they are actually provided.

These problems are typical of capital cities in other developing countries. The large cities are growing very rapidly in area and population, and yet the rural areas are just as deserving of development aid. In the future much will depend on reaching a balance between progress and development in the cities and outside them.

Nairobi (Population 478 000 in 1969) (Fig. 100a, b)

Nairobi is the largest town and industrial centre of East Africa. It has a population of 478 000 (1969 census). As in the case of Kampala it was the town that came first and the industry that followed, to feed the town. So in order to understand why Nairobi developed industry, it is necessary to understand why it developed as a town.

It was very largely a matter of chance that Nairobi became a town at all. It was originally chosen in 1896 as a suitable place for railway yards when the Uganda railway was being built. The Athi Plains were the last considerable area of flattish country before the railway plunged into the more broken hills bordering the Rift Valley. In addition Nairobi had food, and drinking water (if limited). Once a railway settlement was established, the local administration moved in from Machakos in order to be near the railway. The altitude (1 700 m, 5 600 ft) proved suitable for European settle-

A recent aerial picture of downtown Nairobi. The large multi-storey buildings are government offices, business houses and hotels. The large building in the left foreground is the headquarters of the East African Railways organisation. The wide road on the right is Government Road. Compare this photograph with Fig. 100b.

ment, so later the town became the capital. As the country to the north and east developed, Nairobi became a marketing and shopping centre and the point at which goods were put on the train for the coast. All this happened in spite of the place being at the beginning marshy and unhealthy and in other ways unsuitable as the site of a large city.

As so often happens, once a town gets to a certain size, the size itself becomes an attraction. The bigger it becomes, the better it is as a market. It is this fact that attracts industry to Nairobi, despite the lack of coal and the presence of only a small amount of hydro-electric power. The industry that has developed can be summarised as follows:

1. Processing of raw materials for export—sisal, coffee, tea.
2. Processing for local consumption—bacon, meat, beer, shoes, metal beds, timber, cement.
3. Industries in connection with transport—motor repairing, tyres, batteries.

Industrial siting has, in the past, been planned and will be more so in the future. The main industrial areas are and will be to the south-east of the city next to the commercial centre and near the railway. The noxious industrial area (producing

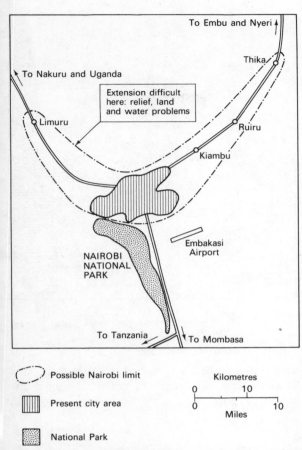

To Embu and Nyeri

Thika

To Nakuru and Uganda

Extension difficult here: relief, land and water problems

Limuru

Ruiru

Kiambu

NAIROBI NATIONAL PARK

Embakasi Airport

To Tanzania

To Mombasa

⌐ ⌐ Possible Nairobi limit

Present city area

National Park

Kilometres
0   10

0   10
Miles

Fig. 101   The future development of Nairobi—a linear city. It now seems likely that the western 'horn' of the city, towards Limuru, will not be extended

unpleasant fumes or smells) is confined to the extreme south-east, so that odours will be carried away from the city by the prevailing north-east winds.

The growth of Nairobi

Immigration from rural areas has caused Nairobi to grow very rapidly. The built-up area had become so large by 1964 that the boundary had to be placed farther out. The city is now 700 sq km (268 sq miles) in area compared with 90 sq km (35 sq miles) before 1964. Estimates of population growth show that Nairobi will become a very large city indeed by the year 2000. It is expected that there will be 875 000 people by 1980, 1 500 000 by 1990, and 2 500 000 by the year 2000. There is danger that such rapid growth could result in a very haphazard

urban sprawl, with difficult communications and a lack of 'breathing space', that is, parks and gardens for recreation. To prevent this, the planners have already worked out a plan for the systematic and orderly development of the Nairobi Metropolitan Region, as it will be called.

It is expected that Nairobi will eventually extend to Limuru in the north-west and to Thika in the north-east. Some of the main reasons for the shape of this growth are summarised on the sketch map (Fig. 101). The pattern of this development is known as the 'Linear City', since it is based on one main line of communication running between two main centres. In this case the centres are present-day Nairobi, and Thika. Between the two will be a series of alternating residential and industrial neighbourhoods, strung out like beads on a necklace. Between these will be green 'wedges' of land which are deliberately left free of development. Their main use will be for recreation.

It may be asked whether it is worthwhile to have a plan for the development of a town when there is not enough money to carry the plan very far. The answer is 'yes', without any doubt. All over the world countries have realised when it is too late, that unplanned development creates problems.

It is wise to have long-term policies for development, both for towns and for the countryside. In this way blunders can be avoided and the very best use is made of resources. The Kampala and Nairobi plans are very far-seeing, and there are other examples in East Africa. By their foresight and wise spending, the governments are ensuring that limited resources are used as efficiently as possible.

The tourist industry

It is impossible to view the skyline of Nairobi without being impressed by the number of hotels reaching into the sky. These buildings are symbolic of one of the most important single developments in Kenya, and in East Africa as a whole, tourism. Nairobi has traditionally been the centre for foreign travellers wanting to hunt and photograph wild animals. The numbers of such people were small until less than ten years ago. Then there began the system of travel known as 'package holidays'. Chartered aircraft from European countries, mainly Germany, Switzerland and England, brought more and more people to East Africa, for relatively inexpensive holidays and 'camera safaris'. Nairobi had the advantage that it already had a number of good quality hotels and could accommodate quite large numbers. Its neighbouring game park and central position were other advantages, so that it continues to hold first place. However, all three countries offer great opportunities to tourists for game-viewing, water sports, scenery, mountain climbing and sunshine. Although Kenya still has the largest slice of the tourist cake, Uganda and Tanzania are making rapid strides to develop their tourist potential. New hotels are springing up, not only in the main cities, but at game parks and along the coast, a favourite place with holiday-makers.

Tourism is a very important asset. It is sometimes called an 'invisible export', because it earns foreign exchange just as crop exports do. Tourists pay to stay in hotels, enter game parks and travel in the country. In doing so they give employment to considerable numbers of hotel staff, drivers and game wardens. Indirectly tourism benefits agriculture, fishing, manufacturing and commerce. This is a result of tourists' demand for food, accommodation, purchases of handicrafts and other products. The tourist trade constitutes about ten per cent of Kenya's foreign earnings each year. In

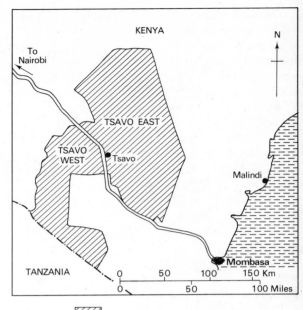

Tsavo National Park, Kenya

Main Mombasa to Nairobi road

Fig. 102 Tsavo national park

1968 £16·4 million was earned from tourism. This is more than was earned by coffee, the most important export crop!

Tourists watching elephants at Kilaguni Lodge in the Tsavo National Park. The landscape is typical of much of Kenya's nyika, with isolated residual hills rising above the plateau

162

Tanzania plans to triple the number of foreign visitors in the current Five-Year Plan. By 1974 it is estimated that foreign exchange earnings from tourism will reach £7 million. At present Uganda gets by far the smallest share of the tourist business in East Africa, but there is nothing to stop its development in the future. Because of the potential income from tourism, much effort is being made by all the government Ministries concerned to expand facilities as rapidly as possible.

Game parks in East Africa contribute significantly to the overall economy. They are situated for the most part on the dry or very dry plateaus. These areas have in the past been of little economic value. They are important in terms of 'conservation', that is, the preservation of resources. They are also a major tourist attraction. Now they are paying their way, and bringing improved communications and job opportunities to remote places.

In the old days numbers of wild animals were kept in check by the natural hazards of life, because each is preyed upon by other animals. Local hunters for meat and skins, and commercial hunters and poachers of ivory and valuable furs, kept the numbers down. Now game parks give protection. While this is good conservation where species are dying out, in some places game park country is becoming over-populated. In Tsavo East for example there are so many elephants that they have over-grazed, and have uprooted and killed the natural vegetation. They have created an 'elephant desert'.

Tsavo National Park (Fig. 102) is quite typical of the game parks in East Africa. It covers an area of 20 000 sq km (7 700 sq miles), and is one of the biggest of its kind in the world. It offers a great variety of scenery and game animals of all kinds, especially elephant and lions. Access to the park is excellent, since the main Mombasa to Nairobi road runs directly through it. There are excellent hotels near the main entrances. Elsewhere there are small lodges, some offering less expensive 'self-help' accommodation. Others are being constructed to provide even fuller facilities for the growing number of tourists who visit Tsavo each year. In the season 1967–8 over 52 000 people visited this one park, while there were over 250 000 visits made to Kenyan game parks as a whole.

It may seem strange that one of the most valuable 'exports' need not leave the country at all. But East Africans are realising that tourism is a wonderful natural resource. It is even possible that it may one day become the most valuable economic resource. With careful planning and management the tourist industry will thrive and develop. There are many signs that tourist traffic is only beginning, and that far more people will travel in the coming years. If this is so the East African countries are assured of a valuable income.

Work to do

1. Explain why many people think that East Africa is more likely to become prosperous as a result of agricultural, rather than industrial, development.
2. In East Africa the following kinds of settlement often develop into towns.
    (i) A marketing centre in a rich agricultural area.
   (ii) A good port.
  (iii) A centre of good communications.
   (iv) A place with industrial possibilities in raw materials, power or labour.
    (v) A centre of administration.
   For your own town, or nearest town, work out which of the above factors have been important in its growth.
3. Make an annotated diagram of the photograph of Mwadui mine (page 150). Refer to Figures and photographs on pages 155–159 for help.

Chapter 15: A regional approach to the distribution of population

This chapter discusses the reasons why some parts of East Africa are more thickly peopled than others. At the same time it gives a summary of the regional geography of each country. Keep an atlas map of East Africa handy while you are reading it, or refer to Fig. 103.

In many cases it is not difficult to understand why one district has many inhabitants or another only a few. A good rainfall, a fertile soil or rich mineral resources will attract people. Deserts, poor soil and the tsetse fly will do the opposite. If too many people try to live in a poor area, they die. Thus the number of people living in a place is often an *indicator* of its desirability. It indicates either that its present resources *can* or *cannot* support many people, or whether people see it as a place where they want to live.

It is not, however, always a simple question of rich land having many people and poor land few. There are parts of Southern Tanzania where good land lies almost unused. Yet in the Central Region much dry and seemingly unsuitable country is quite thickly peopled. Tanzania provides some very interesting studies in population distribution.

The following description relates to the regions shown on the map on page 46 and the population map on this page. Each country is taken in turn.

Kenya

If you look at the population map you will see that the distribution of population in Kenya is fairly simple: the highest density zone forms a broad belt in the centre of the country stretching eastwards from Lake Victoria and the Uganda border for 500 km (300 miles). This area coincides almost exactly with the area of higher land, and provides an excellent example of a key fact in the geography of East Africa: higher land, rising well above the drier main plateau, supports more people. This is partly because of the higher rainfall totals, but also because

volcanic soils produce better crops; because the cooler climate on the mountains is healthier, so people live longer; and because people *want* to live there. The rainfall and crops vary in sequence with height. Some parts have population densities of over 150 per sq km (400 per sq mile) and the city

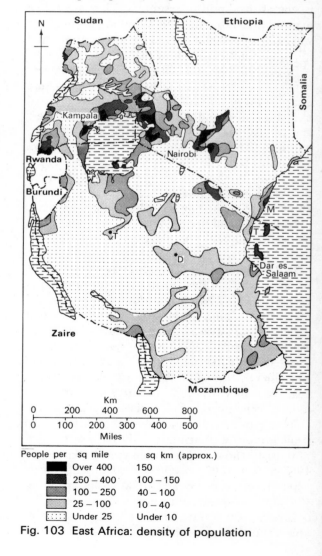

People per	sq mile	sq km (approx.)
■	Over 400	150
	250 – 400	100 – 150
	100 – 250	40 – 100
	25 – 100	10 – 40
	Under 25	Under 10

Fig. 103 East Africa: density of population

and suburban areas have still higher densities. The only other considerable area of population borders the coast.

The remaining three-quarters of the country is dry, sparsely inhabited and likely to remain so, unless irrigation water can be provided. Average densities are less than 4 per sq km (10 per sq mile). However, this is one of the places where the wildlife population is very high and famous game reserves such as Tsavo attract many tourists. The game is therefore protected; but in parts of Tsavo the elephant population has become so large that the vegetation has been overgrazed, and the area has become an elephant-made desert.

The coastal lowlands

This area forms a narrow belt from Lamu south to the Tanzania border with an average of 20–80 people to the sq km (50–200 to the sq mile). About 30 km (20 miles) from the sea the rainfall decreases and the country becomes barren dry bush. To the north of Lamu the desert of Somalia begins. The activities of the people resemble those found along much of the coast. Coconuts and maize are important crops, and sugar and sisal estates are found. There is fishing and market gardening to supply Mombasa Island itself, where the sea terminus of the Kenya-Uganda railway and the branch to Moshi provide plenty of work.

The highlands

West of the coastal strip, the population is very scanty, except in the Taita Hills, an area of higher rainfall. The number of people only really begins to increase when the Highlands are reached. The Kenya Highlands can be subdivided into smaller units.

The highlands east of the Rift Valley

Mount Kenya itself rises to 5 200 m (17 000 ft). It is a snow-capped volcanic cone. Below the snow-line is a belt of alpine vegetation and below that bamboo. Further down comes the forest which circles the entire mountain. The north-western slopes are in a rain shadow, so that Nanyuki district makes better grazing than cultivated land. All the foregoing areas are thinly populated.

To the east and south the population densities are very high in the Kikuyu, Embu and Meru districts. Population growth has been rapid. Although some Kikuyu and related peoples have settled new areas under resettlement schemes, the land shortage there is as severe as anywhere in East Africa. This area and the plateau areas of Machakos and Kitui have already been referred to in chapter 12.

On the eastern side of the Rift Valley the Aberdare Mountains are high, cold and wet. Forest reserves cover a considerable area, but mixed farms and settlement areas go up to 2 700 m (9 000 ft), growing wheat and pyrethrum and raising dairy cattle and pigs.

The Rift Valley

The highest part of the Rift Valley, between Longonot and Nakuru, has a rainfall of over 750 mm (30 ins), although drier than the mountains on either side. South of Lake Naivasha the rainfall is very much less. Much of the area is included in Rift Valley Province.

As a whole the densities of population in the Rift Valley are not very high. It was formerly an area of large European-owned farms, and is now mostly resettled as a mixed farming area.

The highlands west of the Rift Valley

West of the Rift Valley there is another area of higher land. The Mau Hills are largely forest-covered and sparsely inhabited.

The western flanks of the Kenya Highlands, like the eastern, contain African smallholdings and some large farms and plantations. The area is only moderately populous by contrast with the high density of population in parts of the Kikuyu country. The two chief tribal groups are the Nandi and the Kipsigis. The Nandi were a very vigorous pastoral tribe which has now turned successfully to cultivation and cattle rearing. The Kipsigis of the Kericho district are notable as a Nilo-Hamitic group who in recent years have made remarkable progress in the enclosure of their land for cultivation and for managed pasturage.

The Highlands area therefore shows considerable variations in population density. In general, the areas formerly owned by Europeans, though now broken down into smaller farms, are still less densely settled than other areas.

The Lake Victoria Basin

This forms part of what has already been described

as the *cotton–maize–millet belt*. The Luo and the Abaluhya, two very large tribes, inhabit the area. In the Maragoli country, just south of Mount Elgon, the population densities are extraordinarily high, up to 400 to the sq km (1 000 to the sq mile). As in Kikuyu there is pressure on the land. The Kano plains, east of Kisumu, are drier and have fewer people, but are being irrigated to extend cultivation. To the south the hills of Kisii are closely cultivated and settled.

Tanzania (mainland and islands)

The coast and islands

The true coastal plain is quite a narrow belt of country. Most of it has sufficient rainfall to support agriculture but for various reasons the density of population is very uneven. It is at its highest in the neighbourhood of the towns of Dar es Salaam, Tanga and Lindi. There sisal and coconut plantations provide work. They are also found in the lower Rufiji valley, although rice growing is more important. Along the coast itself there is a good deal of coral rock which does not produce a very fertile soil and coral reefs make approach by sea difficult. Hence people do not regard these as especially good places in which to live.

The areas are like the coral *wanda* of Zanzibar and Pemba. In more favourable areas and in some parts of the islands the population densities are the highest found on the coast, reaching 150 per sq km (400 per sq mile).

The plateaus

In Tanzania these fall into two groups:
1. The plateaus of south-eastern Tanzania.
2. The western plateaus.

1. The plateaus of south-eastern Tanzania (Fig. 104)
These plateaus are found between the Southern Highlands, the Central Railway line and the Mozambique border. Their position is shown in Fig. 104.

The first of the plateaus lies near the coast. It rises gradually to a height of 600 m (2 000 ft). Then there is a steep west-facing escarpment with a drop of 580 m (1 600 ft). This coastal plateau is formed of a series of sedimentary rocks, mainly limestones, sandstones and grits. It has a rainfall of 900 mm (35 ins), most falling between December and May.

The northern part of this plateau is thinly peopled, and covered with tsetse-infested miombo woodland. The southern section, especially the Makonde Plateau, is surprisingly thickly populated. The soils are poor, and until a pipeline was opened there was no water on its surface. The main reason for the high population density seems to be the system of agriculture used by the Makonde (see chapter 3). The main crops grown are cassava, rice and millets, with sisal and cashew nuts as cash crops. Timber is exported from the Rondo plateau to the north of the Makonde.

Between the coastal plateau and the Southern Highlands is the interior plateau, a vast stretch of country only a few hundred metres above sea level in the east. It rises gradually to the west, reaching over 1 200 m (4 000 ft) in the Matogoro Mountains. The eastern part is dotted with isolated hills called inselbergs. The hills are higher and closer together towards Songea.

Except in a few areas, the plateau is thinly peopled, for once again it is tsetse-infested miombo woodland. The country was formerly more populous but the Angoni slave-raiding attacks and the Maji Maji rebellion against the Germans were responsible for the deaths of a large number of people.

Round Songea and Masasi the land has been cleared and there is a fair population density. Away from the coast tobacco and groundnuts are the main cash crops (see chapter 7).

2. The western plateaus
A broken belt of highland country runs north-east from Njombe to the Usambara Mountains. To the

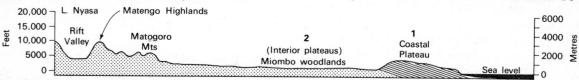

Fig. 104 Section through south-east Tanzania

west of this are the great western plateaus of Tanzania. They are, on the whole, higher than the plateaus of the south-east. They can be further divided on the basis of rainfall.

Immediately to the west of the highland belt is a zone of very dry country. This is a continuation of the dry zone of Kenya and north-east Tanzania. The northern part is part of Masailand, and the centre is occupied by the Wagogo (see chapter 12). Further south the dry country ends in the Buhoro Flats. The only part of this area which has a population density of over 2 per sq km (5 to the sq mile) is that occupied by the Wagogo and even this suffers periodically from drought and hunger despite government help. This area is now the centre of considerable development in ranching (see chapter 8) and ujamaa villages.

The western part of the plateaus receives more rain. Like most of southern Tanzania this area is covered with tsetse-ridden woodland. Again, as in southern Tanzania there are clearings in the miombo woodland. The clearings are of various sizes, the most important of them being round Tabora. Apart from these clearings the population density is low, averaging less than 4 per sq km (10 per sq mile).

Between the dry east and the tsetse-ridden west is found a block of more densely populated country with up to 100 people per sq km (250 per sq mile). Its southern end is near Nzega and its northern on Lake Victoria. Much of this belongs to Sukumaland, already discussed in chapter 8. Although Sukumaland is not a well-endowed region, we have already discovered the reasons why it has been possible for people to make a success of living there. Mwadui diamond mine and the Shinyango district come within this area.

To the west of Lake Victoria the shores are in some ways like Buganda. Coffee and bananas are grown by the Bahaya. Like Buganda it has a high rainfall and is very green although the dry season is more marked. Instead of flat-topped hills Bukoba has a series of east-facing sandstone escarpments. Although the Bukoba area has heavy seasonal rainfall the land away from the lake is drier, and is less productive. But although the Bahaya country is less uniformly fertile than Buganda, it is still rich and populous by comparison with some other areas.

The highlands

The highlands of Tanzania are found mainly around and within the plateaus. From the north there is a continuation of the Kenya Highlands which projects into the heart of the country. This is broken up by two branches of the Eastern Rift Valley. The one containing Lake Manyara is more directly in line with the Kenya rift. The other containing Lake Eyasi goes off at an angle.

North of Lake Eyasi lie the Serengeti plains at a height of 1 500 m (5 000 ft). Few people live in this high plateau country. The Serengeti plains are famous as one of the world's finest game reserves. This area and Lake Manyara and the Ngorongoro Crater have a great future as a wildlife park and tourist attraction.

The Singida and Kondoa Highlands are found south of Lake Eyasi. Because these are above the general level of the plateau they have a slightly higher rainfall. The density of population is therefore greater, rising to 40 per sq km (100 to the sq mile). In fact, these highlands are probably over-populated and soil erosion is serious (see Fig. 14).

East of the Rift Valley are the volcanic cones of Kilimanjaro and Meru, which are described in chapter 9. The southern slopes of these mountains form one of the most densely peopled areas of Tanzania with densities of 150 per sq km (400 per sq mile).

The Southern Highlands form another large block of mountain country. As a whole the Southern Highlands are not densely populated and it is not clear why this is. Mountain areas in East Africa usually support more people. The volcanic soils of Tukuyu and the Poroto Mountains support a greater density of population (80 per sq km, 200 per sq mile) but the Iringa, Njombe and Ufipa plateaus only have a moderate number of people. The Livingstone Mountains have very few indeed.

Southern Tanzania is likely to see great changes in the near future. Suddenly after years of frustration the area is being opened up through its new links with Zambia. These include the improved and surfaced road, the Tazama pipeline already operating and the Tan-Zam railway which should be opened by 1975.

Parts of the mountains of Rwanda and Burundi project into Tanzania. In Ngara district the population density is 40 per sq km (100 to the sq mile).

Round Kasulu there is also a high population density.

In eastern Tanzania there are several isolated blocks of highland including the Pare, the Usambara and the Uluguru Mountains. On account of their nearness to the sea these areas receive a high rainfall and are able to support as many as 100 per sq km (250 per sq mile).

Uganda

Uganda is a country mainly made up of plateau. To the south this plateau ends in the flat-topped hills of Buganda and in Lake Victoria. To the east there are mountains along the Kenya border, the highest of them being of volcanic origin. West of the plateau the mountains form a higher and wider barrier.

The country can be divided into three regions.

The hills and mountains of western Uganda

The high land of western Uganda lies near the western rift valley. There are many signs of former volcanic activity: old volcanoes, groups of crater lakes, and lava flows. Lower parts of the valley are occupied by Lakes Albert, Edward and George. The valley is interrupted by the block mountains of the Ruwenzori, reaching a height of 5 000 m (nearly 17 000 ft) above sea-level. The rift valley itself is 80 km (50 miles) across and thinly peopled by Uganda standards. The rainfall is low. Much of the area is tsetse-infested. Part of the rift valley is now a game reserve and National Park. Fishing is an important occupation especially in Lake George. Salt is extracted from Lake Katwe. Farming may develop with irrigation.

The Ruwenzori Mountains do not support many people. They are too high, cold and rugged.

The bordering hills are much more fertile. They are high enough to get a rainfall of 100–150 mm (40–60 ins). The extension of the railway to Kasese the provision of bus and lorry transport, and the hard-surfacing of main roads, have made it worthwhile to grow more coffee, tea, tobacco and other crops in this fertile country. Some sections are very densely peopled. Kigezi, in the south-west, averages 80 per sq km (200 to the sq mile). The West Nile hills have a population of 43 per sq km (112 to the sq

mile). The hills of Ankole, north Kigezi and Bunyoro have fewer people. In Bunyoro the low density is partly a result of the fierce wars with Buganda and partly due to the tsetse fly.

The central plateau

The plateau contains most of the people of Uganda, but the number of people living in the area to the north of Lake Kioga is very different from that to the south. Although there is a good scatter of people, the average density in the north is usually not more than 80 per sq km (200 per sq mile). In the south bordering Lake Victoria there are some areas with densities over 200 per sq km (500 per sq mile). Indeed, as the population map shows, some of the highest population densities in the whole of East Africa are found in a zone about 160 km (100 miles) wide round the northern shores of Lake Victoria in Uganda and Kenya. Nevertheless notable changes in the northern part of Uganda have followed the building of the railway. This reached Gulu in 1967 and already bridges the River Nile to Pachwach. Later it will be extended further into West Nile to Arua.

Many aspects of life and development have been assisted by the introduction of the railway. The transport of cotton is easier by rail than by the old river barges. Groundnut production is rising. Parts of the area are ideal for ranching. Private ranches along the railway line now 'ship' live cattle to Kampala for slaughter. Labour is also more mobile, and feeder roads move crops to the railway.

The banana–coffee zone
The cultivation that takes place on the shores of Lake Victoria has already been described in detail in chapter 7. Some parts of this zone are as fertile as any in the world. The density of population and cultivation varies according to the distance from the lake. Within about 50 km (30 miles) of the lake densities of about 150 per sq km (400 to the sq mile) are met. Southern Buganda and Busoga have other advantages in addition to their natural fertility. For a long time they have had a stable government. They have also acquired good rail, road and water communications.

East of Iganga and further from the lake the rainfall is not so reliable and the population density falls. But it is rarely below 40 to the sq km (100 to the sq mile). Mubende suffered from the same tribal warfare that depopulated south-east Bunyoro.

The cotton–millet–maize zone

Although many parts of this zone get as large a total rainfall as the banana–coffee zone, the distribution through the year is not so favourable. The countryside is much more open and drier in appearance. Hence there are great variations in density. On both sides of the Nile, east to the slopes of Mount Elgon and north into Teso, the population density averages 40 per sq km (100 to the sq mile). In the far north low densities may in part be due to a difference in way of life. The Nilotic Acholi and Lango until recently preferred pastoralism to agriculture. The Wateso and Basoga have a stronger tradition of cultivation and so can feed a larger number of people to the square kilometre.

The hills of eastern Uganda

These are less favoured than those of western Uganda. In the north Karamoja has neither a very high nor very reliable rainfall. The district is therefore better suited to cattle rearing than to cultivation. There is an average of only 4 people per sq km (12 per sq mile).

In contrast the southern and western slopes of Mount Elgon support very many people. The rainfall is high and the volcanic soil fertile. Bananas and coffee, as elsewhere in East Africa, allow an intensive use of the land.

In conclusion, only isolated areas of East Africa are closely settled, and these are usually mountain lands or coastal cities and islands. The plateaus of East Africa are not usually regions of great population density except where they lie within the Lake Victoria Basin. The western, northern and north-eastern shores of the lake are especially well populated.

Work to do

1. The following are among the most densely peopled parts of East Africa. Make sure that you can give the *reasons* for the exceptional density in the Kikuyu area, northern Nyanza, Mombasa Island, southern Buganda and Busoga, Bugisu, Sukumaland, the southern slopes of Kilimanjaro and Meru and in the Rungwe district.

2. Compare the population density map on page 164 with the rainfall map on page 12. Which thinly peopled parts of East Africa from the point of view of rainfall look most promising for future development? Suggest reasons why they remain undeveloped.

Chapter 16: Conclusions

When the first edition of this book was written in the late 1950s the authors said that they hoped to do more than to bring together widely scattered material that could help students to pass examinations 'for many of the things discussed affect the lives of all of us'.

Then two subjects were of very great interest to all young people in East Africa. The first was the reaching of a higher standard of living than was known by their parents. The second was the independence of their home countries. Both of these required resources. Independence without the money to do things could be a very empty prize.

The way to greater wealth involves, among other things, an understanding of the resources and opportunities of one's own country: a land can be used well or badly. A farmer who lets his ground suffer from soil erosion is not only destroying his own wealth: he is preventing his son from having a good farm; he is robbing his country of something that cannot be easily replaced. A man who cultivates well can improve his land and leave his sons and his country richer than before.

The study of geography is, in part, a study of the way in which a country is used. If we know the quality of the soil, we can improve it and grow the crops that are best suited to it. If we understand the rainfall, we do not make the mistake of trying to grow the wrong crops at the wrong time. It is necessary to work with nature, not against it.

Since that time remarkable progress has been made, but people are now aware of other problems. One group might be called 'the problem of gaps'. These are the dangers that can arise in a country from the widening gaps between city dwellers and country people, between limited food production and rapidly increasing numbers of people to be fed, between nations that 'have' and nations that 'have not', and so on.

The governments of Kenya, Tanzania and Uganda are giving careful thought and planning to solving or reducing some of the problems. Much of this book is occupied with ways in which people are working to increase production from farms, workshops and larger industries. The 'gap' between the well watered and the seasonally dry districts is illustrated by the weather calendars for west Uganda and southern Tanzania (Fig. 48 and Fig. 53). Co-operative marketing is an attempt to reduce the gap between the country producer and the merchant or exporter; but even co-operative marketing can fail to give the farmer his just rewards unless the sale and distribution of his product is carefully organised.

All three countries are concerned about the difficulty of bringing amenities such as schools, clinics, electric light and power to scattered country districts. President Nyerere especially among the East African leaders is trying the experiment of communal work and living in the ujamaa villages, but there are 'self-help' programmes in the other countries too.

Another thing we can learn from our geographical studies concerns peoples. To most of us, strangers appear odd, sometimes stupid, sometimes rather frightening or dangerous. We are often suspicious of them. Many newly independent countries find that their different peoples disagree. If we wish to overcome these difficulties, one way to help is to study other peoples. Then we begin to understand *why* people have different customs, traditions and points of view, and if we know more about them we realise that what seems strange in others is often related to the conditions of the place in which they live.

It is especially hard to understand another person's point of view if their language is different from our own. The many different peoples in East Africa speak many different languages. This is also a problem in education: it is easier to provide books and train teachers when everybody speaks a common language. Opportunities for education are needed for many older people who did not finish their schooling. But it all costs money.

All countries are anxious to increase their trade, especially with other countries. But there is some evidence that it will pay better to develop internal production and trade and that of the East African Community, rather than chasing the international market, except in those products for which East Africa is especially notable. There is a splendid internal market (or demand) for all kinds of goods and services from the 31 million people of the East African Community provided they have money in their pockets to spend.

East Africa is in many ways most fortunate. Few East Africans suffer from the extreme poverty of the more crowded parts of Asia. Most East Africans who wish to do so can be better off than their parents were. There is hope and opportunity for an even better future. It would be a great pity if the possibilities were never realised because of lack of understanding between its peoples or failure to recognise the way the resources of the earth can best be used.

Glossary

Alluvial, soil or rock laid down by water.

Arable, cultivated (as opposed to pasture) land.

Bacteria, extremely small living creatures which help to break up vegetable and animal matter.

Balance of trade/payments, record of how much comes into a country, in goods or money, compared with what goes out.

Banana, a tropical fruit, usually sweet; in this book the word is used to include non-sweet plantains as well.

Baobab, a large tree, with a thick trunk and pulpy fruit.

Basement complex, the lowest rocks which lie under each country.

Bilharzia, a worm disease of human beings, caught from infected snails living in still, shallow water.

Blackquarter, a disease of cattle.

Boma, a place protected by a strong hedge: a place for cattle: a term used for administrative headquarters.

Bush fallow, land formerly cultivated allowed to return to bush to give it a rest.

Capital, money or goods saved, used to produce more money or goods.

Coir, fibre produced from the vegetable covering round a coconut.

Copra, dried coconut kernels from which oil is obtained.

Creek, a small inlet of a sea, lake or river.

Dhow, an Arab boat, usually with one mast and sail.

Environment, surroundings within which people live.

Escarpment, the steep edge of bedded rocks that have been tilted and eroded; also formed by faulting.

Euphorbia, a type of plant; it grows well in dry and high places.

Fallow, land left uncultivated or unsown in order to rest.

Flux, limestone mixture used in copper smelting to help keep the metal liquid.

Fodder, food for grass-eating animals.

Ghee, a clear oily form of butter, originally from India.

Granite, a crystalline type of rock, once molten.

Hullery, a factory in which the parchment covering of coffee beans in removed.

Kwashiorkor, disease caused by vitamin shortages.

Laterite, a hard, brick-like material formed by the decomposition of rocks under tropical conditions.

Legume, the family of plants to which peas and beans belong. Important because these help to enrich the soil by transferring nitrogen from the air.

Levees, embankments.

Ley, system by which grass is sown for pasture and to rest the soil.

Mangrove, a tree which grows in salt-water swamp.

Margarine, an artificial butter made mainly from vegetable oils.

Masika, a term given to the long rains in Tanzania, Zanzibar and Pemba.

Mbuga, area of black soil in the lowest part of a broad valley. Liable to flood during the rains.

Milkweed (manyara), small fleshy plant, often used for hedges.

Miombo, a form of savanna woodland found in Tanzania.

Mulch, material, often vegetable, laid on the ground to protect the soil from the sun and rain.

Murram, a type of red clay-like rock with hard lumps in it; used to surface roads in East Africa.

Nyika, means wilderness; often used to describe a dry, thorny, bush type of vegetation.

Overstock, to put more animals on a piece of ground than it can really support.

Parastatal, using government money to invest in companies.

Perennial, lasting through the year or years.

Prune, to cut off unnecessary branches or shoots of a tree in order to make it grow and give better fruit.

Quartz, a white hard mineral found in granite and other rocks; used in glass making.

Ranching, keeping cattle in large numbers in big open fields.

Reef: (*a*) a mass of rocks, in the sea, near to the surface; (*b*) rock containing gold.

Resource base, whatever a country can use for its development, its minerals, crops, livestock and people.

Rinderpest, a disease of cattle.

Rotation, growing different crops in a definite order on a piece of ground, in order to preserve the fertility of the soil.

Savanna, a type of vegetation where trees and grass grow mixed together.

Sesamum (simsim), a plant whose seeds yeild a fine oil.

Shamba, a Swahili word meaning 'farm'.

Silt, mud or fine earth deposited by water.

Soil profile, the layer arrangement in a soil.

Sorghum, a kind of millet: a food grain.

Spinach, a vegetable, the green leaves of which are cooked and eaten.

Stud, bulls or other male animals kept for breeding.

Subsistence, that which supplies the means of living.

Thicket, a collection of trees or bushes growing closely together.

Vicious circle, a situation in which conditions tend to get worse and worse.

Water table, the level below which the soil and rock is saturated with water; wells must reach below this level.

Yams, a fleshy root, a type of sweet potato.

Index